ABORIGINAL PEOPLE AND OTHER CANADIANS

SHAPING NEW RELATIONSHIPS

The International Canadian Studies Series
La Collection internationale d'études canadiennes

The *International Canadian Studies Series* offers a unique collection of high-quality works written primarily by non-Canadian academics. The Series includes conference proceedings, collections of scholarly essays, and other material (including poetry, novels, plays, and monographs). The Series publishes works written in either English or French.

La *Collection internationale d'études canadiennes* présente des ouvrages de premier ordre, rédigés surtout par des universitaires non canadiens. Elle comprend des actes de colloques, des séries d'articles et d'autres formes d'écriture comme des recueils de poésies, des romans, des pièces de théâtre et des monographies. La collection publie des ouvrages en français et en anglais.

Editorial Committee/Comité éditorial:
Guy Leclair
Chad Gaffield

International Canadian Studies Series
Collection internationale d'études canadiennes

ABORIGINAL PEOPLE AND OTHER CANADIANS

SHAPING NEW RELATIONSHIPS

Edited by Martin Thornton and Roy Todd

D.N. Collins, G. Mercer, H.N. Nicholson, M. Thornton, R. Todd, D.S. Wall

International Council
for Canadian Studies

University
of Ottawa Press

Université d'
University of
Ottawa

Institut d'études canadiennes
Institute of Canadian Studies

University of Ottawa Press gratefully acknowledges the support extended to its publishing programme by the Canada Council, the Department of Canadian Heritage, and the University of Ottawa.

National Library of Canada Cataloguing in Publication Data

Main entry under title:

Aboriginal people and other Canadians : Shaping new relationships

(International Canadian studies series ; 5)
ISBN 0-7766-3018-0 (bound). – ISBN 0-7766-0541-0 (pbk.)

1. Native peoples – Canada – Social conditions.   2. Native peoples –
Canada – Ethnic identity.   3. Canada – Race relations.
I. Thornton, Martin, 1955– II. Todd, Roy   III. Series.

E78.C2A148 2001   305.897'071   C2001-903733-3

UNIVERSITY OF OTTAWA
UNIVERSITÉ D'OTTAWA

Cover Design: John Beadle

ISBN 0-7766-3018-0 (cloth)
ISBN 0-7766-0541-0 (paper)
ISSN 1489-713X

Printed and bound in Canada

Blackfeet at Earnscliffe, Ottawa, 1886.
Front row, left to right: North Axe, Peigan Chief, One Spot, Blood Sub-Chief. Middle row, left to right: Three Bulls, half brother of Crowfoot, Crowfoot, Blackfoot Chief, Red Cloud, Blood Chief. Back row, left to right: Father Lacombe, John L'Heureux, interpreter.

National Archives of Canada PA-045666

Contents

Contributors

Dr. David N. Collins is Head of the Department of Russian and Slavonic Studies and Deputy Director of the Centre for Canadian Studies at the University of Leeds. His academic interests include the comparative problems of European colonial expansion within the Northern Hemisphere. His publications include "Culture, Christianity and the Northern Peoples of Siberia and Canada" and bibliographic works including *Siberia and the Soviet Far East*.

Dr. Geoffrey Mercer is a Senior Lecturer in the Department of Sociology and Social Policy of the University of Leeds. He is a member of the British Association of Canadian Studies and former Review Editor of the *British Journal of Canadian Studies*. He has published on Aboriginal peoples and the Welfare State and also extensively on disability issues.

Dr. Heather Norris Nicholson is a Senior Lecturer in Geography at Ripon and York (a college of the University of Leeds). Within Canadian Studies she teaches on a range of socio-cultural issues, has research interests in Aboriginal film-making and tourism and is Vice-President of the British Association of Canadian Studies.

Dr. Martin Thornton is Director of the Centre for Canadian Studies at the University of Leeds. His teaching and research interests fall into the area of Canadian foreign policy and the Cold War. His publications include *The Domestic and International Dimensions of the Resettlement of Polish Ex-Servicemen in Canada, 1943-1948* and an edited book of *Nancy Astor's Canadian Correspondence, 1912-1962*.

Dr. Roy Todd is an Executive Committee member and former Director of the Centre for Canadian Studies at the University of Leeds. He is currently Director of Research at Trinity and All Saints, a college of the University of Leeds. His current research is focused on urban Aboriginal people in Canada. Previous Canadian research has covered aspects of multiculturalism and policing and "race" relations.

Dr. David S. Wall is a Senior Lecturer in Department of Law at the University of Leeds. His research interests and publications are in the field of policing, cybercrimes, access to justice and criminal justice professionals. He has conducted research into access to justice related issues within the Canadian criminal justice system.

Acknowledgements

This study of the changing relations between Aboriginal people and other Canadians is based upon research funded by the Canadian High Commission and the Foundation for Canadian Studies in the United Kingdom under their Canadian Society in Transition Sustained Study Award programme (1996-98). The authors are members of the Centre for Canadian Studies, University of Leeds and work at the University of Leeds or at Colleges of the University of Leeds (Ripon and York and Trinity and All Saints). The project was co-ordinated and directed by Roy Todd.

In the course of the research we have appreciated the encouragement and support of Professor Frank Cassidy, School of Public Administration, University of Victoria and Professor Bruce Miller, Department of Anthropology and Sociology, University of British Columbia. Professor Cassidy acted as a discussant, gave a paper on the implications of the Delgamuukw case, and provided an authoritative commentary on presentations at a conference held at the University of Leeds in November 1998 at which earlier versions of these papers were presented. Professor Miller and a group of his postgraduate students participated in a video-link discussion on aspects of the ethics and politics of research with Aboriginal people during the conference.

We are grateful to the Foundation for Canadian Studies and the Canadian High Commission for the financial support that enabled us to undertake this research. We are particularly grateful to the Academic Relations Section of the Canadian High Commission for its continual support and encouragement during the two years in which we have worked on this project.

Finally, we are grateful to those members of Aboriginal and other communities, in cities and elsewhere, who facilitated our data gathering in Canada.

Chapter 1

Introduction

Roy Todd

The televised confrontations between Mohawks and the army at Oka, Quebec, in the summer of 1990 provided high drama which caught the attention of Canadians across the nation. In the following year, after the collapse of the Meech Lake Accord, and in the context of continuing failures to meet the needs of Aboriginal communities, the Royal Commission on Aboriginal Peoples was established. The Commission had a broad mandate to review the situation of Aboriginal people and to make policy recommendations. Now, as we enter a new decade, we can begin to assess whether changes are occurring, and to discern whether the last decade of the twentieth century was a decade of constructive transition. Are relations between Canada's Aboriginal peoples and other Canadians continuing as critically as before? Is a new pattern of relations emerging after the recent challenges to the colonial legacy by Aboriginal people? Are Canadians together creating new structures and negotiating new structures that do not lead to the reproduction of earlier tragedies and difficulties? These questions were amongst those addressed by the research summarised in this volume.

This collection is multi-disciplinary, focusing on themes which incorporate (i) historical developments; (ii) social, demographic, socio-economic and spatial data; (iii) educational developments; (iv) governance, peace keeping and social justice; (v) social and health policy; and (vi) cultural policy, cultural representations and identity. The contributors' disciplinary starting points cover history, sociology, social policy, geography and law.

There are emergent issues within these papers. These include understanding of small rural communities and experience in Canada's cities, leading us to reflect upon objectives for liveable communities in urban and rural contexts. There are themes of social exclusion, marginalisation and identity, topics which are of concern to ethnic and cultural minorities as well as Aboriginal peoples. Concerns with governance, justice, equality and gender are reflected here. Self-help and empowerment in Aboriginal communities and in the cities also have a place. Finally, reflection on methodology, historiography and the representation of the social relations at the heart of these issues leads to engagement with theories and models found in contemporary and historical literature and in policy documents.

The final Report of the Royal Commission on Aboriginal Peoples (RCAP) has inevitably formed a point of reference for almost all of the chapters. The Commission's view of history, its portrayal of the recent past, its account of the present and its proposals for new policies all came under scrutiny. The sense of dialogue at the heart of the final Report of the RCAP is an undeniable achievement. The scope of its recommendations is immense and the contribution to understanding made by the supporting research is very substantial. Also, as a resource for scholars, the Royal Commission's main report and the supplementary reports arising from its research agenda will offer benefits for some considerable time. While it is too soon to judge the long-term outcomes of the Canadian Government's response— "Gathering Strength"—that emerged in January 1998, recognition of the very considerable depth and complexity of the social and other issues to be addressed by government policy is inescapable. Positive change, if any, will not come rapidly but the rhetorical point of the suggestion that "gathering dust" might be a more apt phrase rather than "Gathering Strength" reflects an understandable impatience with an enduring issue. The following chapters have been written with an awareness of the tensions between the hopes and expectations found in the Report of the RCAP and the reactions to the Government response.

In the next chapter, Martin Thornton considers aspects of the history of Aboriginal people in their relationships with national and provincial governments. In the making of modern Canada, non-Aboriginal people committed offences and wrongs against Aboriginal people. Governments at the federal and provincial levels have been at the centre of what he refers to as a perplexing and sad history. Any history of Aboriginal people is faced with the problems of approach, definition, context and selection of important subject matter for analysis. The 1996 Report of the RCAP addressed these difficulties. Martin Thornton includes scrutiny of the Commission's approach to history in his analysis, offering a critical perspective on the embedded view of history in the RCAP's final report.

Social relations between Christian missionaries and Aboriginal people have been a continuous feature of Canada's history since the arrival of Europeans on the continent. As David Collins notes in his opening remarks to Chapter 3, "Discussion of Christian missions to the world's indigenous peoples excites impassioned opinions both for and against." The first part of the Chapter presents a critical analysis of writings about the Christian missionary endeavour to Canada's First Peoples over the last three decades. These sources are analysed within categories ranging from hagiographic and respectful writing, through neutral reporting to severely critical works. The second part of the chapter gives an extensive, classified, bibliography including more than five hundred items.

Whereas the first three chapters are concerned with historical issues, both drawing from and reflecting critically upon historiography and historical methodology, the final four chapters focus on contemporary issues. Their main themes include the complex and increasingly significant situation of Aboriginal people in urban areas, aspects of health and healing, social and criminal justice and finally, through a study of Aboriginal tourism, a potential form of economic regeneration. In each of these chapters the ongoing interaction of Aboriginal and other Canadian cultural and social forms is made clear. To some extent these chapters indicate the invisibility and assimilation that characterise the situation of Aboriginal people at the end of the twentieth century in Canada. On another reading, they reveal how adaptation and change are being negotiated within a context of interplay between Aboriginal traditions and expectations and the responses of non-Aboriginal institutions.

Roy Todd, in Chapter 4, reviews evidence about Aboriginal people in urban areas (almost one-half of the Aboriginal population). He summarises the diversity of their socio-economic situation while making clear the extremely difficult circumstances encountered in some urban areas arising from poverty and a predominantly antagonistic criminal justice system. Drawing upon fieldwork conducted in two major Canadian cities he shows how social exclusion and its consequences are tackled actively by the representatives of Aboriginal organisations through negotiations with police, social, health and educational services. These case studies reveal the strength and resourcefulness that can arise from mutual adaptation and the synthesis of Aboriginal and non-Aboriginal cultures.

The maintenance of Aboriginal traditions is also a part of the next chapter, which explores matters related to health and healing. Geof Mercer begins by summarising the legacy of Aboriginal ill-health, one of the material consequences of the stark realities of social division, during the twentieth century. He then analyses health policy, clarifying critical perspectives and reviewing new developments. Finally, he considers policy recommendations for health services based upon ideas of partnership in the health care system. These incorporate a holistic approach to health, respond to concerns about Aboriginal control and are sensitive to diversity across and within First Nations' groups.

Alternative models of provision also form the basis of the following chapter by David Wall. The criminal justice system has clearly failed to respond to Aboriginal people and one of the responses has been to turn towards the restorative models of justice traditionally practised by Aboriginal people. This chapter explores the impact and effectiveness of these alternative models, raising questions about their consequences and their place within the broader criminal justice system.

Finally, the cultural dimensions of a recent form of economic regeneration—Aboriginal tourism—are discussed in Chapter 7. Heather Norris Nicholson considers some of the multi-layered messages offered by the rise of Aboriginal tourism in Western Canada. This economic growth relates to changes within and beyond Aboriginal communities. Involvement in tourism as an economic niche clearly coincides with broader indigenous struggles to achieve political and socio-cultural recognition as well as economic self-reliance. Yet the federal and provincial governments have also actively encouraged indigenous participation as a means to strengthen tourism's appeal in an increasingly competitive global industry. Diverse forms of activity have arisen from this marriage of convenience, and the analysis of sites of tourism discloses varied aspects of contemporary Aboriginal experience.

As a whole, this collection covers historical and contemporary themes, including concerns with governance and responses to religious institutions. The discussions raise theoretical and methodological issues, matters of social and health policy, criminal justice and economic regeneration. The diverse studies, of contexts, times and situations of negotiation and transition, form a broad basis for further study. They encourage reflection upon the possibility of constructing a new way forward for relations between Aboriginal peoples and other Canadians.

This introduction opened with a reference to the start of the 1990s and the Oka crisis. As we reflect on the first decade of the twenty first century, with the implications of the Delgamuukw case still being assessed and the 1998 treaty with the Nisga'a band still being discussed, a forecast for the new decade would be premature. However, the joint impetus for "restructuring the relationship" (to use a phrase from the RCAP) is considerable. We hope that the research included here will contribute to understanding this momentum of change and to further exploration of the conditions which have fostered its development.

Chapter 2

Aspects of the History of Aboriginal People in their Relationships with Colonial, National and Provincial Governments in Canada

Martin Thornton

The official attitude of the Canadian government towards Aboriginal people has become one of reconciliation and an acceptance of past wrong-doing. Not only has this required some agreement between Aboriginal people about what was wrong in this collective history, but it has also required a methodological understanding of how the past should be perceived and analysed in what is not an exact science. This reconciliation of historical problems and historiographical approaches is exactly what was attempted and put forward in the findings of the Canadian Royal Commission on Aboriginal Peoples (RCAP) published in five main volumes in 1996. By January 1998 the Minister of Indian Affairs and Northern Development, the Honourable Jane Stewart, was to accept the findings of the Royal Commission and acknowledge the sad history of the treatment of Aboriginal People in their relationship with the Government of Canada (Stewart, 1998).[1]

Why evoke the hoary problems of the past at all? As if to answer this question and the historiographical question that has perplexed many a young school student bored by his textbook and/or history teacher: why study history? The *Report of the RCAP* included the eloquent riposte:

> ...the past is more than something to be recalled and debated intellectually. It has important contemporary and practical implications, because many of the attitudes, institutions and practices that took shape in the past significantly influence and constrain the present (RCAP, 1996a, p. 31).

In also accepting that interpretations of history vary with historians, the Commissioners entered into the controversial area of what is objective historical truth.[2] Both Aboriginal and non-Aboriginal historical traditions would appear to involve the creation of myths, although the oral tradition in Aboriginal culture is particularly noted.

The non-Aboriginal historical tradition in Canada is clearly different from Aboriginal approaches towards studying and using history. Having been educated in a tradition of conservative diplomatic history, where the emphasis on scholarly documentation and archival written records is paramount, the contrast with Aboriginal perspectives on historical research could hardly be greater. Where the western social, scientific and humanities approach is for objective distancing from an issue or event, Aboriginal perspectives tend to create an involvement in the past, an approach of empathy and a view that human beings are not necessarily at the centre of the universe. *The Report of the RCAP* accepted the methodological problem at the beginning of its research and discourse, noting:

>...the Aboriginal historical tradition is an oral one, involving legends, stories and accounts handed down through the generations in oral form. It is less focused on establishing objective truth and assumes that the teller of the story is so much a part of the event that it would be arrogant to presume to classify or categorize the event exactly or for all time (*ibid.*, p. 33).

These differences were compounded by western historians, in the nineteenth century and early twentieth century, dismissing the oral tradition as merely myth and legend. Subsequently, substantial Canadian Aboriginal history has been based on government records, economic and military reports and religious documents generated largely by European males and analysed largely by European males. A lack of familiarity with North American Native cultures and languages compounded the problems (Edmunds, 1995, p. 721). Non-Aboriginal authored histories of Aboriginal people were overtly and inadvertently mythic. A view that the western academic historical approach is in some ways non-mythic can also be challenged. The history of Euro-Canadians is beset with problems of myth creation. Some Canadian historians have written about the mythic nature of Canadian identity, including the problem of defining Euro-Canadian identity and what it means to be a Canadian (Reid, 1997; Morton, 1972; Mandel and Taras, 1987).[3] These historians acknowledge that they have been involved in a western historiographical discourse that creates myths. Historians can, and often do, disagree widely about interpretations of the past and the *Report of the RCAP* could hardly be expected to reconcile perplexing historical contradictions. It would nevertheless appear that two or more mythic historical traditions may in fact have been at work in Canada, but the Euro-Canadian approach based on documented findings has dominated. As a consequence of this bias, the Aboriginal population has often been kept at the periphery of historical analysis and its importance marginalised.

In discussing the uses and abuses of history, the eminent Canadian historian Donald Creighton questioned the view that Canada was divided into Quebeckers who had wants and Canadians outside Quebec who wanted to deny these wants, and took to task how these differences were subsequently reinterpreted (Creighton, 1972, p. 65). The history of Aboriginal and non-Aboriginal people appears to have been divided in the same way: Native Canadians with wants, needs and demands and non-Aboriginal people who have tried to deny them. Donald Creighton in 1972 was also to describe those historians who interpreted an unsatisfactory past for current needs as revolutionary (Creighton, 1972, pp.67-68). Aboriginal people would be perceived by such historians as a defrauded people driven through a period of misery and oppression from which a now more enlightened society is trying to escape. This is using the past to try to revolutionise the future. Although the Commissioners of the *Report of the RCAP* may not have been described as revolutionary elsewhere, in terms of historical discourse and Donald Creighton's definitions, the Commissioners could be described as revolutionaries. This is not an entirely flattering description because they could be accused of using or abusing history for current needs.

Aboriginal and non-Aboriginal people, it was argued in the *Report of the RCAP*, had to come to terms with the problems created by past mistakes. In this regard, there are "ghosts of history" explaining the tensions between Aboriginal and non-Aboriginal people in Canada.

The ghosts take the form of dishonoured treaties, theft of Aboriginal lands, suppression of Aboriginal cultures, abduction of Aboriginal children, impoverishment and disempowerment of Aboriginal peoples (RCAP, 1996c, pp. 4-5).

Legacies from these events, it was believed by Commissioners, have determined the attitudes of people today and how they respond to current problems.

Has historical study helped to clarify who the Aboriginal people of Canada are? Today, this generic term tends to apply to people of the First Nations, Inuit and Métis and the Constitution of Canada describes Aboriginal people as such. Some official publications, including those of the Province of Quebec, use the word Amerindian alongside Inuit to refer to Aboriginal people. First Nations is a useful and descriptive title since it refers to those descendants of the "first nations" to arrive in North America, this being thousands of years before the European settlements of the 1600s. Métis, in its broadest sense, has been used to describe people of mixed North American First Nation and European descent but also meaning country-born. Although racial interaction and Métis settlement would occur throughout Canada, it was in the West that Métis became recognised as a people and clearly established in Manitoba and Saskatchewan. As historian Jim Miller has pointed out: a French-speaking and predominately Roman Catholic Métis out-numbered a country-born and largely non-Catholic English-speaking Métis (Miller, 1997, p. 5). Métis were particularly politicised through the life and execution of Louis Riel of the Red River Valley. The Honourable Jane Stewart was to refer to the "sad events" resulting in the death of Louis Riel, and how Canada should reflect on the proper position of Riel in Canadian history, without stipulating exactly what that should be (Stewart, *op. cit.*). Volume 4 of the *Report of the RCAP* was to trumpet the success of the federal government in acknowledging the important role that Métis people have played in the partnership between Aboriginal and non-Aboriginal people (RCAP, 1996b, pp. 199-386). This had clearly been the case since the Constitution Act of 1982 acknowledged the Métis as Aboriginal people.

Given the drive for economic advancement amongst European developers that ran through fur trading, agriculture and mining, the colonial administrators and Britain did not feel inclined to promote indigenous rights. Further, the Confederation of Canada in 1867 did not improve the situation for the Aboriginal population and the normal division of Canada's political history into pre- and post-Confederation appears inappropriate for the Native population. With diseases decimating the Aboriginal population, particularly in the nineteenth century, few incentives appeared to exist for non-Aboriginals to establish rights and treaties for Aboriginal people. This position was notably the situation in British Columbia, an area that joined the Confederation of Canada as a Province in 1871. The fact that Native people in British Columbia did not extinguish their rights by treaty has put them in an interesting legal position today.

The period roughly from 1800 to the ill-fated White Paper of the Pierre Trudeau Government of 1969 is seen by the RCAP as a period of displacement and assimilation. This is notably the product of three official and unofficial developments: the Bible, the plough and the concept of enfranchisement. Ontario provides a useful example of this arrangement.

Many early "reserves" were in fact Christian missions, such as the Methodists' Credit Mission west of Toronto, where the churches evangelized and assisted Natives whose economy was being disrupted by agriculture. In the 1830s a state-sponsored effort at setting up reserves was initiated in the Coldwater-Narrows region, but this attempt to tie Natives to an agricultural setting proved a failure and was abandoned. After 1846 the Colonial government again tried to encourage Natives to relocate and settle, but encountered resistance from Native leaders who feared the loss of the small tracts they still controlled. By Confederation a reserve policy existed in Ontario although its implementation was intermittent at best.

Enfranchisement represented the other significant policy initiative in Ontario (Miller, 1997, pp. 3-4).

Enfranchisement as a tool of assimilation was clearly tried in Ontario and Quebec prior to Confederation. Statutes in 1850 in Quebec and in Ontario in 1857 attempted to allow "Indians" to effectively choose not to be "Indians." This approach was reinvigorated in post-Confederation Canada.

Governmental responsibility for the affairs of First Nations was transferred from imperial control to the province of Canada in 1860.

After Confederation, administrative control of matters pertaining to First Nations was taken by the federal government and the delegated office of the Secretary of State Canada in his capacity as Registrar General and Superintendent General of Indian Affairs. His powers were transferred in 1873 to the Secretary of State for the Provinces, but responsibility for First Nations and the North fell to the Minister of the Interior. Under his jurisdiction, the Department of Indian Affairs was created in 1880.

In the language of the Indian Act of 1876 the difference between status, non-status "Indians" and "Eskimos" (Inuit) became a crucial one for Canada and Aboriginal people. It can also be seen to create a number of problems whilst trying to define the relationship of First Nations to the state. "Indians" were seen as wards of the state and to be protected from corrupting influences. This Act furthered the general Canadian government policy of trying to ensure assimilation: that "Indians" would become like Europeans. It consolidated previous practices and laws towards "Indians," putting them in a separate legal category. Male "Indians" could, if sober and industrious, apply to be British citizens and be enfranchised, but they would give up their status and rights as an "Indian." This did not apply universally throughout Canada, and was notably not applied on the West Coast, but it was, with various amendments (n.b. 1880, 1884), the backbone of Canadian governmental attitudes and a major reason for resentment of First Nations for decades to come.

In a conference in the Northwest Territories at the same time that the Indian Act was being enacted, the Cree band of First Nations were ceding land by treaty to the Canadian Government. This peaceful co-operation in Canada contrasts with events in the USA where a group of Sioux, Cheyenne and Arapaho were warring against American Government treaty violations and inflicted a bloody blow against General George Armstrong Custer and 265 troops at the Battle of the Little Big Horn in Dakota.

As the historical context of the RCAP concluded: the Canadian Government undermined "Aboriginal institutions and life patterns" (RCAP, 1996d, p. 4). This, it was believed, was achieved by a range of instruments or actions by the Canadian Government, in particular: the Indian Act, removing the jurisdiction of Aboriginal governments, creation of residential schools, relocation of Aboriginal communities, loss of land and the "substitution of welfare for an effective economic base" (RCAP, 1996d). Besides the problems caused by the Indian Act, three historical problem areas were highlighted for special consideration: residential schools, the relocation of Aboriginal communities and the issue of Aboriginal veterans of wars.

An area given special attention by the RCAP and criticised by the Minister of Indian Affairs and Northern Development is that of the residential school system. Not only were Aboriginal communities distressed by the separation of children from their communities, native languages and heritage, but the tragedy was worsened by the existence of physical and sexual abuse that has become evident in some parts of this sordid system. Education was an obvious mechanism by which assimilation of Aboriginal people to Euro-Canadian way of life could be promoted. Schools on reserves had proven inadequate in terms of attendance and cultural assimilation, so that by 1883 "industrial schools" of a residential nature were promoted and spread from the Prairies to both British Columbia and Ontario (notably northern Ontario). By the middle of the twentieth century these schools would spread to Quebec and Nova Scotia. In 1923, the Government of Canada no longer officially distinguished between "industrial" and "boarding" schools, but designated both as "residential schools" (Miller, 1997, p. 13). Who actually ran these schools? As historian Jim Miller points out:

> ...at the height of the system's development in the 1920s, there were eighty such operations. Approximately three-fifths were run by Oblates, Jesuits (one institution), and several organizations of female religious such as the Sisters of Charity, Grey Nuns, and Sisters of Saint Ann. Anglicans operated about one-quarter, while Methodists and Presbyterians were in charge of the remainder (*ibid.*).[4]

Can these schools be defended against the evidence of child labour (working half days), dietary inadequacies, prevalence of disease, limited academic standards, excessive physical punishment, lack of emotional support and examples of sexual abuse? Of course, the evidence of these abuses is now very clear and the rather limited defence would appear to be the historical context in which it took place. The type of schooling being offered (be it less individually abusive) was not unlike that of contemporary institutions of the period in Canada and elsewhere. Preparing boys for marketable trades and girls for advanced domestic skills was a common approach to education at this public level. However, what was clearly unforgivable from the view of Aboriginal people is the systematic attempt to attack the cultural and spiritual life of Native peoples. Carol Higham has recently illustrated how Protestant missionaries to Native peoples in both Canada and the United States encouraged the promotion of negative Native stereotypes (Higham, 2000). If negative stereotypes existed then the "redeeming" work of missionaries would consequently be seen in a positive light. The Government of Canada has accepted that this assorted wretched treatment of Aboriginal people cannot be expunged from history, but Canada should "gather strength" in going forwards against the background of this abusive history.

Since the publication of the *Report of the RCAP*, selective apologies have been made to First Nations of Canada over the treatment of Native children at residential schools administered by religious denominations. It is estimated that 125,000 children passed through about 80 residential schools (*The Guardian*, October 29, 1998). Legal cases are also pending since many victims are suing both churches and the federal Government of Canada. The United Church of Canada made an unequivocal apology over the physical and sexual abuse that took place in its schools. Some out-of-court settlements are being made concerning the abuse, but a lawsuit against Roman Catholic and Anglican churches has developed and a substantial financial claim on behalf of children at a First Nations residential school in Brantford, Ontario has been pursued.

Similar to the ethos behind residential schools, land areas "reserved" for Aboriginal people were established which largely helped non-Aboriginals designate land to be occupied by Aboriginal people. This also served as a mechanism to further political, economic and social control of the occupants. Relocations were made on grounds of improving Aboriginal's health and their environment, but also for non-Aboriginals to obtain valuable land for settlement. Aspects of this policy date back to the seventeenth century. However, it was only codified under the Confederated Government of Canada in the nineteenth century. In addition:

In 1885, the Department of Indian Affairs instituted a pass system. No outsider could come onto a reserve to do business with an Aboriginal resident without permission from the Indian agent (RCAP, 1996c, pp.14-15).

Treaty-making, in contrast to the relocation of Aboriginal people, was not a procedure dominated in the same severe way by colonists and the later Canadian Government, but was a process with a long Aboriginal history. For example, alliances had been at the centre of co-operation between the separate Nations of the Iroquois. Aboriginal people brought a strong spiritual association to these proceedings and the Euro-Canadian reciprocating partners did not ignore this. Queen Victoria provided a potent symbol for Aboriginal people as a "Great Mother" to be trusted, and her declarations were evoked in later years when Aboriginal people required support. Both during conscription crises in Canada and during the debates over patriation of the Canadian Constitution, First Nations would evoke treaties for their own purposes.

Differences of interpretation over treaties are particularly apparent with regard to the 1877 Treaties of Canada with the First Nations of Manitoba and North West Territories. Government officials thought they were agreeing to a one-time land deal, whereas, leaders of First Nations, thought they were agreeing to a renewable partnership and even emphasised the spiritual nature of the relationship.

At the heart of relations between provinces and Aboriginal people is the point and problem, notably experienced in Quebec, that "reserves" are not protected from the implementation of provincial laws. Although the Federal "Indian Act" gave special rights for "Indians" on reserves, courts have ruled that such reserves are "...not 'enclaves' shielded from the application of provincial laws" (Government of Quebec in London, 1997, p. 1). However, Native leaders in many provinces have settled or formally extinguished further claims by signing treaties limiting the areas of their land. In contrast, British Columbia has been of interest recently, particularly because few Native leaders entered into treaties and thus did not extinguish their land claims. The case of Delgamuukw (hereditary Chief of the Gitxsan people of northwestern British Columbia) versus British Columbia led to an historic decision, whereby the Supreme

Court voted that Aboriginal title to land could be proven by Aboriginal people showing that their

> ...ancestors occupied the land exclusively and continuously from before the time that Canada claimed sovereignty over the land (Gray, 1998, p. 1).[5]

This ruling has implications for Native legal claims, but also from an historical point of view helps to contradict a previously held Euro-Canadian view of the nineteenth century that the Americas were *terra nullius* (empty land) when the Europeans arrived. This legal notion of Canada being vacant land when European settlers arrived was declared factually, morally and legally wrong by the *Report of the RCAP* (Plaitel, 1998, p. 3). The Delgamuukw ruling does, nevertheless, reinforce a Royal Proclamation of 1763 by King George III that:

> ...the several Nations or Tribes of Indians with whom We are connected, and who live under Our Protection, should not be molested or disturbed in the Possession of such parts of Our Dominions and Territories as, not having been ceded to or purchased by Us, are reserved to them, or any of them, as their Hunting Grounds...(Ministry of Aboriginal Affairs, British Columbia, 1998, p. 1).

Given the high profile cases of First Nations, perhaps it is a surprise that Canada's biggest move towards self-government for its Native communities should come with the creation of Nunavut (translated from Inuktitut as "Our Land") on the 1st of April, 1999. The central and eastern parts of the Northwest Territories, an area that has an 85% Inuit population, became an area of Aboriginal self-government. It was the product of the Nunavut Land Claims Agreement signed in 1993. The Inuit have also had a chequered history where suicide rates have been higher than the national average and the residential school system exhibited features of physical and sexual abuse. The inhospitable nature of the physical environment in Nunavut in many ways assisted the development of self-government and perhaps makes this political, economic, territorial and legal change less of a surprise. Although political and economic control rests with the inhabitants of Nunavut, much of the annual budget still comes from the federal government.

Both the issues of reserves and Aboriginal land claims in an historical and contemporary context have led to a stereotyping of Aboriginal people and in some cases self-stereotyping. In considering Aboriginal people as a special case within Canada, and with attempts to invest them with a clear legal and cultural identity, the fact that a marginal majority live in an urban environment with all the cultural and social problems of modern market economies can become lost.[6] In evoking the issues of Aboriginal rights on reserves and for fishing rights, the image of Aboriginal people as hunters and gatherers of food in a rural environment becomes evoked. Yet, as the *Report of the RCAP* and the 1996 Canadian census clearly show, the contemporary problems of Aboriginal people are in many ways dominated by issues of urban living.[7] Ghislain Otis has written about the difficulties of modernity and Aboriginal life. He has suggested that a more traditional Aboriginal rights model perpetuated in court cases needs to be juxtaposed against the fact that a substantial number of Aboriginal people live in cities and have had to adapt to the problems of modernity (Otis, 1997, pp. 182-194).

In the twentieth century, two world wars caused particular consternation and long-term grievances for Aboriginal people, particularly those who directly participated in these conflicts. Although over 3,000 "registered Indians" volunteered for the Canadian Armed Forces during the Second World War, adequate records were not kept on Métis, Inuit and non-status "Indians" (RCAP, 1996c, p. 16). Despite cultural and historical differences amongst Aboriginal and non-Aboriginal people in Canada, many of the economic and social reasons for registering for military service appear similar. Clearly a disproportinate number of Aboriginal people, in comparison with those from the general population, were rejected from military service on health grounds, including severe conditions of tuberculosis and pneumonia. A lack of formal educational attainment kept numbers of Aboriginal people out of the Navy and Air Force. Aboriginal people also found new opportunities in wartime domestic employment that had previously been unattainable for them and this clearly reduced the incentive to volunteer.

Fishing caused a problem in British Columbia, since during the fishing season it became difficult to locate fishermen of the First Nations who were liable for military service. They appeared to be out on long fishing trips during the summer and trapping and hunting during the autumn and winter. The Indian Agent for Bella Coola, British Columbia, also noted what he was to describe as an "inferiority complex" *(R.G. 10. Vol. 6768, File 452-20, pt. 4*, NAC - National Archives of Canada.). It became apparent that the Bella Bella's of British Columbia did not wish to be placed amongst a majority of Euro-Canadian soldiers. A different interpretation of this is that they expected discrimination from "white soldiers,"—a view not believed to be evident amongst interior First Nations of British Columbia (*ibid.*). Indian Agents believed that the contact between Euro-Canadians and First Nations interior tribes made them less worried about discrimination.

The conscription issues of the First and Second World Wars not only caused problems for Quebec, but also for Aboriginal people, some of whom questioned whether First Nations should ever be obliged to register for military service. Some First Nations felt that the National War Mobilisation Act of the Second World War should have exempted them from war service. Even if it did not, previous legal precedent and governmental promises should have been upheld to support this view. An organised opposition to registering for military service was established amongst First Nations of British Columbia and Quebec (also evident in the Oka crisis of 1990).

First Nations of Manitoba were to take up the case of military service with their sympathetic Indian Agent, A. G. Smith, in May 1943. They quoted freely from a book: *The Treaties of Canada With the Indians of Manitoba and the North-West Territories* by the Honorable Alexander Morris, P.C. (*ibid.*). It was widely quoted by the leaders of Manitoba's First Nations that the Lieutenant Governor, Alexander Morris, in October 1873 made the following promise:

> The English never call the Indians out of their country to fight their battles. You are living here and the Queen expects you to live at peace with the white men and your red brothers and with other Nations (*ibid.*).

In June 1943, First Nations delegates from Quebec and British Columbia lobbied Parliament for exemption from war service and also income tax (although status "Indians" on reserves did not pay tax). Delegates were from Caughnawaga, Loretteville and Oka Reservations of Quebec, and also Vancouver in British Columbia.[8] First

Nations of Quebec, Ontario, Manitoba, Nova Scotia and British Columbia registered complaints with the Indian Affairs Branch of the Department of Mines and Resources (responsible for First Nations since 1936). The Appeals Court of the King's Bench was forced to rule against First Nation opposition in 1943.

In contrast to the compulsion to register for military service for First Nations, no Canadian law compelled Inuit to register and take up arms. There is no easy comparison here since Inuit were largely nomadic, did not accept tribal laws and often did not speak either English or French. Enforcement of any similar law for Inuit would have been very problematic in the rather inhospitable environment of the North. Some enforcement of military service regulation for First Nations in the northern reaches of most provinces also proved a problem since the population often could not be found. Inuit were also not signatories to treaties with the Canadian government and by implication not wards of the state in the same way as First Nations. The Department of Mines and Resources unofficially informed *The Evening Citizen* newspaper of Ottawa in June 1943 that Inuit: "...just don't know or understand anything about wars" (*R.G. 10. Vol. 6768, File 452-20, pt. 5*, NAC).

Over 200 Aboriginal people died in the Canadian military services during the Second World War, a rough figure that again excludes Métis and "non-status Indians." Much pride has been garnished from this sacrifice and in particular the heroism of Charles Bryce, a soldier from the First Nations. Charles Bryce, of the Lake Superior regiment, was among 162 Canadians to win the Distinguished Conduct Medal. He was also awarded the French Medaille Militaire for his bravery during the Second World War. Many other Aboriginal men received the Military Medal, some of whom died abroad serving Canada. It can be argued that the sacrifices of the Aboriginal communities were particularly severe since the war dead were often the most healthy, strong and educated and the community could ill-afford to lose them.

To a large extent the Indian Affairs Branch of Mines and Resources avoided responding positively or negatively to the issue of military service and Canada's First Nations by disclaiming responsibility for military matters. Of course, with regard to mobilising military personnel, the Department of National War Services and the National Selective Service were technically responsible. In 1943, a Superintendent Watson of the Indian Affairs Branch of the Department of Mines and Resources did correspond with the Royal Canadian Mounted Police of St. Regis, Quebec and provided a blanket response that was to persist throughout the war:

There is nothing in the Regulations excepting indians from service and it is not considered necessary to have a letter from the Indian Affairs branch...(R.G. 10, Vol. 6769, File 452-20-10, pt. 1, NAC).

On returning to Canada, First Nations veterans of the First and Second World Wars (and to a lesser extent the Korean War), found that they were denied many of the benefits provided for other Canadian veterans, including access to land and financial loans. The Veteran's Land Act and the abuses of discretionary powers by the Indian Agents have been prominent grievances held by Second World War veterans from First Nations. Like African-Americans who fought in the Second World War for the USA, the irony of fighting for liberty and democracy and against tyranny, despotism and arguably against racism was not lost on Aboriginal people from Canada. The irony that the Canadian Government eventually apologised and financially compensated Japanese Canadians interned during the Second World War was not lost on Aboriginal veterans of wars. Since the benefits of peace were seen not to be shared equitably between Aboriginal and non-Aboriginal people and there was an inequality of treatment and a lack of acknowledgement for all of Canada's war veterans, Aboriginal people have felt particularly aggrieved.

Conclusions

Like the *Report of the RCAP*, this historical introduction only provides snapshots or aspects of problems that have bedevilled the relationships between Aboriginal and non-Aboriginal people. Like modern news coverage, historical study often emphasises the disharmony and crisis that provide interesting subject matter. Choosing seminal events for academic analysis often artificially elevates certain events for academic purposes. However, the range and depth of issues relating to a sordid and difficult history between Aboriginal and non-Aboriginal people in Canada justifies a rather negative emphasis.

Clearly, the Government of Canada has taken substantial responsibility for what it now accepts as a range of misguided policies of non-Aboriginal people towards First Nation, Métis and Inuit in Canada. However, a western scholarly approach still pervades the study of Aboriginal people in Canada. Acknowledging Aboriginal approaches to history has not seen the replacement of linear approaches or the sectionalisation of history on a chronological continuum. Even with the development of ethnohistory, difficulties of historical perspective, methodology and cross-cultural differences pervade the problem of understanding the history of Aboriginal people in relation to colonial, national and provincial governments in Canada. Rather than a synthesis of ideas and approaches on the study of Aboriginal history, a peaceful co-existence has developed between what are very different approaches to explaining the past.

The *Report of the RCAP* has been criticised in Canada as too costly to produce (58 million Canadian dollars) and too expensive as a set of documents (250 Canadian dollars). It has also been criticised as rather naive in suggesting that more money and more self-government should be thrown at Aboriginal people. It has also met some criticism for its recounting of a bankrupt historical relationship between Aboriginal people and the Canadian Government. As the journalist John Gray in the *Globe and Mail* suggested:

If recent history has proved anything, it is that the country is too complex to be seen through a single prism. There are too many peoples, too many histories, too many scores to settle. A single prism did not work for English-French relations, it will not work for the aboriginal peoples (Gray, 1998, p. 5).

A self-criticism of what has been covered here and also a criticism of the *Report of the RCAP* is the observation that the history of Aboriginal people emphasises what Janet Chute calls "victimhood." This concerns the problem of portraying Aboriginal people as almost entirely victims of decisions. The neglected approach has been that of "Native agency"—putting Aboriginal people at the centre of much decision making. Aboriginal people in Canada can be seen throughout periods of history and even pre-Confederation history as working in concert with other non-Aboriginal groups and organisations. This can in fact be seen in a

...wide range of Native behaviours; among them fur-trade negotiating dexterity, calculated compliance in fighting in intercolonial wars, willingness to invite missionaries to reside in Native villages and, during the settlement era, sporadic protest against political encapsulation (Chute, 1996, p. 56).

In defence, the attempt to rectify the problems of the past by the RCAP has led to a victim approach for which clearly evidence and material exists. Aspects of the history of Aboriginal people in their relationships with colonial, national and provincial governments covered here parallels material covered by the RCAP. It also parallels the grievances of Aboriginal people in Canada, for which Aboriginal people have now been given a public apology from the Canadian Government.

John Gray has used an anecdotal story to show the difficulty of setting an historical context for Aboriginal people in Canada. In the *Globe and Mail* he cited Professor Newhouse from Trent University in Ontario who has plaud a "simple" question before first-year Native Studies students over a number of years (Gray, *op. cit.*, p. 1). The question is: "What contribution have Aboriginal people made to Canadian life?" Some 600 students have so far failed to provide a single example. It is, of course, a loaded question and very difficult to answer. The *Report of the RCAP* inadvertently explains why it is a difficult question by posing and answering the reverse question: What has Canada contributed to Aboriginal life? The answer is a much more straight-forward and sorry one.

Notes

1. Address by the Honourable Jane Stewart on the unveiling of *Gathering Strength—Canada's Aboriginal Action Plan*, January 7, 1998.
2. The Commissioners were: René Dussault, George Erasmus, Paul L.A.H. Chartrand, J. Peter Meekison, Viola Marie Robinson, Mary Sillett and Bertha Wilson.
3. The Centre of Canadian Studies at the University of Edinburgh held a conference in 1990 on: "Limitless Identities: Is there a Canadian History?"
4. Also see Collins, D. (chapter 3), "Relations between First Nations and Christian Missionaries."
5. On other Supreme Court cases, notably the Van der Peet trilogy of cases, see Berry, D. S. (1997) "'Where Politicians Fear to Tread': The Supreme Court of Canada and Aboriginal Rights," *British Journal of Canadian Studies*, vol. 12, no. 2, pp. 165-181.

6. See Mercer, G. (Chapter 5) "Aboriginal Peoples: Health and Healing."
   Also see Todd, R. (Chapter 4) "Aboriginal People in the Cities."
7. As the census was to illustrate:
   "About three of every 10 Aboriginal people lived on rural reserves, and
   another three in 10 lived in census metropolitan areas. One-quarter lived
   in urban areas other than census metropolitan areas, and one-fifth in rural
   areas other than reserves..."
   "About one-fifth of Aboriginal people...lived in seven of the country's
   25 census metropolitan areas in 1996..." in "1996 Census: Aboriginal
   Data," www.statcan.ca.
8. Delegates were: Peter K. Jacobs, Joseph Delisle, Jules Sioui, George A.
   Cree, Tom Skye, Paul K. Diabo, Thomas Bordeaux, Andrew Paull and
   Thomas Assu. *R.G. 10, Vol. 6768, File 452-20, pt. 5*, NAC.

References

Armitage, A. (1995) *Comparing the Policy of Aboriginal Assimilation:
Australia, Canada and New Zealand*, Vancouver: University of British
Columbia Press.

Berry, D.S. (1997) "'Where Politicians Fear to Tread': The Supreme Court of
Canada and Aboriginal Rights," *British Journal of Canadian Studies*,
vol.12, no. 2.

Cassidy, F. Editor (1991) *Aboriginal Self-Determination*, Montreal: The
Institute for Research on Public Policy.

_____, Bish, R.L. (1989) *Indian Government: Its Meaning in Practice*,
Halifax, Nova Scotia: The Institute for Research on Public Policy.

Chute, J.E. (1998) *The Legend of Shingwaukonse: A Century of Native
Leadership*, Toronto: University of Toronto Press.

_____. (1996) "A Unifying Vision: Shingwaukonse's Plan for the
Future of the Great Lakes Ojibwa," *Journal of the Canadian Historical
Association*, New Series, vol. 7.

Coates, K.S. (1991) *Best Left as Indians: Native-White Relations in the Yukon
Territory, 1840-1973*, Montreal: McGill-Queen's University Press.

Creighton, D. (1972) *Towards the Discovery of Canada*, Toronto: Macmillan
of Canada.

Edmunds, R.D. (1995) "Native Americans, New Voices: American Indian
History, 1895-1995," *American Historical Review*, June.

Gaffen, F. (1985) *Forgotten Soldiers*, Penticton, B.C.: Theytus Books.

Granatstein, J.L., Morton, D. (1989) *A Nation Forged in Fire: Canadians and
the Second World War, 1939-1945*, Toronto: Lester and Orpen Dennys
Limited.

Gray, J. (1998) "Not a Word About Natives," <www.theglobeandmail.com>,
June 29, 1998.

Higham, C.L. (2000) *Noble, Wretched, and Redeemable. Protestant
Missionaries to the Indians in Canada and the United States, 1820-1900*,
Albuquerque: University of New Mexico Press.

Hylton, J., Editor (1994) *Aboriginal Self-Government in Canada: Current
Issues and Trends*, Saskatoon: Purich.

Kulchyski, P., McCaskill, D., Newhouse, D. (1998) *In the Words of the Elders: Aboriginal Cultures in Transition*, Toronto: University of Toronto Press.

Mandel, E. Taras, D. (1987) *A Passion for Identity: An Introduction to Canadian Studies*, Toronto: Methuen.

Miller, J.R. (1997) *Canada and the Aboriginal Peoples 1867-1927*, Canadian Historical Association Booklet, no. 57, Ottawa: Canadian Historical Association.

_____. (1991) *Skyscrapers Hide the Heavens: A History of Indian-White Relations in Canada*, Toronto: University of Toronto Press.

Morton, W.L. (1972) *The Canadian Identity*, Toronto: Toronto University Press.

National Archives of Canada, *R.G. 10, Vol. 6768, File 452-20, pt. 4* and *pt. 5*, *R.G. 10, Vol. 6769, File 452-20-10, pt. 1*.

Otis, G. (1997) "Opposing Aboriginality to Modernity: the Doctrine of Aboriginal Rights in Canada," *British Journal of Canadian Studies*, vol. 12, no. 2.

Plaitel, R. (1998) "Vast Changes sought to Aid Natives," <www. theglobeandmail.com>, June 29, 1998.

Reid, J. (1997) "'A Society Made by History': The Mythic Source of Identity in Canada," *Canada Review of American Studies*, vol. 27, no. 1.

Royal Commission on Aboriginal Peoples (1996a) *Report of the Royal Commission on Aboriginal People, Volume 1, Looking Forward, Looking Back*, Ottawa: Minister of Supply and Services.

Royal Commission on Aboriginal Peoples (1996b) *Report of the Royal Commission on Aboriginal People, Volume 4, Perspectives and Realities*, Ottawa: Minister of Supply and Services.

Royal Commission on Aboriginal Peoples (1996c) *People to People, Nation to Nation, Highlights from the Report of the Royal Commission on Aboriginal Peoples*, Ottawa: Minister of Supply and Services.

Royal Commission on Aboriginal Peoples (1996d) *Guide to the Principal Findings and Recommendations*, Ottawa: Minister of Supply and Services.

Royal Commission on Aboriginal Peoples (1994) *Public Policy and Aboriginal Peoples 1965-1992, Volume. 3, Summaries of Reports by Provincial and Territorial and Other Organizations*, Ottawa: Minister of Supply and Services.

Sawchuk, J. (1998) *The Dynamics of Native Politics: The Alberta Métis Experience*, Saskatoon: Purich.

Stevenson, M.D. (1996) "The Mobilisation of Native Canadians During the Second World War" *Journal of the Canadian Historical Association*, New Series, vol. 7.

Stewart, J. (1998) *Gathering Strength—Canada's Aboriginal Action Plan*, <www.inac.gc.ca/info/speeches>.

Chapter 3

The Historiography of Christian Missions to
Canada's First Peoples since 1970

David N. Collins

This paper has two sections. The first part presents a critical analysis of
writings about the Christian missionary endeavour to Canada's First
Peoples published since 1970. It is based on the second part, which
takes the form of a bibliography.

Discussion of Christian missions to the world's indigenous
peoples excites impassioned opinions both for and against. Christians
themselves hold a wide range of views, depending on denominational
differences, disagreements between the traditional and liberal wings
within denominations and even rivalries between mission agencies.
The vast variety and amount of literature about missions and
missiology (the study of mission) may be gauged by glancing at the
pages of a few journals.[1] Adherents of other faiths and non-religious
people hold views that are sometimes violently antipathetic to
Christian proselytism. In addition academics writing from
anthropological, sociological, feminist, Marxist, postmodernist, new
age and other viewpoints, not to speak of the proponents of "political
correctness," present more or less hostile critiques of the history and
present state of Christian missionary activity.

Very few writers approach the subject dispassionately, though
often the confident way in which people express themselves seems to
imply that as professionals they are writing objectively. It is not at all
clear that complete "objectivity" about such a subject is either possible
or desirable. It is, however, important that writers on the subject should
be honest about their particular religious, political or ideological

standpoint both to arouse their awareness of their own bias and to aid others' assessment of their work.[2]

Analysis of the large amount of literature directly concerned with Christian missions to Canada's First Peoples published since 1970[3] is complex given the multifarious approaches and diversity of subjects studied. Roman Catholic missions have received the most attention, both positive and negative. A considerable number of studies investigate developments during the heyday of New France, the seventeenth century. Naturally the Jesuit missions predominate, though some accounts detail the role of the Récollets and women missionaries. Then follows an hiatus with very little about the eighteenth and early nineteenth centuries. The exploits of the Oblates of Mary Immaculate in the mid-nineteenth century, who spread Catholic influence beyond the limits of New France to the outermost parts of Canada, have given rise to a considerable and growing literature. Anglican missions have received less attention than those of the Catholics, but a respectable body of research is devoted to their activities from the mid-nineteenth century onwards. Coverage of the Protestant free churches (Moravian, Presbyterian, Methodist and so on) is sporadic. Despite a few noteworthy studies, much remains to be done in this area. As for the small Evangelical churches whose activities began in the 1940s, the Pentecostals and the Charismatics who came on the scene from the 1960s, very little work has been done.

The historiographical survey will be divided into the following sections, each of which will be subdivided to facilitate analysis:

a) Hagiographical Publications, Autobiographies and "Respectful" Biographies
b) Broadly Neutral Studies and Primary Source Publications including Letters
c) Moderately Critical Studies
d) Severe Criticisms and Works Imbued with Strong Ideological Convictions

Hagiographical Publications, Autobiographies and "Respectful" Biographies

This section investigates "hagiographic descriptions of the work of...wilderness saints...[which] lauded the efforts of the back-country clerics" (328, pp. 27-28. Citations from the Bibliography will be given in this form.), that is, items written from a generally uncritical position by Christians themselves in order to inform and inspire their co-religionists through tales of the heroic endeavours of their brothers and sisters in distant lands. Such works are unashamedly partisan and propagandistic, intended to foster greater belief among the faithful and to stimulate increased support for the missions. They are generally confident, unselfcritical and superficial. Theologically rigid, they tend to gloss over many of the problems which beset missionary activity, except that they highlight their heroes' battles against savage environments, disease and superstition. Some of them show a keen sense of the grandeur and exotic state of nature, and on occasion manifest a somewhat grudging admiration for the hardiness of indigenous peoples. On the whole, though, they are eurocentred, with a lack of sympathy for local cultures and pity for the benighted state of the objects of the enterprise. They are usually based on a range of sources chosen to illustrate their main contentions. Many examples exist apart from the few cited in the footnote below (Young, 1899, 1903; Gould, 1917; Tucker, 1856).

This section also includes biographies and autobiographies of missionaries. In the past these were often hagiographic, particularly in the Victorian period. Such an approach could still be found particularly among Catholic writers up to the 1960s when the Québécois *révolution tranquille* (the quiet revolution) began and the Second Vatican Council initiated much rethinking.[4] However, signs of a more sensitive and sophisticated, yet still committed, approach were already evident in the first half of the twentieth century in autobiographies written by Sir Wilfred Grenfell, medical missionary to Labrador, Gabriel Breynat, o.m.i., first Catholic Vicar Apostolic of Mackenzie, and Archibald Lang Fleming, the first Anglican Bishop of the Arctic (Grenfell, 1920; Breynat, 1945-48; Fleming, 1957).

One of the distinguishing characteristics of missions historio-graphy since 1970 is that hagiography is far rarer than in the past, except in some accounts by evangelicals. The development of secular humanism, the anti-colonial movement and theological liberalism, not to say neo-marxist liberation theology, has resulted in the prevalence of a far more critical attitude. Hence, though bibliographies of literature written as late as the 1960s would have included large numbers of blatant hagiographies, relatively few have appeared since

1970 (See, for instance nos. 019, 077, 103, 449). Most items, which I have rather arbitrarily assigned to this category, tend to be more sensitively written than in the past.

Roman Catholic Missions

The French Catholic Church, active in Canada from the earliest days of New France, has generated a substantial hagiographical literature, much of it relating to the activities of the two main missionary orders, the Jesuits, active in the seventeenth century, and the Oblates of Mary Immaculate, who have spearheaded Catholic missionary outreach in the Canadian North and West from 1845 to the present. Augustin Brabant's *Mission to Nootka*, covering the period 1874-1900, was reissued in the 1970s, and is so clearly a product of its time that it sits rather uncomfortably with many of the items in the Bibliography. The editor admits that "Father Brabant's writing was atrocious, few of his statements corresponded to the known facts and the book was written for propaganda purposes," but correctly sees it as an authentic expression of opinion at the time when it was written (007, p. 5).

The Oblate Order has been particularly active in recording the lives of its missionary priests. As well as individual biographies and obituaries there is a multi-volume *Biographical Dictionary* (016, 018 ["a respectful testimony by a knowledgeable colleague, to Kajuualuk's constant pursuit of his two life-goals: personal sanctity and the Christianization of the Inuit," *Musk-Ox*, 1987, no 35], 019, 028, 035, 084, 097, 315, 394, 412, 426, 543). Other items include an "authorized" popular illustrated biography of Emile Jungbluth (1908) by a writer specializing in drama and juvenile books, studies and obituaries of the famous fathers Pandosy, Guy Marie-Rousselière and Théophile Didier, brief studies of nuns who worked alongside the Oblates, a popular illustrated account of Father Turquetil's mission at Chesterfield Inlet, occasional popular articles on missions, mission ships, etc. and Gaston Carrière's study of Oblate medical care to their Aboriginal parishioners (015, 051-2, 066, 311, 324, 342, 355, 386, 437, 416, 433, 448, 536, 573, 596). James MacGregor's biography of father Lacombe, the 14th book by this highly readable western historian, though not an official version in any respect, demonstrates a good deal of affection and respect for Lacombe whose 67 years as an Oblate missionary made him a significant figure in late 19th-century Prairie history (062; cf584). Father Nicolas Coccola, who worked in the British Columbian interior and left considerable memoir material, has been the subject of three accounts, the latest of which has a fine scholarly apparatus by Margaret Whitehead (105, 330-1). Committed studies of the Oblates have also occasionally been presented to the Study Sessions of the Canadian Catholic Historical Association (326, 453-4, 485).[5] Guy Marie-Rousselière published a sketchy overview of European northern endeavours including missionary activities (411). I have not as yet been able to see the recently published memoirs of Father Segundo Llorento's time in the Yukon, or Father Brown's journal of his first seven years in the Mackenzie Valley (058, 536). There are also a biographical dictionary of the Récollets and a few accounts of missionaries in the Maritimes, such as l'Abbé Maillard, Joseph de Cozangue (an Abenaki) and the early 19th-century Acadian Antoine Gagnon (417, 532, 568, 582).

Anglican Missions

David Carter wrote a study of Rev. Samuel Trivett (1852-1931), an Anglican working among the Bloods of present-day Alberta on behalf of the Church Missionary Society (CMS). This was based on materials in the CMS archives and the Glenbow Alberta Institute. It is useful to read this in conjunction with Georgeen Barrass's edition of Harry Stocken's memoirs of work among the Blackfoot and Sarcee, 1885-1923, (017a, 094. See also 030).

Donald Marsh, the second Anglican Bishop of the Arctic, left some extremely valuable and fascinating memoirs full of human interest and love for his largely Inuit flock. They provide a superb evocation of mid-twentieth century mission work and attitudes. They were edited and published by his wife, Winifred, some of whose brilliantly evocative watercolours of the Padlimiut among whom they worked have also been published but are unfortunately out of print now (063-5).[6] A recently published account by Rev. Arnold Ruskell, and an Anglican missionary from Ireland,—which contains bright colour photographic reproductions—is excellent in evoking life in Canada's North in the 1950s but sadly lacks any spiritual content. A privately memoir published by J. Webster in the mid-1990s has been unavailable to me (086, 102).

A children's book by Constance Savery, a derivative biography of William Bompas, adds nothing of significance to the historiography

(089).[7] Phylis Bowman's study of William Duncan's endeavours in British Columbia, *Metlakatla, the Holy City* is placed here because of its stress on the religious aspects of Duncan's work (006; cf589). A detailed study of the indefatigable medical missionary to Labrador, Wilfred Grenfell, published recently is also included here since in his own words he remained "a communicant member 'in good standing' of the Episcopal Church" despite developing rather unorthodox opinions (Rompkey, 1991see no. 085).[8]

Nonconformist, Free-Church Missions (Methodist, Moravian, Presbyterian, United Church, etc.)

Though hagiographical publications about missions from these churches abounded in earlier years, there is little recent material to place in this category. Theological liberalism and decline in the denominations led to doubt, self-criticism and reassessment even in the 1960s. There is a brief article about a Methodist missionary, Henry Bird Steinhauer, an Ojibway from Lake Simcoe (469). A recent book on Methodist women missionaries says little about missions to Canada's First Peoples, merely remarking that the Port Simpson, BC, and Alberta missions received the less educated applicants for missionary work "on the assumption that one did not need a fine education to teach Indian girls how to sew" (Gagan, 1992, p. 151).

As regards Presbyterian missions, a pamphlet and an article by William Smiley provide useful, though rather antiquarian, accounts of the mission established at Prince Albert, Saskatchewan, by James Nisbet (091, 470).

Evangelical Missions

Contemporary Evangelical missions (consisting of people from independent free churches and smaller groups such as the Mennonites who believe in baptising believers rather than infants) came on the scene far later than their mainstream Catholic, Anglican and nonconformist counterparts, beginning roughly in the 1940s. They have been little studied as yet.[9] Consequently, the relatively small amount of literature available is from a committed perspective, and much of it consists of propaganda for the missions. Apart from brief explanatory pamphlets published by the smaller groups, most of the material has been published by the Northern Canada Evangelical Mission (NCEM). Phil Du Frene's *The Best of Northern Lights* (029) includes reprints of articles from the Mission's newsletter. Bernard Palmer, a well-known American author of children's Christian books, has written a popular account of Marshall Calverley and his wife's work among the northern Cree and a rather episodic and flimsy account of the NCEM's early history printed on poor quality paper (079-80). Far more substantial, and a valuable source in its own right, is the illustrated fiftieth anniversary compilation, *Light on the Horizon* (056), printed on the NCEM's impressive machinery in Prince Albert, Saskatchewan. This is by far the best study of any northern Evangelical mission, though it does tend to skirt delicately round problems experienced by the Mission at one stage.

Other publications provide brief hagiographic biographies of missionaries and native converts (087-8, 095-6). Leslie Garrett's 1977 autobiography is particularly interesting in that it traces his move from evangelical Anglicanism to a far more radical position, which resulted in him moving to work with the NCEM (035). A final item which I wish to draw to the reader's attention despite its non-Canadian subject matter is an account of evangelism among the Alaskan Iñupiat: clearly committed, it nonetheless provides a lively and atmospheric introduction to the lives of contemporary evangelical workers among northern indigenous peoples (093).

The only readily available survey of Mennonite missions to Canada's indigenous peoples which I have discovered is a series of small sections in the third volume of the magisterial *Mennonites in Canada* (Regehr, 1996, pp. 332-9, 355-81, 370ff.).

Pentecostal and Charismatic Missions

Pentecostals and Charismatics (evangelical in theology, but differing from the Evangelicals in the section above by their belief that the baptism and gifts of the Holy Spirit are a contemporary reality received through a separate "baptism of the Spirit")[10] are relatively recent arrivals. They have as yet left little trace in the historiography of missions. Ken Birch, Executive Director of Canadian Ministries of the Pentecostal Assemblies of Canada (PAOC) stresses that there is great diversity in Native Pentecostal experience, explaining that "...there has been...little reflection in this area. We are better at doing than reflecting."[11] Early Pentecostal endeavours in the Canadian North were chronicled, excitedly but without any scholarly pretensions, by Mildred Brown (008). Two books have been published vividly depicting the activities of Rev. Kayy Gordon of Glad Tidings Fellowship among the Inuit (037-8).

Broadly Neutral Studies and Primary Source Publications including Letters

This section includes secondary works, published letters and documents which may well be written by believers, but are neither overtly propagandistic nor excessively critical in intent. They are informative, and do sometimes discuss problems arising in the course of missionary work. However, such criticisms as they contain are muted, especially in comparison with those voiced by authors included in categories C and D below.

General

Several publications about missionary teaching methods are denomination-specific, but have a wider relevance. One fascinating example is a rare study of early "visual aids" given in a book which is both art history and a commentary on Europeans' faltering attempts to put their views across: *La conversion par l'image: un aspect de la mission des Jésuites auprès des Indiens du Canada au XVIIe siècle.* The connection of this with Leahey's "Comment peut un muet prescher l'évangile?" and Raymond Gilles' study of the first catechism produced in New France is very close: the establishment of communication with the objects of mission was crucial to success. Also of interest is a study of the introduction of 17th century liturgical chant in amerindian languages, reminiscent of the film *The Mission* (033, 217, 398, 553; cf595). Also concerned with art is a critique of the contemporary Ukrainian Canadian artist William Kurelek's paintings of the early missions (083). Another noteworthy publication, this time predominantly architectural in content, but with much relevance to missionary activities in British Columbia, is John Veillette and Gary White's *Early Indian Village Churches*. A great contrast to this is a report of archeological investigations into the early Jesuit mission at Sillery (Veillette and White, 1977, in 215 and 594).

Other items survey linguistic activities, such the Anglican Edmund Peck's studies of Inuktitut, the printing of the Cree Bible and the activities of the Rossville Mission Press and the Church Missionary Society (CMS) press at Moose Factory in the 1850s (305-6, 345, 590). A list of Native language imprints in the Anglican Church of Canada's holdings, not all of which are of strictly Anglican provenance, gives us a clear indication about the extent of missionary linguistic and translation endeavours by the early 1980s (031). This translation work continues and is subject to critical investigation by linguists (611).

Roman Catholic Missions

More attention has centred on Catholic missions than any others. Guy-Marie Oury has edited the correspondence of the seventeenth-century nun Marie de l'Incarnation, and Pauline Dubé's 1991 Laval University literature thesis consisted of a critical edition of an early Récollet text (076, cf his 2 volume biography, 077; 552). Here I also include the magisterial series of publications about the early Jesuit missions laboriously prepared by Lucien Campeau, S.J. His *chef-d'oeuvre*, the six volumes of *Monumenta Novae Franciae* published between 1967 and 1992, are each around 850 pages in length, and contain a very rich source base, though they are condemned by some for continuing to "manifest a considerable amount of ethnocentric bias" (010-4).[12] A very erudite survey of relations between the Holy See and missions in North America, based on considerable work in the Vatican Archives, was published by Luca Codignola in 1995 (211).

There is very little about eighteenth-century Catholic missions, which can perhaps be explained by the parlous state of the Church in Quebec after the fall of New France, theological and political developments within the Catholic Church outside Canada and the French Revolution.[13] Exceptions are studies of Fathers Léo-Paul and Jean-Baptiste de la Brosse, and Father Edmund Burke (221, 374, 454).

Grace Nute's set of documents about missions to the northwest between 1815 and 1827 is predominantly Catholic, much of it relating to the present USA, whereas Brian Owens and Claude Roberto's *Diaries of Bishop Vital Grandin*, an Oblate active in the Prairie west from 1854, who became the first Bishop of Saint-Albert near

Edmonton in 1871, provide a really vital introduction to Catholic developments in the old Northwest Territories (074, 078).

The inauguration of a series of monographs on the Oblates of Mary Immaculate "the first attempt to produce a comprehensive and critical history of the western Oblates"[14] is most welcome. It was established by the Oblate Order and edited by Professor Raymond Huel of Lethbridge University. The initiative has already led to the publication of several extremely interesting books, the proceedings of a colloquium (558) and a periodical *Western Oblate Studies/Études oblates de l'Ouest*. The first book, a narrative overview by Donat Levasseur, a member of the Order, gave the view from the inside, with the strengths and weaknesses of one intimately associated with the subject of his research (055). Hence it has been included in section B. The others, more critical, are included in section C. Raymond Huel has produced articles on specific subjects (the development of a mission strategy, the life-cycle in one representative mission station) for another Oblate journal (380-1).[15]

Claude Champagne studied the life and works of Vital Grandin in a detailed work with many quotations from primary sources. Added to the published diaries mentioned above this gives a very clear idea of Catholic attitudes towards evangelism, catechesis and culture change in the late 19th century. Champagne also produced a relatively brief overview article on the northwestern Oblates. Perhaps more valuable in this respect are the numerous articles by Gaston Carrière, some of which publish documentary material. Other studies of specific Oblate activities have been published by Rod Fowler (the New Caledonia Mission), Jacques Johnson (the Kisemanito training school for Native priests)—which it is well to compare with Zimmer's historical study of attempts to train priests, and Mary McCarthy, the Providence Mission (016, 326, 319-23, 351, 389, 408, 494). This section might well include Kay Cronin's popular study of Catholic work in British Columbia (024).

Father Choque published a brief, illustrated, 75th-anniversary history of the mission to Chesterfield Inlet (Igluligaarjuk) with the text in English and Inuktitut (020). The quality of the illustrations hardly bears comparison with Barbara McConnell and Michael Odesse's richly illustrated volume about the reconstructed buildings of Ste. Marie des Hurons, near Midland, Ontario. The value of the latter derives from the ethos of the museum itself: it provides a highly accessible insight into the conditions under which the early Jesuits would have lived. A video or CD rom version of this would be most useful as an educational aid (061). There are also several brief articles on individual missions scattered through Canada (308, 520, 538-40, 546, 549, 570-1, 585-87, 606).

Anglican Missions

The *Journal of the Canadian Church Historical Society* (JCCHS) continues to provide a most valuable service as an outlet for studies of missions in Canada. Though it concentrates on Anglican activities, it has on occasion ventured beyond denominational confines. Extremely important are the numerous contributions by Frank Peake, whose work over many years has strengthened the historiography of Anglican missions immeasurably. A whole issue of the journal was devoted to essays by Peake in 1989 (439-45). Other articles of note, each of which contribute materially to the historiography, are by John Archer, Brenda Hough—a sensible discussion of mission policy in the 1840s, John Long, David Nock, Winona Stevenson, Ian Whitaker, J. Wilson and Richard Lonsdale (303, 379, 406, 430, 474, 487, 493, 533, 545, 574, 598, 610).

As a representative example of these articles I will take John Long's study of Edwin Watkins, Anglican missionary to the Crees of Fort George (Chisasibi) in the 1850s. Long states that he has used CMS materials

> ...to document Watkins' activities and accomplishments in attempting to introduce new beliefs and regular patterns of worship and formal education among HBC employees and Cree hunters.

His article chronicles "a story of missionary frustration and failure, of one white man's maladaptation in a northern Algonquian environment." Fully aware of Watkins's failings, Long nevertheless writes in a non-disparaging way, providing quite a poignant insight into a man who was "unable to plumb the depths of his clients' minds and comprehend their motives or understanding" and was "frequently tempted to despair" (229).

There have also been a few broadly neutral articles about Anglican missions in other journals, including the texts of four letters by William Cockran about the Red River colony in the 1830s (350), John Long's study of George Barnley among the James Bay Cree (similar to his study of Watkins mentioned above), Robert Johns' brief overview of St. Peter's Hay River and a fragment on English missionaries among the Inuit of Baker Lake (383, 388, 407). Two articles provide positive assessments of the missionaries' influence in protecting Native people from the deleterious effects of whalers (475, 488).

The Reverend Henry Budd, one of the Anglican Church's early native clergy, left most interesting diary material, which was edited by Katherine Pettipas, who had done a Ph.D. on Budd, and published in the Manitoba Record Society series in 1974 (082, 510). A special issue of the JCCHS was devoted to him and his contemporaries (376). A less well-known employee of the CMS was an Inuk Peter Okakterook, active in the decade 1848-58, whose biography has been reconstructed by François Trudel (482).

Nonconformist, Free-Church Missions

Preeminent among items in this category is Donald Smith's thorough and scholarly study of the life of the Reverend Peter Jones (Kahkewaquonaby), who worked for the Methodist Church among the Mississauga (092). Smith's work is in many ways a model for other biographies. Whilst not lacking sympathy with its subject, it is not swept up by sentimentality. In fact, where necessary it points to grave deficiencies in mission attitudes and policies.

William Brooks' convenient but rather slight overview of British Wesleyan activities in Hudson's Bay Company territory from 1840 to 1854, published as long ago as 1970, is one of the few other dispassionate studies of non-conformist missions. More valuable as an historical source is Hugh Dempsey's edition of the Rundle journals, which has an expert introduction by Gerald Hutchinson clearly placing the papers in their historical context (026, 312; cf565). Vera Fast's comparison between James Evans and William Mason is helpful in that it reveals something of the problems of missionary personalities which are so often concealed (346, 554).

Moderately Critical Studies

Works included in this section are those whose authors, while not totally denying the legitimacy of Christian missions in principle, are critical of the thinking behind and the practical outcome of missions given the perceived effects on the First peoples. However, the criticisms are made in a balanced way. An example of this is the following passage by Ken Coates:

> The suggestion that the missionaries' efforts were of dubious or negative benefit to the...Indians...is not made in order to belittle the clergy's efforts or, even less, to challenge their sincerity. Instead, like much of the recent literature on native-missionary activities, this article is designed to move beyond hagiographic descriptions...which have so dominated the historiography in past generations. Writing on missionary activities, long the preserve of the religious community, has attracted an increasing number of secular scholars. The simultaneous expansion of work on native-white relations, both polemical and analytical, has resulted in a decidedly less favourable, though unquestionably more comprehensive, treatment of missionary activities (Coates, 1984-5, p. 27).

General

There have been several attempts at general accounts of Christian missions to the indigenous peoples of the USA, which shed some light on developments in the somewhat different conditions of Canada (003, 005, 057, 206).[16] There have also been a few interesting surveys of theories and practices adopted by missionaries to Canada ranging from the seventeenth to the twentieth centuries (352, 414, 428, 435, 438, 451, 458, 523, 592, 602, 609). However, the only general academic study of Christian missions to Canada's First peoples published since 1970 is *Moon of Wintertime* by Professor John Webster Grant, an associate of the Department of Religious Studies at the University of Toronto, who has published widely on other aspects of Canadian church history (040). Using a plethora of archival sources, Grant put together a thorough overview of the main denominations' activities. Particularly successful was his balanced and judicious final chapter, his conclusion being that the Indians had not so much rejected Christianity *per se,* but rather the "cultural genocide that seemed inseparable from it" (040, p.263). Grant acknowledged that his work was a pioneering effort which would have to be built on later. This is true, particularly since he did not look at missions to the Inuit at all, and could find very little data on the evangelical, pentecostal and charismatic missions (040, pp. vii, 202, 213). Incidentally, Grant highly approved of a far shorter study by John Badertscher, writing that it provided an "incisive analysis of early missions in Manitoba" (304, quotation from 040, p. 281). John Stackhouse wrote of Grant's groundbreaking study of condemnation of white influence upon Indians:

> Beyond Grant's lucid and often graceful writing, the book stands as exemplary history in its concern to present the players in the drama in the context of their times and cultures. Grant steadily refuses to take sides in his judgements, but also refuses a simpleminded relativism that sees everyone as just "doing their own thing" (Stackhouse, 1988, p. 70).

Instead, he consistently, if sometimes didactically, exhorts the reader to see missionary, trader, government official, or Indian within the choices available to him or her as historical characters and describes them (yes, and sometimes praises or condemns them) accordingly

> ...Grant shows the complexities of judging the effects of the encounter between missionaries—and the white colonial powers behind them—and Indians: as the native cultures were eroded, so did the Indians increasingly embrace Christianity as well as European civilization. Grant neither rejoices over nor laments this development: but it is an important fact to consider in the face of anthropologists' almost wholesale condemnation of white influence upon the Indians (*ibid.*).

I have myself grappled with defining the different categories of Christian approaches to mission and Native culture in a theoretical way recently. Other useful contributions in this area are scattered throughout the literature. I will just draw attention to contributions by Antonio Gualtieri and David Nock in this regard (332, 073a, 371-2).

Several studies combine to give us a fairly detailed knowledge of church-government relations in the Mackenzie Valley, which is clearly a fruitful field of research (200-2, 208-10).[17]

One general problem which is pointed out with some incredulity is the ferocity of nineteenth-century denominational rivalry. This usually refers to Catholic-Anglican competition in the northwest, but also to other denominations in central Canada. The most telling of these concerns the place of religious competition in the death of a girl from tuberculosis in 1931 (400, 420, 432, 465, 484).

Roman Catholic Missions

Father René Fumoleau, well known for his championing of the Native cause in the 1970s, has produced a brief but really revealing testimony plus poems about his work among the Dene (032, 353).[18] In 1953, he set off for Canada unprepared:

> It was a particular era in history. My previous training, or the lack of it, didn't seem to matter much. As long as I was an ordained priest and I could say Mass in Latin, it seemed that I didn't need any notion about anthropology, race relations, local history, culture, etc....I knew that the Dene had much to learn from me, and I was willing to give my life in order to educate them into my western values, to civilize them into the only economic and political system I knew, and most of all, I was going to save them from eternal damnation. With a bit of luck I could even recreate in Denendeh the Christendom which had disappeared in Europe...I believed that I was the one who had the truth and the whole truth. I looked at the people as at an emptiness that I could fill, and I still wanted to teach more than to listen (353, pp. 140-3).

He goes on to chart his personal transformation over the years as he evolved a far more radical understanding of the situation, and to present a balanced, sober and repentant assessment of the good and bad in missionary history, advocating the establishment of a self-reliant Dene church.

Particularly important for Catholic missionaries was the influence of the Second Vatican Council and statements by several popes that though missions were a legitimate activity, many mistakes had been made. Perhaps one of the key points in the process of reassessment and readjustment which followed was Pope John Paul II's declaration during his visit to the sanctuary to the seventeenth-century martyrs in

Huronia in 1984 (387). The struggles to adapt to the new era, and the crisis of conscience experienced by many Catholics (for instance, the Oblates were led to apologize publicly to the First Nations) may be followed in the pages of *Kerygma*[19] and in a tentative call for the Church to share the reality of the lives of previously oppressed peoples "through a ministry of presence" (602). This could be interpreted as a denial of all the Oblate Order has stood for since the 1840s. However, while there has been a change of emphasis, of mood, of approach, the Oblates are in no sense advocating a wholesale ditching of Catholic doctrine and practice. Incidentally, the recent spate of studies of Oblate history have in large part been possible because of Oblate funding for that very purpose.

The second volume of the Western Oblate series [see section on Roman Catholic Missions above], a development of a Ph.D. on the mission to the Dene by Mary McCarthy, shows the influence of these changed attitudes. She concluded that:

...the history of the Oblate missions to the Dene is one of enormous zeal, of caring and suffering, of incomprehension and understanding, of sorrow, pain and joy on both sides...the old way of "doing" missions, by charitable work combined with evangelization...must be replaced by a new way.

She supports the fashioning of a new church, the result of "a cooperative effort between priests and people" (059, quoting p. 190).[20] Her critique, therefore, whilst powerful, suggests a positive way out, though some will undoubtedly be unhappy with the extent of syncretism implied.

The third volume in the series, "an introduction to the missions of the prairie provinces" during the first century—1845-1945—is by Raymond Huel. John Foster in the foreword claims that it continues a study of the Oblates "in a positive and scholarly beneficial manner." Forthrightly yet emphatically he confronts the issues arising out of the history of the Oblates...in the process Huel has created a study that will become the hallmark against which other studies of this nature will be judged (046, p. x).

Huel himself points to the "intricate" nature of the subject, stressing that similar studies of British Columbia, the Yukon, the

Northwest Territories and the Arctic regions will have to be written to provide a complete overview, not to mention the need for in-depth studies of individual mission stations and up-to-date biographies of the missionaries themselves (*ibid.*, p. xii). It is rather ironical, therefore, that Donald Smith in reviewing Huel's book criticizes him for not probing into the personalities of individual Oblates, and providing a "dry" section on finance with the human face of the missionaries emerging rarely (Smith, 1998, pp. 343-4).

The sophistication of Huel's methodology and intellectual approach may be judged from the following passage which I quote at length. It raises issues which must be taken into account if a balanced and relatively objective mission historiography is to be developed as opposed to a descent into prejudiced polemical diatribes.

A history of Oblate [or any other DC] missionary efforts would be incomplete without an examination of the response of First Nations people to the apostolic process and the establishment of a missionary edifice...At the time of initial contact the First Nations were preliterate and left no written records but they possessed an oral tradition that provides an accurate account of its [*sic*] past. The Oblates provided an extensive chronicle of their encounter with Indians and by utilizing the canons of ethnohistory as elaborated by specialists such as James Axtell and Bruce Trigger, it is possible to use these sources to gain valuable insights on the interaction of those who were being evangelized. Axtell has suggested "a good working principle" for studying missions and missionaries: "each side of the Christian curtain has to be studied from its own perspective." From the perspective of a missionary, conversion was motivated by Christianity's superior spirituality and the desire to be redeemed. For Indians, the motives for conversion were far more complex and rooted in the "elemental fact of ethnic survival" in the face of social, cultural and economic challenges. If these two fundamental viewpoints are ignored the end result will not be a "more objective understanding" of the missionary process but the substitution of a contemporary politically correct terminology for "old prejudices" (046, pp. xii-xiii, quoting Axtell, 1985).[21]

Despite the fact that Robert Choquette's study of the Oblate experience was published only one year before Huel's, the books complement rather than clash with each other. Choquette, writing from the bilingual University of Ottawa/Université d'Ottawa has other emphases, particularly the extent to which the "love-hate relationship between Catholic and Protestant Christians in Canada" has affected French-English relations in the northwest. His overall view is that Protestant missionaries (he has in view mainly the Anglicans) were "culturally arrogant," and succeeded well only where native catechists and clergy were employed, whereas Catholic missionaries, who lived longer among their flock, learned their languages and had been brought up in a cultural and linguistic minority were more successful (021, pp. 225-33).

Whilst concluding that the Oblates played the same role as the Jesuits in seventeenth-century New France as agents of European cultural change and the suppression of indigenous religions, Choquette comes to the rather unfashionable view that:

...in both cases missionaries frequently proved to be the best allies the Indian people had among the white men. Many...devoted their entire adult careers to their Indian charges, developing lasting friendships and ties of love and affection that were severed only in death, and not even then in the eyes of the devout. Frequently the same missionaries who sought to crush and eradicate native religions lobbied and worked tirelessly for the economic, social, and communal welfare of their aboriginal flock. The French Catholic missionary frequently became a trusted adviser, leader, and friend to the people of the Northwest. That trust rested on long years, and in many cases lifetimes, of disinterested devotion and service by the missionaries. These missionaries of both seventeenth century New France and nineteenth-century Canada had committed themselves to the best interests of their aboriginal flock, as they saw them...only in the latter part of the twentieth century would the Euro-Canadians put sufficient critical distance between their own culture and religion to realize that the evangelization of Canada's Indian people need not have been the bearer of such heavy cultural baggage (021, quoting p. 236).

Other moderately critical studies of Catholic missions, varied in content and approach, include: (for the early period) Dominique Deslandres's investigations of Marie de l'Incarnation's educational policies, Claire Gourdeau's analysis of Marie's attitude to Indian culture and David Blanchard's study of catholicism at Kahnawake, 1667-1700 (309, 337-9,364). For the later period there are: Margaret Whitehead's *The Cariboo Mission*; John Foster's investigation of clashes between missionaries and Métis leadership at Red River; Thomas Lascelles's study of Léon Fouquet among the Kootenay, 1876-1887 and Jacqueline Gresko's reassessment of the Lemert thesis in the case of British Columbia (014, 349, 505; cf also 049, 069, 072, 213, 327, 486).

Anglican Missions

A book to which attention should be drawn is David Nock's "case study of different policies used by whites in their dealings with North America's native peoples." Nock follows Hobart and Brant in detecting three possible strategies for dealing with Native peoples: cultural replacement, cultural synthesis and cultural continuity. The book takes the form of an investigation of strands of the former two in the work of Rev. Edward Wilson (1844-1915), a missionary sent to the Ojibwa in 1868 by the Church Missionary Society to establish a Native church as advocated by the influential Henry Venn, who envisaged a form of cultural synthesis. The book details Wilson's failure, contributing to the explanation of why Venn's ideas did not work. It also looks at Wilson's attempts, after leaving the CMS in 1873, to apply cultural replacement by educating pupils in assimilationist schools, such as the Shingwauk and Wawanosh residential schools, whilst at the same time dreaming of "Indian self-government and the native Indian church supported by themselves" (073a, pp. 1-5). The book outlines Wilson's anthropological ideas (developed when the science was in its infancy), then poignantly assesses his dreams, experiments and eventual disillusionment. Though Nock has been criticized for failing to come to grips with Wilson the man (Rawlyk, 1988; 580), nevertheless the book is a must for understanding the motivations and actions of CMS personnel in the Victorian era.

William Duncan, another rather controversial figure, became extremely well-known in the late Victorian period for his establishment of Metlakatla, a model village for Christian Indians in

British Columbia, which he then moved to Alaska. A positive study of his work was included under the first section, second subsection above (006). There are two more critical appraisals, which are best read in conjunction with Bowman: one by Peter Murray, the other by Jean Usher. An additional short evocation is included in an issue of the popular regional historical periodical *Raincoast Chronicles* (071, 098, 489).[22]

Brett Christophers investigated the activities of John Good, an Anglican missionary sent to British Columbia by the high church Society for the Propagation of the Gospel (SPG). The book traces Good's work with the Nlha7kápmx (Thompson) people of the Fraser River valley in British Columbia, examining "why it was that the Nlha7kápmx first solicited Good in 1867, what it was about his mission that absorbed them through the 1870s, and why they deserted him towards the end of the decade." He studied Good's methods, his influences on the Nlha7kápmx and vice versa and Good's role in dealings with the authorities as a spokesperson for the Nlha7kápmx (022, quoting p. xix). Particularly interesting is the section dealing with the Mission's decline and collapse in the late 1870s, which is blamed partly on Bishop Hills' insistence on enforcing rigorous monogamy, Good's financial and family problems, social changes brought about by the influx of railway construction gangs and Good's inability, however hard he petitioned, to prevent Nlha7kápmx land being lost to settlers (022, chapter 7). This is a rather sad story told within the context of mission developments in other parts of the British Empire. Note also an article on Good by Frank Peake, whose subtitle "The Trials and tribulations of the Church, 1861-1899" neatly sums up Good's dilemmas (444).

A very balanced and well-researched study is E. Palmer Patterson's *Mission on the Nass*, a study of Anglican and Methodist work among the Nishga from 1860 to the 1890s, which has a postscript bringing the account into the twentieth century (588).

Several unpublished research dissertations about Anglican missions testify to the existence of a large quantity of easily obtainable, original sources in English (500, 502, 503, 508, 510).

Consequently, though less worked on than Catholic missions, Anglican mission historiography is by now reasonably thorough, particularly when the following substantial and helpful articles are taken into consideration: Ian Getty's study of the failure of the CMS native church policy in the northwest, which goes very well with an article by David Nock covering southwest Ontario and Algoma; Ken Coates's studies of the Yukon; John Long's look at the pluses and minuses of Anglican influence in James Bay; Barry Gough's studies of missionaries in British Columbia who opposed customs both Native (potlach) and white (rum) of which they disapproved; Jean Usher's critique of CMS social policy; Kerry Abel's moderately critical survey of the relationship between Bishop Bompas and the Canadian Anglicans; and Nancy Saxberg's unusual *Archeology and History of an Anglican Mission* (090, 200, 208-210, 216, 328, 357-8, 404, 431, 483). Very recently Christopher Trott of Concordia University published two extremely interesting articles on the rival Anglican and Catholic attempts to convert the Baffin Island Inuit (1929-47), and the upheaval caused by a prophetic experience which happened to an Inuit woman (480-1).

Nonconformist, Free-Church Missions

Jacqueline Gresko in her review of Clarence Bolt's *Thomas Crosby and the Tsimshian* expressed considerable satisfaction that this book had been written: "Historians have long hungered for a book-length study of Methodist missions to the First Nations of British Columbia to compare with work available on other missionaries" (004).[23] The book investigates why half the Port Simpson Tsimshian became Methodists during Thomas and Emma Crosby's term there (1873-97), the others continuing to follow their traditional practices, and why they eventually clashed with him and invited the Salvation Army as replacement leaders. Bolt concluded that when Crosby had to offer what the Indians wanted, they followed him, the Indians determining their own religious future, and not being mere missionary dupes.[24] As Gresko points out, Margaret Whitehead came to a similar conclusion about the Carrier and Gitksan's reaction to Father Adrien Morice's Catholic mission (*Canadian Historical Review*, 1994, pp. 101-2).

Gerald Hutchinson's study of British Methodists and the Hudson's Bay Company demonstrates the influence of denominational divisions on mission successes (223). Isaac Makindisa's Ph.D. on Henry Bird Steinhauer, the Ojibway Methodist preacher, adds considerably to the historiography of Methodist mission methods and personnel, as does

H. Maclean's MA on Methodist schooling for the Indians of Upper Canada (507-8). Jennifer Brown's two articles probe into the issue of encounter, exchange and dependency (313-4). Whereas Jennifer Brown uses Methodist lantern slides to evaluate Victorian attitudes towards the Native peoples, Sarah Carter presents a really illuminating analysis of attitudes revealed in publications by the foremost Methodist ministers of their day: John McDougall, John MacLean and Egerton Ryerson Young (325). Philip Smith's brief excursion into the failure of Methodist missions to go among the Beothuks, which wistfully asks whether the presence of missionaries would have prevented this people's extermination, is one of very few contributions about the Maritime region (471). Another slant is the attempt by John Badertscher to see missions of the (now) United Church as other people saw them, to admit to and learn from errors in the past (204).

Very welcome because of their rarity almost as much as their content are recent studies of Moravian missions (422, 534-5, 560, 562, 600) and two studies on the role of women in Methodist and Presbyterian missions (218, 240). An article about the Society in Scotland for Propagating Christian Knowledge (SSPCK) is of interest in revealing a "colonialist" Anglican attitude towards missionary outreach in the remote Scottish Highlands, which was used as a model for missions to North American. However, the missions in question took place in the eastern United States and not Canada (415).

Severe Criticisms and Works Imbued with Strong Ideological Convictions

Publications placed in this category are written from a position of hostility towards Christianity in general and missions in particular, a group John Foster has called "'politically correct' secularists" (Huel, 1996, p. x). The declared aim of some of these studies is to delightedly carry out an autopsy on a failed enterprise (203).[25] Because of their general approach they tend to ignore or severely downplay spiritual and theological issues. Far removed in worldview from the mindset of missionaries they tend to misjudge missionary motives, or interpret them in an alien way. Nevertheless, their use of disciplinary approaches does yield important new information, and provides an array of new angles from which the whole process can be assessed. As regards historians of the Prairie west, Frits Pannekoek, following views expressed earlier by Philip Goldring, presents a critique of this "secular skepticism," holding that by "taking sides" post World War II historians have sometimes "compromised the possibility of a careful dispassionate view of the impact of the clergy." There is an acceptance of the secular bias of secondary sources and a lack of consultation of church documents, though Pannekoek admits that some historians recognize that:

> ...the missionary record does offer insight into the social conditions of those not likely to figure largely in the correspondence of the influential and literate.

He suggests that church historians should "encourage their colleagues to jump the barriers of secular prejudice" (Pannekoek, 1991, pp. 29-35).

It is also pertinent to quote John Stackhouse's remark about Bruce Trigger's repudiation of European "ethnocentricity" in his celebrated *Natives and Newcomers*. Stackhouse writes:

> First, he never defined this frequently used term, and does not discuss the basic hermeneutical problems involved, leading one to wonder whether Trigger really believes that he and his fellow anthropologists can study the Indians "objectively," and, if not, what he would posit as the correct alternative approach to this study. And second, the book virtually establishes a new ethnocentricity, this one centred upon the Indians, and the traders who had the most contact with their cultures...(Stackhouse, 1988, p. 72).

General

Carol Devens writes from a strongly feminist, anti-colonial viewpoint. Two of her most forcibly put arguments are that (a) in pre-contact, indigenous, North-American societies the sexes were equal and missionaries from various denominations ruined the position of Aboriginal women by introducing patriarchalism and (b) women were less likely to accept Christianity than men and were less ardent as believers (340). Ruth Brouwer in a review of the book criticizes the "ideologically fashionable introduction," and contends that:

...neither argument is as original, or as convincing, as the book's dust-jacket copy would have us believe...generalizations about all Native people on the basis of a study that deals mainly with Ojibwa communities should provoke scepticism.

Yet she does allow that Devens's work provides some fascinating insights into the role gender could play in influencing Native acceptance of Christianity (Brouwer, 1993, pp. 623-4). In 1996, a whole issue of *Ethnohistory* was devoted to Native women's responses to Christianity. Most germane to this paper are the articles by Jo-Anne Fiske on Carrier women. Earlier, Eleanor Leacock had published two articles on Montagnais women and the Jesuits, Myra Rutherdale investigates the colonial role of women in Anglican missions and Margaret Whitehead investigates Protestant ideas about what would make Native women "useful Christian women" (227, 397, 427, 466, 490).[26] Interestingly enough Christophers investigated Devens's main contentions in his study of the Nlha7kápmx, and failed to find corroborating evidence (022, p. 133).

Assimilationist policies tend to be attacked throughout the literature. Elmer Miller's contends that missionaries were in reality agents of secularization, as does Hilary Rumely's MA on religious and social change among the Indians of British Columbia (418, 511).

The investigation of syncretist developments among First Peoples communities has provoked a great deal of investigation by critics of mission, many of whom have been anthropologists interested in acculturation and the protection of cultural diversity. Particularly significant studies undertaken by Antonio Gualtieri, who visited 16 Inuit and Dene communities in the western Arctic during 1971 concluded that there had been relatively little "indigenization" of Christianity in the region. I have looked at Gualtieri's conclusions in my comparative article (040, 371-2, 332). Certain other studies point to a great deal of syncretism, especially among nominally Catholic groups (361), while others cast a very critical eye at the extent of acculturation brought about by the missionaries' deliberate policies of culture change (038, 047, 212, 215, 336, 368, 373, 375, 382, 384-5, 425, 462-4, 481, 522, 526, 530-1, 547, 564, 567, 604).

Anthropologists and historians are also intrigued by the phenomenon of prophetic movements among Native peoples, a "neo-shamanism" arising subsequent to missionary encounters, which often contains elements taken from Christianity whilst reacting strongly against its exponents. Some are actively promoting the reintroduction of shamanic practices (222, 230, 302, 307, 354, 366, 390, 405, 434, 459, 461, 477, 481, 492).

A particularly strong form of syncretism was developed by an Oblate, Father Vandersteene, who experimented with a "noble attempt to synthesize a genuinely Cree Catholic Church" but ended up leading his adherents into a religious and cultural dead end. A study of this experiment by Earle Waugh has recently been published by Wilfrid Laurier University Press (101).[27]

Some researchers investigate "medical" competition between missionaries and shamans. On occasion this is linked with disapproval of the introduction of European medical methods into societies which had a functioning traditional medicine system. Sometimes well-intentioned interventions are held to be disastrous, particularly in the case of Brother Hooker in Alaska (302, 347, 392, 395, 429, 461, 467, 566).

There are a couple of Japanese investigations into why it was ever considered necessary for indigenous peoples, Inuit and Indian respectively, to become Christians. These are interesting because a certain distance from eurocentred thought patterns gives them an unusual point of approach (225, 233).

On the vexed question of Native residential schools, James Miller's recent *Shingwauk's Vision*, has received a somewhat mixed reception. Though the majority of reviews have been positive, hailing it as "balanced, comprehensive, timely," a "substantive history" and "fair in its assessment of the schools," the *Canadian Catholic Review* reviewer said that it raised questions about the extent to which professional historians should set aside any pretence at objectivity in their eagerness to attack those they thought were to blame (Choquette, 1996, pp. 21-3).[28] Elsewhere his study has been denounced as "a partisan essay" lacking in systematic data about the schools. Robert Choquette writes:

What is most striking about Miller's book is his unrelenting criticism, concern for people. indeed condemnation of just about all the actions of white people in the matter of residential schooling...and he repeatedly and repeatedly and repeatedly reiterates the judgement that these schools, which simply did not work, had just about everything wrong with them...the stories that show the schools in a more favourable light are dismissed out of hand...had Miller's research been as thorough in French sources as it was in English ones, he would have discovered much more evidence of positive evaluations of Indians by missionaries, of devotion by missionaries to their charges, of lives sincerely given over to the welfare of Indians, not out of some warped interest in assimilating them but out of authentic care and concern for people.[29]

Kerry Abel, on the other hand, holds that "advocacy is a legitimate role for historians," but argues that:

...we need to be more open in communicating such purposes to a general public that still believes history is about uncovering truth, and facts are facts with no room for interpretation

and cautions that:

...it is also easy to twist ahistorical interpretations from our evidence if we become too involved in drawing information from the past purely for the purpose of constructing an argument that speaks to a contemporary issue (Abel, 1996, p. 97).

Other more or less critical studies of the schools issue, either in seventeeth-century New France or in nineteenth- and twentieth-century Canada, have been written by at least a dozen scholars (043, 047, 209, 219-20, 226, 231, 234-6, 241, 318, 328, 340, 344, 388, 402-3, 419, 450, 456, 476, 479, 504, 506, 557).[30]

One article which stands out is Allison Mitcham's investigation of contemporary (to the early 1970s) French- and English-language fiction about "northern mission, priest, parson and prophet" (421). The only follow-up to this so far seems to be Jamie Scott's "Colonial,

Neo-Colonial, Post-Colonial: Images of Christian Mission" which investigates works by Hiram Cody, Rudy Wiebe and Basil Johnston (468). Incidentally, the latter is a fine evocation of life in a residential school by one Indian (048).

Roman Catholic Missions

Kerry Abel completed a Ph.D. on the Dene, ethnohistorical in nature, and very critical of Oblate and Anglican Church Missionary Society influence. This has since been published (001, 500). I quote a response to it from Mary McCarthy:

> Writing as an ethnohistorian, trying to consider both sides of the missions, she emphasized the Dene independence in religion, and claimed that previous writers, including myself, had given too much weight to the missionary side of the equation. Leaning heavily on anthropological scholarship, she concluded that "ultimately...the Christian missions have not made profound changes in the daily lives or cultural outlook of the Dene." (p. 326)

> I disagree with this conclusion and believe that the Catholicism preached to the Dene by the Oblates, and accepted by them almost on their own terms, did have a profound impact on their lives and outlook. This does not mean that they completely altered themselves; no one would expect such a result. The history of their acceptance of Catholicism shows that these spirit-guided people were able to integrate the spirituality of catholicism into their lives, fit its rules of conduct into their society like the traditional guidance of the elders, and find in its rituals and sacraments helpful spiritual contacts in times of trouble or joy. The catholicism they incorporated became theirs; no one has the right to define it out of existence (059, pp. xxi-xxii).

Naturally, both these scholars are speaking from committed positions. It would be difficult to find a median position of agreement between them.

Criticism of the Jesuits' policies and activities in New France have been sustained and wide-ranging (047, 227, 373, 384-5, 397, 462-4).

This reached a new level of ferocity recently with *Rhétorique et conquête missionnaire*, a series of essays edited by Réal Ouellet (075; cf528, 576, 601). Ramsay Cook wrote in a review of the collection, much of which focusses on Father Lejeune:

> The...writers utilize literary and cultural criticism, rhetorical analysis, feminism, and psychoanalysis as interpretative tools. None...seems much interested in theology...The Lejeune that emerges from this analysis is neither the intelligent, stubborn, dedicated servant of Christ depicted by Father Lucien Campeau nor the crypto-humanist Father Laforgue of Brian Moore. Instead we are introduced to a sado-masochistic (perhaps even a closet homosexual) priest excited by bloody violence and even cannibalism, whose propagandistic writings are filled with images of militant, even bellicose Christianity and a blind inability to comprehend the native people of the St. Lawrence region...such a hostile account...until recently, could only have come from a Protestant polemicist, and *orangiste*. But in contemporary Quebec these attitudes are commonplace. The weakness of this new orthodoxy is that it often ignores historical context (Cook, 1994 pp. 280-1).

Anne-Hélène Keribiou's *Les Indiens de l'Ouest canadien vus par les Oblats* is an analysis of a collection of 280 photographs which purports to tell us about the ideological presuppositions of the photographers, but it falls down because:

> Keribiou adopte, sans la moindre critique, les interprétations de certains auteurs...le texte contient des inexactitudes historiques...et l'interprétation que l'auteur fait sienne est souvent simpliste et superficielle, voire fantaisiste, quand il n'invente pas tout bonnement (049).[31]

I felt that I had to mention a couple of novels here, both of which attack the seventeenth-century Catholic missionary enterprise. Brian Moore's *Black Robe* (since made into a film) explores the misunderstandings, trials and sexual frustrations of Father Laforgue. Based on research into the *Jesuit Relations*, it uses particularly explicit vocabulary to convey the coarseness of the language used by the Algonkians, and explores ritual cannibalism to some extent. William

Vollman's novel provides a curious, haunting and rather peculiar attempt to encapsulate on paper a "tragic tale of secular and religious imperialism," the "economic and cultural rape of Canada" by seventeenth-century fur traders and Jesuits. This labyrinth is certainly worth exploring (068, 100).

Equally injurious, not least to the reputation of one well-advertised nineteenth-century missionary to British Columbia, has been the severely critical psychological/historical study of Father Adrien Morice by David Mulhall (070). Clearly, investigation of the psychological effects of an alien environment and cultural milieu on the missionaries is a legitimate form of study, but the results seem to reflect the preconceptions of the investigators as much as those of the objects of that study. For instance, a startling contrast with the Ouellet findings mentioned above is provided by Anya Mali, writing from the Hebrew University of Jerusalem. She concludes her 1996 study like this:

The missionaries were impressed and influenced by the natives. Paul Le Jeune's rueful comment that if Christians were to execute "all their divine inspirations with as much care as our savages carry out their dreams, no doubt they would very soon become great Saints", indicates that native culture gave the missionaries ample food for thought regarding both the harvest of souls and the sanctification of souls. What missionary writings from New France make clear is that in order to make sense of strange encounters it was becoming increasingly important for individuals to trust personal experience rather than relying exclusively on prevailing conceptions or traditional rules. Indeed, the case of the missionaries and contemplatives in New France suggests that at a time when the Catholic Church was busy delegating watch-dogs to monitor and regulate all spheres of Catholic life—from basic morals to complex theological points, from mystical claims of individuals to the collective enterprise of the overseas missions—there was still room for individuals to follow their own instincts and listen to their own dreams with regard to religious experience, be it the conversion of others, or their own ongoing spiritual conversion (576, p. 88).

Anglican Missions

The Anglican Church in Canada signalled a reexamination of its relations with the First peoples as early as 1969, at a time when activists like Harold Cardinal were first voicing the Indians' displeasure with their colonial treatment. *Beyond Traplines: Does the Church Really Care?* opened a debate which has never ceased since (044). At the extreme liberal end of the Anglican debate there have been attempts to formulate a radical new approach in which an amalgamation of Christian and traditional native beliefs would be welcomed (045).[32] To the more evangelical wing of the Church this is unacceptable, since it appears to dump the Church's traditional values and beliefs in favour of a new syncretism. Many traditional Anglicans would not be at all happy, for instance, with the approval of sweat lodge rituals.[33]

Nonconformist, Free-Church Missions

A very interesting article by Dacree McLaren from McMaster University discusses the role of two Dakota men, Peter Hunter and John Thunder, employed by the Presbyterian Church of Canada to minister to their own people. McLaren argues that

> ...both men used the office of missionary and the symbols of Christianity to communicate their needs to the dominant white society and to achieve their goals on behalf of the Dakota people...willingly adapting to Euro-Canadian institutions if those institutions were useful to the Dakota...They appropriated mission work and Christianity to serve as a platform, manipulated Christian symbols and concepts to attract attention and reinforce their personal status, and capitalized on the economic advantages of Christian conversion (409, quoting pp. 277, 298).

The problem with this type of analysis is that it makes no allowance for the supernatural or for the internalization of faith, assuming that human beings are basically utilitarian. It is a bleak way of looking at people.

Christian Missions to Canada's First Peoples: A Bibliography of Works Published since 1970

A bibliography of Christian missions to the North-American Indians was published in 1978 (Ronda and Axtell, 1978), but since then no systematic survey has appeared in print.[34] This bibliography contains directly relevant books, articles and essays in books published since 1970. I have also included unpublished theses. Several journals of Christian provenance have been indispensable in compiling this list. The historiography of Anglican missions has been well served for many years in the pages of the *Journal of the Canadian Church Historical Society*. Catholic missions (and particularly the exploits of the Oblates) have had several periodicals devoted to them, not all of which I have been able to mine systematically. They include *Études Oblates*, *Vie Oblate* and *Kerygma*, a pastoral journal published since 1967 by the Institute of Mission Studies of St. Paul's University, Ottawa, intended to be: "a communication medium between missionaries on the one hand, [and] between the missionaries and the Institute of Missiology on the other" (Kerygma, 1981), which includes interesting letters from missionaries. Recently they have been joined by *Western Oblate Studies/Études oblates de l'Ouest* [unfortunately unavailable to me]. The publications of the *Study Sessions of the Canadian Catholic Historical Association/Sessions d'études de la société canadienne d'histoire de l'Église catholique* have also included very relevant material over the years. The more important of the non-Christian journals have been *Ethnohistory*, *Études/Inuit/Studies* and *Studies in Religion/Sciences Religieuses*.

However, the booklist is not exhaustive. It omits denominational and diocesan histories, and works containing short sections on missions, like Part 2 of Miller (James) (1989) *Skyscrapers Hide the Heavens* (Revised ed., Toronto: U. of Toronto Press), Chapter 6 of Fisher (Robin) (1977) *Contact and Conflict: Indian-European Relations in British Columbia, 1774-1890* (Vancouver: UBC Press) and Chapter 5 of Trigger (Bruce) (1985) *Natives and Newcomers* (Kingston/Montreal: McGill-Queen's U. Press). I have omitted most pamphlet and newsletter material (such as, for instance, contributions to *Eskimo*, the magazine of the Catholic Diocese of Churchill-Hudson Bay, or *Arctic News* published by the Anglican Diocese of the Arctic), even though these contain many useful and interesting items. Nor have

I included general studies of the theory and practice of cross-cultural mission.

Information about archive materials and earlier publications may be found both in reference sources such as MacDonald (Wilma) (1986) *Guide to the Holdings of the Archives of the Ecclesiastical Province and Dioceses of Rupert's Land* (Winnipeg: St. John's College Press; Records of the Anglican Church of Canada, no. 1) and in many of the items listed below. Luca Codignola's meticulously researched paper on the Holy See (item 211) contains particularly impressive details of finding aids to Vatican records and references to publications on early European-Amerindian contacts.

It is important to include a word of caution about some mission agency publications. Assessing two journals produced by the high church Anglican Society for the Propagation of the Gospel (SPG), Brett Christophers writes:.

> ...the letters contained in these volumes have been heavily censored...Simon Carey points out that the printed extracts of Bishop Hills's journal "have been edited by missionary society secretaries with such loyalty and tact that the human and courageous figure of the original tends, in the published version, to emerge as a sanctimonious prig."...Editors actually cut out contentious material, such as conflicts among missionary churches, disputes between missionaries and colonial officials, so on (022, quoting Carey, (Simon) (1982) "The Church of England and the Colour Question in Victoria, 1860" *Journal of the Canadian Church Historical Society*, vol. 24, 63.

Notes

1. I have in mind publications such as the World Council of Churches' *International Review of Mission*, the South African Missiological Society's *Missionalia*, the American Society of Missiology's *Missiology: An International Review*, the *International Bulletin of Missionary Research, Mission Studies*, the Journal of the International Association for Mission Studies, the *Evangelical Missions Quarterly* and *Bibliografia Missionaria*, published in the Vatican by the Pontifical Mission Library of the Congregation for the Evangelisation of Peoples.

2. Writing as an historian educated in the western liberal Anglophone conviction that objectivity and even-handedness is an ideal to be aimed at, I am nevertheless aware that my approach is bound to be affected by my Pentecostal Christian beliefs.

3. The Bibliography, which is undoubtedly incomplete, contains 445 entries.

4. See, for instance, in date order of first publication, Laut, (1905) "Père Lacombe: A Wilderness Apostle of the North" *Outing Magazine* April, reprinted with its illustrations in Oppel, compiler, (1984) *Tales of the Canadian North*, Secaucus, NJ: Castle, pp. 75-89; Talbot, (1935) *Saint Among Savages: the Life of Isaac Jogues*, New York: Harper; Ferland, (1944) *Sentinelles du Christ: les soeurs grises de Montréal à la Baie d'Hudson* (Montréal: Imprimerie de l'Hôpital Général, Sœurs grises de Montréal), whose 1944 English translation was entitled *Arctic Angels: An Enthusiastic Account of the Grey Nuns' Heroic Work Among the Eskimos of the Northern Waters*; Talbot, (1949) *Saint Among the Hurons: the Life of Jean de Brébeuf* (New York: Harper)—which appeared in Spanish (1951) Barcelona: L. Miracle and German (1952) Salzburg: Müller; Charron, (1950) *Mère Bourgeoys 1620-1700*, Montréal: Beauchemin; Groulx, (1962) *Le Canada Français. Missionnaires: une autre grande aventure*, Montréal: Fides.

5. It would be a useful exercise to compare their approaches to the subject, given the changes in public perceptions during the twenty years separating their publication, with each other and with Lamirande, (1990), published in the new periodical *Western Oblate Studies/Études oblates de l'Ouest*. I have unfortunately not had access to the latter.

6. See also Pattison, (1995) "Images of Another Time: Winifred Marsh Among the Padlimiut," *Up Here Magazine* September/October, pp. 30-37, 53 which reproduces some of them. The originals are in the Prince of Wales Heritage Centre in Yellowknife.

7. Based on Cody, (1908) *Apostle of the North* (London: Seely, Service) and Archer, (1929) *A Heroine of the North: Memoirs of Charlotte Selina Bompas, with Extracts from the Journals and Letters*, compiled by S. A. Archer (London: SPCK). Constance Savery wrote more than thirty other brief "Stories of Faith and Fame," including one about Wilfred Grenfell.

8. I have not read this (it should probably be in the second or third category). Grenfell wrote of his religious beliefs in chapter 26 of his 1920 autobiography.

9. My article "Christian Missions and First Peoples: Fifty Years of the Northern Canada Evangelical Mission," item 333, contains brief details of the missions in question.

10. There are people in most denominations now who are theologically pentecostal/charismatic. For instance, there are charismatics in the Anglican Diocese of the Arctic. The discussion here, however, is about groups outside the main denominations.

11. Correspondence with author, July 1998.
12. Critique in Trigger, (1985) *Natives and Newcomers,* Kingston: McGill-Queen's University Press, p. 46. A review by Luca Codignola is slightly more positive: "Bien que Campeau ait ignoré d'une manière superficielle et injustifiée un siècle d'historiens et de débats historiographiques, le volume IV des *Monunenta Novae Franciae* deviendra un outil essentiel pour le spécialiste de la Nouvelle-France et de l'époque de la rencontre entre Européens et Amérindiens, comme l'est d'ailleurs déjà toute la série." *Revue d'histoire de l'Amérique française* vol. 44, no. 1, (1990), quoting p.103. Elsewhere (item 542) the quality of these sources has been compared with the vast, but somewhat dated, edition of the Jesuit Relations by Reuben Thwaites. Incidentally, Thwaites has come under attack recently for biased editorial work (item 564).
13. See, for instance, the short survey in Francis *et al.,* (1992) *Origins: Canadian History to Confederation,* 2nd. ed. Toronto: Holt, Rinehart and Winston of Canada, pp. 175-7.
14. Quoted from a promotional leaflet.
15. See also an article by Gilles Lesage, 401.
16. 003 and 005 are fairly critical of Christian missions in principle, and could perhaps be assigned to the fourth category.
17. The work by Coates was published in greater detail in 1991, *Best Left as Indians: Native-White Relations in the Yukon Territory, 1840-1973,* Montreal, Kingston: McGill-Queen's University Press, chapters 6, 7 and 10.
18. See also Fumoleau, (1973) *As Long as This Land Shall Last: A History of Treaty 8 and Treaty 11, 1870-1939,* Toronto: McClelland and Stewart.
19. Published by the Institute of Mission Studies of St. Paul's Catholic University, Ottawa. See nos. 300, 335, 343, 359-60, 363, 377, 403, 423. See also nos. 053, 081.
20. See also her earlier, less mature study 060, covering Manitoba.
21. See also Axtell, (1982) "Some Thoughts on the Ethnohistory of Mission," *Ethnohistory* vol. 29, pp. 35-41 and Trigger, (1986) *Natives and Newcomers: Canada's "Heroic Age" Reconsidered,* Montreal: McGill-Queen's University Press.
22. There are substantial sections on Duncan's work in Fisher, (1977) *Contact and Conflict,* Vancouver: UBC Press, and in no. 040.
23. Gresko's review (1994) *Canadian Historical Review* (*CHR*) vol. 75, pp. 100-3 is generally favourable, but points out many leads, particularly in respect of women, that Bolt did not follow up.
24. See the article no. 310 for a clear statement of this conclusion.
25. See also critical studies such as 205, 207.
26. Other items which stress the issue of gender are: 025, 341, 391, 546, 567. Contrast these with 478 about missionary wives.
27. Quotation from "Review" (1998), *CHR,* vol. 79, no. 2, pp. 348-9.

28. 067; "Review" (1998), *CHR*, vol. 79, no. 1, pp. 130-1.
29. Donald Smith's review of 046 makes a related point: A Sarcee elder, Lucy Big Plume Tsuu T'ina, who had been at Dunbow Industrial School expressed approval of the missionaries' help in establishing education, (1998) *CHR*, vol. 79, no. 2, p. 344.
30. Incidentally, the last of these, Elizabeth Furness's *Victims of Benevolence*, now published (553) has been slammed as "disappointing...inadequate and often misleading", (1997) *CHR*, vol. 78, pp. 690-2. See also 539, 574, 590, 598.
31. The quotation is from a "Review." (1997) *CHR*, vol. 78, pp. 360-1.
32. See also the very radical appeal in no. 473 to engage in another mission, this time to bring the Native Americans back to their previous beliefs.
33. From personal conversations.
34. A considerable database, particularly for the earlier period, has been established by researchers working for the North Atlantic Missiology Project (NAMP), based at the faculty of Divinity in Cambridge. A CD rom containing over 70 "position papers" of related researchers is being published soon. See www.divinity.cam.ac.uk/carts/namp/ or visit the discussion site: Missions-namp@mailbase.ac.uk.

References

Abel, K. (1996) "Tangled, Lost and Bitter: Current Directions in the Writing of Native History in Canada," *Acadiensis*, vol. 26, no. 1.
Axtell, J. (1985) *The Invasion Within: The Contest of Cultures in Colonial North America*, New York: Oxford University Press.
Brouwer, R. (1993) "Review," *Canadian Historical Review*, vol. 74.
Choquette, R. (1996) "Partisan History," *Canadian Catholic Review*, November.
Cook, R. (1994) "Review," *Canadian Historical Review*, vol. 75.
Ferguson, B., Editor, (1991) *The Anglican Church and the World of Western Canada, 1820-1870*, Regina: Canadian Plains Research Centre.
Fisher, R. (1977) *Contact and Conflict*, Vancouver: UBC Press.
Francis, D. *et al.*, (1992) *Origins: Canadian History to Confederation*, Toronto: University of Toronto Press.
Fumoleau, R. (1973) *As Long as This Land Shall Last: A History of Treaty 8 and Treaty 11, 1870-1939*, Toronto: McClelland and Stewart.
Gagan, R. (1992) *A Sensitive Independence: Canadian Methodist Women's Missionary Work*, Montreal, Kingston; McGill Queen's University Press.
Gould, S. (1917) *Inasmuch. Sketches of the Beginnings of the Church of England in Canada in Relation to the Indian and Eskimo Races*, 2nd ed., Toronto: Missionary Society of the Church of England in Canada.
Grenfell, W. (1920) *A Labrador Doctor: The Autobiography of Wilfred Thomason Grenfell*, London: Hodder & Stoughton.
Grenfell, W. (1933) *Forty Years for Labrador*, London: Hodder & Stoughton.
Oppel, F. (1984) *Tales of the Canadian North*, Secaucus, NJ: Castle.
Pannekoek, F. (1991) "'Insidious Sources' and the Historical Interpretation of the Pre-1870 West" in Ferguson, B. Editor, *The Anglican Church and the*

World of Western Canada, 1820-1870, Regina: Canadian Plains Research Center.

Rawlyk, G. (1988) "Review," *Canadian Book Review Annual.*

Regehr, T. (1996) *Mennonites in Canada, 1939-1970: A People Transformed*, Toronto: University of Toronto Press.

Ronda, J. and Axtell, J. (1978) *Indian Missions: A Critical Bibliography*, Bloomington: Indiana UP.

Smith, D. (1998) "Review," *Canadian Historical Review*, vol. 79, no. 2.

Stackhouse, J. (1988) "Pioneers and Revisionists," *Fides et Historia*, vol. 20, no. 3.

Trigger, B. (1985) *Natives and Newcomers*, Kingston: McGill-Queen's University Press.

Tucker, S. (1856) *The Rainbow in the North: A Short Account of the First Establishment of Christianity in Rupert's Land by the Church Missionary Society*, London: James Nisbet.

Young, E. (1899) *The Apostle of the North: Rev. James Evans*, London: Marshall Brothers.

Young, E. (1903) *By Canoe and Dog Train Among the Cree and Saulteaux Indians*, London: Charles Kelley.

Young, E. (1903) *My Dogs in the Northland*, London: S. W. Partridge.

Bibliography

Books

001   ABEL (Kerry) (1993) *Drum Songs. Glimpses of Dene History* (Montreal: McGill-Queen's UP)

002   ANDERSON (Gerald) Ed. (1988) *Biographical Dictionary of Christian Missions* (New York: Macmillan Reference/Simon & Schuster and Prentice Hall International)

003   BERKHOFER (Robert) (1976) *Salvation and the Savage: An Analysis of Protestant Missions and American Indian Response, 1787-1862* 2nd ed. (New York: Atheneum)

004   BOLT (Clarence) (1992) *Thomas Crosby and the Tsimshian: Small Shoes for Feet too Large* (Vancouver: UBC Press)

005   BOWDEN (Henry) (1981) *American Indians and Christian Missions: Studies in Conflict* (Chicago, U. of Chicago Press)

006   BOWMAN (Phylis) (1983) *Metlakatla - the Holy City* (Chilliwack, BC: Sunrise Printing)

007   BRABANT (Augustin) (1977) *Mission to Nootka, 1874-1900*, ed. by Charles Lillard (Sidney, BC: Gray's Publishing)

008   BROWN (Mildred) (1977) *The Top of the World: the Story of Ken and Sarah Gaetz, Dan and Grace Priest and many Other Missionaries in the Northwest Territories* (Saskatoon: Modern Press)

009   CADIEUX (Lorenzo) (1973) ed. *Lettres des nouvelles missions du Canada, 1843-1852* (Montréal: Bellarmin/Paris: Maisonneuve et Larose)

010   CAMPEAU (Lucien) (1983) *Gannetaha. Première mission iroquoise (1653-1665)* (Montréal: Éditions Bellarmin) Cahiers d'histoire des Jésuites, 6

011   CAMPEAU (Lucien) (1987) *La mission des Jésuites chez les Huron (1634-1650), suivi de la formation des noms de peuples et de bourgades en Huron par Perrette-L. Lagarde* (Montréal: Éditions Bellarmin); Rome: Institutum Historicum Societatas Iesu) Bibliotheca Instituti Historici Societatis Iesu, vol. 46

012/1-6 CAMPEAU (Lucien) (1967-1992) *Monumenta Novae Franciae* (Rome/Québec: Monumenta Historia Societatis Iesu/Presses de l'Université Laval): vol. 1 (1967) *La première mission d'Acadie (1602-1616)*. Monumenta Missionum Societatis Iesu vol. 23; vol. 2 (1979) *Établissement à Québec (1616-1634)*. Monumenta Missionum Societatis Iesu vol. 37; vol. 3 (1987) *Fondation de la mission huronne (1635-1637)*. Monumenta Missionum Societatis Iesu vol. 46; vol. 4 (1989) *Les grandes épreuves (1638-1640)*. Monumenta Missionum Societatis Iesu vol. 50; vol. 5 (1990) *La bonne nouvelle reçue (1641-1643)*. Monumenta Missionum Societatis Iesu vol. 53; vol. 6 (1992) *Recherche de la paix (1644-1646)*. Monumenta Missionum Societatis Iesu vol. 57.

013   CAMPEAU (Lucien) (1972) *La première mission des Jésuites en Nouvelle-France (1611-1613), et les commencements du Collège de Québec (1626-1670)* (Montréal: Éditions Bellarmin). Cahiers d'histoire des Jésuites, 1

014   CAMPEAU (Lucien) (1994) *Les témoignages du sang (1647-1650)* (Rome: Institutum Historicum Societatis Iesu)

015   CANTWELL (Margaret) and Edmond (May George*) North to Shore: The Sisters of Saint Anne in Alaska and the Yukon Territory* (Victoria: Sisters of Saint Anne, 1992)

016   CARRIÈRE (Gaston) (1976-79) *Dictionnaire biographique des Oblats de Marie Immaculée au Canada* vols 1-3 (Ottawa: Éditions de l'Université d'Ottawa) [for vol. 4 see GILBERT...]

017a   CARTER (David) (1974) *Samuel Trivett: Missionary with the Blood Indians, or What's a Nice Boy Like You Doing in a Place like This?* (Calgary: Kyle Printing & Stationery)

017b   CHAMPAGNE (Claude) (1983) *Les débuts de la mission dans le Nord-Ouest canadien: Mission et Église chez Mgr Vital Grandin, o.m.i., 1829-1902* (Ottawa: Éditions de l'Université d'Ottawa/ Éditions de l'Université St-Paul)

018   CHOQUE (Charles) (1985) *Kajualuk. Pierre Henry, Missionary Oblate of Mary Immaculate, Apostle of the Inuit, 1904-1979: From Brittany to the Canadian North* (n.p.)

019   CHOQUE (Charles) (1994) *Mikilar: Lionel Ducharme, o.m.i,*
        apôtre des Inuit (Churchill: Corporation épiscopale)
020   CHOQUE (Charles) (1987) *Seventy-Fifth Anniversary of the First*
        Catholic Mission to the Hudson Bay Inuit, Chesterfield Inlet,
        1912-1987 (Igluligaarjuk: Diocese of Churchill Hudson Bay)
021   CHOQUETTE (Robert) (1995) *The Oblate Assault on Canada's*
        Northwest (Ottawa:University of Ottawa Press)
022   CHRISTOPHERS (Brett) (1998) *Positioning the Missionary: John*
        Booth Good and the Confluence of Cultures in Nineteenth-Century
        British Columbia (Vancouver: UBC Press)
023   COCCOLA (Raymond) [and] KING (Paul) (1986) *The Incredible*
        Eskimo: Life among the Barren Land Eskimo (Surrey: Hancock
        House)
024   CRONIN (Kay) (1976) *Cross in the Wilderness* (Toronto: Mission
        Press) [first published Vancouver: Mitchell Press, 1959 and
        Toronto: Mission Press, 1960]
025   DAVIS (Natalie) (1995) *Women on the Margins: Three*
        Seventeenth Century Lives (Cambridge, MA: Harvard U. Press)
        [one of the women is Marie de l'Incarnation]
026   DEMPSEY (Hugh) ed. (1977) *The Rundle Journals, 1840-1848,*
        introduction and notes by Gerald Hutchinson (Calgary: Historical
        Society of Alberta/Glenbow-Alberta Institute)
027   DEVENS (Carol) (1992) *Countering Colonization: Native*
        American Women and the Great Lakes Mission, 1630-1900
        (Berkeley: U. of California Press)
028   DOLPHIN (Frank) (1986) *Indian Bishop of the West: Vital Justin*
        Grandin, 1829-1902 (Ottawa: Novalis)
029   DU FRENE (Phil) Ed. (1990) *The Best of Northern Lights* vol. 1
        (Prince Albert: NCEM)
031   EVANS (Karen) (1985) *Massinikikan: A Bibliography of the*
        Native Language Imprints in the Holdings of the Anglican Church
        of Canada (Toronto: Anglican Book Centre)
032   FUMOLEAU (René) (1996) *Here I Sit* (Ottawa: Novalis)
033   GAGNON (François-Marc) (1975) *La conversion par l'image: un*
        aspect de la mission des Jésuites auprès des Indiens du Canada au
        XVII siècle (Montréal: Bellarmin)
034   GARNET (Eldon) (1977) *Brébeuf: A Martyrdom* (Erin, ON: Press
        Porcépic)
035   GARRETT (Leslie) (c.1977) *My Album of Memories* (Saskatoon:
        [n.p.])
036   GILBERT (Maurice) and MARTEL (Normand) eds. (1989)
        Dictionnaire biographique des Oblats de Marie Immaculée au
        Canada vol. 4 (Montréal: Maison provinciale)
037   GORDON (Kayy) (1977) *God's Fire on Ice*, with Lois Neely
        (Plainfield, NJ: Logos International)

038   GORDON (Kayy) (1990) *Arctic Ablaze*, with Lois Neely
       (Burlington, ON: Welch Publishing)
039   GRAHAM (Elizabeth) (1975) *Medicine Man to Missionary:*
       Missionaries as Agents of Change Among the Indians of Southern
       Ontario, 1784-1867 (Toronto: Peter Martin)
040   GRANT (John) (1984) *Moon of Wintertime: Missionaries and the*
       Indians of Canada in Encounter since 1534 (Toronto: U of
       Toronto Press)
041   GUALTIERI (Antonio) (1984) *Christianity and Native Traditions:*
       Indigenization and Syncretism among the Inuit and Dene of the
       Western Arctic 2 vols. (Notre Dame: Cross Cultural Publications,
       Cross Roads Books)
042   HADLEY (Michael) (1995) *God's Little Ships: A History of the*
       Columbia Coast Mission (Madeira Park: Harbour Publishing)
043   HAIG-BROWN (Celia) (1988) *Resistance and Renewal: Surviving*
       the Indian Residential School (Vancouver: Tillacum Library)
044   HENDRY (C.) (1969) *Beyond Traplines: Does the Church Really*
       Care? (Toronto: Anglican Book Centre) esp. pp. 21-43
045   HODGSON (Janet) and KOTHARE (Jay) (1990) *Vision Quest:*
       Native Spirituality and the Church in Canada (Toronto: Anglican
       Book Centre)
046   HUEL (Raymond) (1996) *Proclaiming the Gospel to the Indians*
       and the Métis (Edmonton: University of Alberta Press/Western
       Canadian Publishers)
047   JAENEN (Cornelius) (1976) *Friend and Foe: Aspects of*
       French-Amerindian Cultural Contact in the Sixteenth and
       Seventeenth Centuries (Toronto: McClelland & Stewart)
048   JOHNSTON (Basil) (1988) *Indian School Days* (Toronto: Key
       Porter Books)
049   KERIBIOU (Anne-Hélène) (1996) *Les Indiens de l'Ouest*
       canadien vus par les Oblats, 1885-1930 (Sillery: Septentrion)
050   KNOCKWOOD (Isabelle) (1992) *Out of the Depths: the*
       Experiences of Mi'kmaq Children at the Indian Residential School
       at Schubenacadie, Nova Scotia (Lockeport, NS: Roseway
       Publishing)
051   KOWRACH (Edward) (1992) *Charles Pandosy, o.m.i, A*
       Missionary of the Northwest. Missionary to the Yakima Indians in
       the 1850s and Later with the British Columbia Indians (Fairfield,
       WA: Ye Galleon Press)
052   LASCELLES (Thomas) (1984) *Mission on the Inlet: St. Paul's*
       Indian Catholic Church, North Vancouver, BC, 1863-1984
       (Vancouver)
053   LASCELLES (Thomas) (1990) *Roman Catholic Indian Residential*
       Schools in British Columbia (Vancouver: Order of Oblates of
       Mary Immaculate in British Columbia)

054   LaVIOLETTE (Forrest) (1973) *The Struggle for Survival: Indian
        Cultures and the Protestant Ethic in British Columbia* (Toronto: U.
        of Toronto Press) [1st ed. 1961]
055   LEVASSEUR (Donat) (1994) *Les Oblats de Marie Immaculée
        dans l'Ouest et le Nord du Canada, 1845-1967* (Edmonton: U. of
        Alberta Press)
056   Light on the Horizon (1996) *Light on the Horizon: Northern
        Canada Evangelical Mission's Fifty Years of Ministry to Canada's
        First People* (Prince Albert: NCEM)
057   LIPPY (Charles), CHOQUETTE (Robert) and POOLE (Stafford)
        (1992) *Christianity Comes to the Americas, 1492-1776* (New
        York: Paragon House)
058   LLORENTO (Segundo) (1990) *Memoirs of a Yukon Priest*
        (Washington, DC: Georgetown UP)
059   McCARTHY (Mary) (1995) *From the Great River to the Ends of
        the Earth: Oblate Missions to the Dene, 1847-1921* (Edmonton: U.
        of Alberta Press)
060   McCARTHY (Mary) (1990) *To Evangelize the Nations: Roman
        Catholic Missions in Manitoba, 1818-1870* Papers in Manitoba
        History, Report no. 2 (Winnipeg: Manitoba Culture, Heritage and
        Recreation Historic Resources)
061   McCONNELL (Barbara) and ODESSE (Michael) (1980)
        Sainte-Marie Among the Hurons (Toronto: U. of Toronto Press)
062   MacGREGOR (James) (1975) *Father Lacombe* (Edmonton:
        Hurtig)
063   MARSH (Donald) (1987) *Echoes from a Frozen Land,* edited by
        Winifred Marsh (Edmonton: Hurtig)
064   MARSH (Donald) (1991) *Echoes into Tomorrow,* edited by
        Winifred Marsh (Three Hills, AB: Prairie Graphics and Printing,
        Prairie Bible Institute)
065   MARSH (Winifred) (1976) *People of the Willow* (Toronto: Oxford
        University Press)
066   MATHESON (Shirlee) (1986) *Youngblood of the Peace: the
        Authorized Biography of Father Emile Jungbluth, o.m.i.*
        (Edmonton: Lone Pine Publishing)
067   MILLER (James) (1996) *Shingwauk's Vision: A History of Native
        Residential Schools* (Toronto: U. of Toronto Press)
068   MOORE (Brian (1985) *Black Robe* (Toronto: McClelland &
        Stewart)
069   MOORE (J.) (1982) *Indian and Jesuit: A Seventeenth-Century
        Encounter* (Chicago: Loyola U. Press)
070   MULHALL (David) (1986) *Will to Power: The Missionary Career
        of Father Adrian Morice* (Vancouver:UBC Press)
071   MURRAY (Peter) (1988) *The Devil and Mr. Duncan: A History of
        the Two Metlakatlas* (Vancouver: Sono Niss Press)

072 NEBEL (Richard) (1991) *Die Huronenmission in Kanada nach den "Relations des Jésuites de la Nouvelle-France" (1632-1673)* (Bamberg: Universität Bamberg) Kleine Beiträge zur europäische Überseegeschichte, 12

073a NOCK (David) (1988) *A Victorian Missionary and Canadian Indian Policy: Cultural Synthesis vs. Cultural Replacement* (Waterloo: Wilfrid Laurier UP, Editions SR/9)

073b Northern Canada Evangelical Mission (1996) *Light on the Horizon: Northern Canada Evangelical Mission's Fifty Years of Ministry to Canada's First People* (Prince Albert: NCEM)

074 NUTE (Grace) ed. (1972) *Documents Relating to Northwest Missions, 1815-1827* (Saint Paul: Minnesota Historical Society)

075 OUELLET (Réal) ed. (1993) *Rhétorique et conquête missionnaire: le jésuite Paul Lejeune* (Sillery: Éditions du Septentrion)

076 OURY (Guy-Marie) (1971) *Marie de l'Incarnation: Correspondance* (Solesmes: Abbaye de Saint-Pierre de Solesmes)

077 OURY (Guy-Marie) (1973) *Marie de l'Incarnation, 1599-1672* (2 vols. Tours: Abbaye de Saint-Pierre de Solesmes). Mémoires de la Société archéologique de Touraine, 59

078 OWENS (Brian) and ROBERTO (Claude) Eds. (1989) *The Diaries of Bishop Vital Grandin, 1875-1877* vol. 1, trans. by Alan Ridge (Edmonton: Historical Society of Alberta, Amisk Waskahegan Chapter)

079 PALMER (Bernard) (1971) *Journey to a Lonely Land: the Birth and Growth of the Northern Canada Evangelical Mission* (Prince Albert: NCEM)

080 PALMER (Bernard) (1970) *So Restless, So Lonely: A Fascinating, True Account of One Couple's Efforts to Reach a Canadian Indian Tribe* (Minneapolis: Bethany Fellowship)

081 PEELMAN (Achiel) (1992) *Le Christ est amérindien: Une réflexion théologique sur l'inculturation du Christ parmi les amérindiens du Canada* (Ottawa: Novalis)

082 PETTIPAS (Katherine) ed.(1974) *The Diary of the Reverend Henry Budd, 1870-1875* (Winnipeg: Hignill Printing) Publications of the Manitoba Record Society

083 POMEDLI (Michael) (1991) *William Kurelek's Huronia Mission Paintings* (Lewisburg, NY: E. Mellon Press)

084 ROCHE (Claude) (1989) *Monseigneur du Grand Nord. Isidore Clut, évêque-missionnaire, coureur des bois, chez les indiens et les esquimeaux du Nord-Ouest américain (de 1858 à 1903)* (Rennes: Ouest France) Collection "Voyage jusqu'au bout"

085 ROMPKEY (Ronald) (1991) *Grenfell of Labrador: A Biography* (Toronto, Buffalo: U. of Toronto Press)

086 RUSKELL (Arnold) (1997) *Breaking the Ice: An Arctic Odyssey* (Ste-Anne-de-Bellevue: Shoreline)

087   SALWAY (Owen) (1979) *The Bushman and the Spirits* by Barney
       Lacendre as told to Owen Salway (Beaverlodge, AB: Horizon
       House Publishers)
088   SALWAY (Owen) (c.1990) *The Lonely Search: The Life Story of
       Albert Tait* (Winnipeg: Life Books)
089   SAVERY (Constance) (1973) *God's Arctic Adventurer: The Story
       of William Bompas* (Guildford/London: Lutterworth Press)
090   SAXBERG (Nancy) (1993) *The Archeology and History of an
       Anglican Mission: Herschel Island, Yukon* (Whitehorse: Heritage
       Branch, Government of Yukon)
091   SMILEY (William) (1993) *James Nisbet (1823-1874) Founder
       [of] Prince Albert, 1866* (Prince Albert: Prince Albert Historical
       Society)
092   SMITH (Donald) (1987) *Sacred Feathers: The Reverend Peter
       Jones (Kahkewaquonaby) and the Mississauga Indians* (Toronto:
       U. of Toronto Press)
093   STEVEN (Hugh) (1982) *Good Broth to Warm our Bones (Two
       Courageous Men, Roy Ahmaogak and Don Webster Meet at the
       Top of the World the Bring the Gospel to Alaska's Inupiat People)*
       (Westchester, IL: Crossway Books)
094   STOCKEN (Harry) (1976) *Among the Blackfoot and Sarcee*, with
       an introduction by Georgeen Barrass (Calgary: Glenbow Museum)
095   TANIS (Alta) (1996) *God's Warrior: the Life Story of Ray Prince*
       (Winnipeg: Intertribal Christian Communications)
096   TARRY (Arthur) and TARRY (Martha) (1981) *The Way He Chose*
       (Prince Albert: NCEM)
097   TOUPIN (Robert) (1991) *Arpents de neige et robes noires. Brève
       relation sur le passage des Jésuites en Nouvelle-France au XVIIe
       et XVIIIe siècles* (Québec: Éditions Bellarmin)
098   USHER (Jean) (1974) *William Duncan of Metlakatla: A Victorian
       Missionary in British Columbia* (Ottawa: National Museum of
       Man)
099   VEILLETTE (John) and WHITE (Gary) (1977) *Early Indian
       Village Churches: Wooden Frontier Architecture in British
       Columbia* (Vancouver: UBC Press)
100   VOLLMANN (William) (1992) *Fathers and Crows* [second part
       of] *Seven Dreams: A Book of North American Landscapes*
       (London: Andre Deutsch)
101   WAUGH (Earle) (1996) *Dissonant Worlds: Vandersteene Among
       the Cree* (Waterloo: Wilfrid Laurier U. Press)
102   WEBSTER (J.) (c.1995) *Arctic Adventure* (Ridgetown, ON: G.C.
       & H.C. Enterprises)
103   WEISER (Franz) (1987) *Das Mädchen der Mohawks. Die selige
       Kateri Tekakwitha (1956-1680)* (Stein am Rhein: Christiana)

104   WHITEHEAD (Margaret) (1982) *The Cariboo Mission: A History of the Oblates* (Victoria, BC: Sono Nis)
105   WHITEHEAD (Margaret) ed.(1988) *They Call Me Father: Memoirs of Father Nicolas Coccola* (Vancouver: UBC Press)

Papers published in books

200   ABEL (Kerry) (1991) "Bishop Bompas and the Canadian Church" in FERGUSON (Barry) Ed. *The Anglican Church and the World of Western Canada, 1820-1970* (Regina: Canadian Plains Research Centre, University of Regina), pp. 113-25
201   ABEL (Kerry) (1989a) "'Matters are Growing Worse': Government and the Mackenzie Missions, 1870-1921" in COATES (Ken) and MORRISON (William) Eds. *For Purposes of Dominion: Essays in Honour of Morris Zaslow* (North York: Captus University Publications), pp. 73-85
202   ABEL (Kerry) (1989b) "Of Two Minds: Dene Response to the Mackenzie Missions, 1858-1902" in COATES (Ken) and MORRISON (William) Eds. *Interpreting Canada's North: Selected Readings* (Toronto: Copp Clark Pitman), pp. 77-93
203   AXTELL (James) (1975) "The European Failure to Convert the Indians: An Autopsy" in COWAN (William) Ed. *Papers of the Sixth Algonquian Conference, 1974* (Ottawa: National Museum of Man, Canadian Ethnology Service, Mercury Series)
204   BADERTSCHER (John) (1985) "As Others Saw Us" in BUTCHER (Dennis) et al., Eds. *Prairie Spirit: Perspectives on the heritage of the United Church of Canada in the West* (Winnipeg: U. of Manitoba Press), pp. 44-64
205   BEAUCAGE (Marjorie) and LaROQUE (Emma) (1983) "Two Faces of the New Jerusalem: Indian-Métis Reactions to the Missionary" in SMILLIE (Benjamin) Ed. *Visions of the New Jerusalem: Religious Settlement on the Prairies* (Edmonton: NeWest), pp. 27-38
206   BEAVER (R.) (1977) "The Churches and the Indians: Consequences of 350 Years of Mission" in BEAVER (R. Pierce) Ed. *American Missions in Bicentennial Perspective* (South Pasadena, William Carey Library), pp. 275-332
207   CAMPEAU (Lucien) (1991) "La rencontre des Indiens du Canada avec la foi chrétienne au XVIIe siècle" in LANGEVIN (C.) Ed. *Le Christ et les cultures dans le monde et l'histoire* (Montréal: Bellarmin)
208   COATES (Ken) (1991) "Asking for All Sorts of Favours: the Anglican Church, the Federal Government and the Natives of the Yukon Territory, 1891-1910" in FERGUSON (Barry) Ed. *The Anglican Church and the World of Western Canada, 1820-1970*

(Regina: Canadian Plains Research Centre, University of Regina), pp. 126-42

209   COATES (Ken) (1986) "A Very Imperfect Means of Education: Indian Day Schools in the Yukon, 1890-1955" in BARMAN (Jean) et al., Eds. *Indian Education in Canada*, vol. 1 *The Legacy* (Vancouver: UBC Press), pp. 132-49

210   COATES (Ken) and MORRISON (W.) (1986) "More Than a Matter of Blood: the Federal Government, the Churches and the Mixed Blood Populations of the Yukon and the Mackenzie River Valley, 1890-1950" in BARRON (Laurie) and WALDRAM (James) Eds. *1885 and After: Native Society in Transition* (Regina: Canadian Plains Research Centre, U. of Regina), pp. 253-77

211   CODIGNOLA (Luca) (1995) "The Holy See and the Conversion of the Indians in French and British North America, 1486-1760" in KUPPERMAN (Karen) Ed. *America in European Consciousness, 1493-1750* (Chapel Hill, NC: U. of North Carolina Press, Published for the Institute of Early American History and Culture, Williamsburg, Virginia), pp. 195-242

212   COUTTS (Robert (1991) "Anglican Missionaries as Agents of Acculturation: the Church Missionary Society at St. Andrew's, Red River, 1830-1870" in FERGUSON (Barry) Ed. *The Anglican Church and the World of Western Canada, 1820-1970* (Regina: Canadian Plains Research Centre, University of Regina), pp. 50-60

213   DESLANDRES (Dominique) (1992) "Femmes missionnaires en Nouvelle-France: les débuts des Ursulines et des Hospitalières à Québec" in DELUMEAU (Jean) Ed. *La religion de ma mère: les femmes et la transmission de la foi* (Paris: Les Éditions du Cerf), pp. 209-24

214   *Dictionary of Canadian Biography* (1966-90) (12 vols. Toronto: U. of Toronto Press). There are biographies of several missionaries in this work, including, for instance, "Guyart, Marie" vol. 1, pp. 353-6 and "William Cockran" vol. 9, p. 134

215   FISHER (Robin) (1981) "Missions to the Indians of British Columbia" in WARD (W. Peter) and McDONALD (R.) Eds. *British Columbia: Historical Readings* (Vancouver: Douglas & McIntyre), pp. 113-26 [first published in VEILLETTE (John) and WHITE (Gary) (1977) *Early Indian Village Churches* (Vancouver: UBC Press), pp. 1-11]

216   GETTY (Ian) (1974) "The Failure of the Native Church Policy of the CMS in the North-West" in ALLEN (Richard) Ed. *Religion and Society in the Prairie West* (Regina: University of Regina), Canadian Plains Studies, 3, pp. 19-34

217   GILLES (Raymond) (1986) "Le premier catéchisme de la Nouvelle-France: celui de Jean de Bréboeuf, S.J." in BRODEUR (Raymond) and ROULEAU (Jean-Paul) Eds. *Une Inconnue de*

*l'histoire de la culture: la production des catéchismes en Amérique
française* (Sainte-Foy: Éditions Anne Sigier) Collection
catéchismes et sociocultures, no. 1, pp. 17-49

218   GRANT (John) (1995) "Two-Thirds of the Revenue: Presbyterian
Women and Native Indian missions" in MUIR (Elizabeth) and
WHITELEY (Marilyn) Eds. *Changing Roles of Women Within the
Christian Church in Canada* (Toronto: U. of Toronto Press), pp.
99-116

219   GRESKO (Jacqueline) (1986) "Creating Little Dominions within
the Dominion: Early Catholic Indian Schools in Saskatchewan and
British Columbia" in BARMAN (Jean) et al., eds. *Indian
Education in Canada*, vol. 1 *The Legacy* (Vancouver: UBC Press),
pp. 88-109

220   GRESKO (Jacqueline) (1975) "White "Rites" and Indian "Rites":
Indian Education and Native Responses in the West, 1870-1919"
in RASPORICH (Anthony) Ed. *Western Canada Past and Present*
(Calgary: McClelland and Stewart West), pp. 163-82 [also in
JONES (D.), SHEEHAN (N.) and STAMP (R.), Eds.(1979)
Shaping the Schools of the Canadian West (Calgary: Detselig), pp.
84-106]

221   HÉBERT (Léo-Paul) (1986) "Le Nehiro-Iriniu du Père de la
Brosse ou l'Influence d'un livre'" in BRODEUR (Raymond) and
ROULEAU (Jean-Paul) Eds. *Une Inconnue de l'histoire de la
culture: la production des catéchismes en Amérique française*
(Sainte-Foy: Éditions Anne Sigier) Collection catéchismes et
sociocultures, no. 1, pp. 57-83

222   HUEL (Raymond) (1992) "The Chipewyan Prophets, Louis Riel,
and the Oblates of Mary Immaculate: Who Were the True Heralds
of the Word in the Canadian North West?" in GREENSHIELDS
(M.) and ROBINSON (T.) Eds. *Orthodoxy and Heresy in
Religious Movements: Discipline and Dissent* (Lewiston: Edwin
Mellon Press), pp. 93-119

223   HUTCHINSON (Gerald) (1985) "British Methodists and the
Hudson's Bay Company, 1840-1854" in BUTCHER (Dennis) et
al., Eds. *Prairie Spirit: Perspectives on the Heritage of the United
Church of Canada in the West* (Winnipeg: U. of Manitoba Press),
pp. 28-43

224   JAENEN (Cornelius) (1986) "Education for Francization: the Case
of New France in the Seventeenth Century" in BARMAN (Jean) et
al., Eds. *Indian Education in Canada*, vol. 1 *The Legacy*
(Vancouver: UBC Press), pp. 45-63

225   KISHIGAMI (Nobuhiro) (1994) "Why Become a Christian?
Hypotheses on the Christianization of the Canadian Inuit" in
IROMOTO (T.) and YAMADA (T.) Eds. *Circumpolar Religion
and Ecology* (Tokyo: University of Tokyo Press), pp. 221-235

226   LADD (George) (1991) "Father Cockran and his Children:
       Poisonous Pedagogy on the Banks of the Red" in FERGUSON
       (Barry) Ed. *The Anglican Church and the World of Western
       Canada, 1820-1970* (Regina: Canadian Plains Research Centre,
       University of Regina), pp. 61-71

227   LEACOCK (Eleanor) (1980) "Montagnais Women and the Jesuit
       Program for Colonization" in ETIENNE (Mona) and LEACOCK
       (Eleanor) Eds. *Women and Colonization: Anthropological
       Perspectives* (New York: Praeger/Bergin & Garvey), pp. 25-42;
       also in STRONG-BOAG (Veronica) and FELLMAN (Anita) Eds.
       (1986) *Rethinking Canada: the Promise of Women's History*
       (Toronto: Copp Clark Pitman), pp. 7-22

228   LONG (John) (1991) "The Anglican Church in Western James
       Bay: Positive Influence or Destructive Force" in FERGUSON
       (Barry) Ed. *The Anglican Church and the World of Western
       Canada, 1820-1970* (Regina: Canadian Plains Research Centre,
       University of Regina), pp. 104-12

229   LONG (John) (1985) "Rev. Edwin Watkins: Missionary to the
       Cree, 1852-1857" in COWAN (William) Ed. *Papers of the
       Sixteenth Algonquian Conference* (Ottawa: Carleton University),
       pp. 91-117

230   McKAY (Stanley) and SILMAN (Janet) (1997) "A First Nations
       Movement in a Canadian Church" in BAUM (Gregory) and
       WELLS (Harold) Eds. *The Reconciliation of Peoples: Challenge
       to the Churches* (Maryknoll: Orbis Books), pp. 172-83

231   McKAY (Stanley) (1995) "Healing in Communities Following an
       Experience of Mission as Oppression" in ADAMS (C.) Ed.
       Violence Against Women and Children, pp. 404-11

232   MACLEAN (Hugh) (1974) "The Niagara Mission" in RUGGLES
       (R) Ed. *Some Men and Some Controversies*, pp. 11-27

233   MITSURO, Shimpo (1976) "Native Religion in Sociocultural
       Change: the Cree and Saulteaux in Southern Saskatchewan,
       1830-1900" in CRYSDALE (Stewart) and WHEATCROFT (Les)
       Eds. *Religion in Canadian Culture* (Toronto:Macmillan/Maclean-
       Hunter), pp. 128-40

234   MUIR (Elizabeth) (1988) "The Bark School House: Methodist
       Episcopal Missionary Women in Upper Canada, 1827-1833" in
       MOIR (John) and McINTYRE (C.) Eds. *Canadian Protestant and
       Catholic Missions, 1820s-1960s: Historical Essays in Honor of
       John Webster Grant* (New York: Peter Lang), pp. 23-74

235   PERSSON (Diane) (1986) "The Changing Experience of Indian
       Residential Schooling: Blue Quills, 1931-1970" in BARMAN
       (Jean) et al., Eds. *Indian Education in Canada*, vol. 1 *The Legacy*
       (Vancouver: UBC Press), pp. 150-68

236   TITLEY (E.) (1986) "Indian Industrial Schools in Western
       Canada" in SHEEHAN (Nancy), WILSON (J.) and JONES (D.)
       Eds. *Schools in the West: Essays in Canadian Educational History*
       (Calgary: Detselig Enterprises), pp. 133-53
237   TURNER (Edith) (1994) "The Effect of Contact on the Religion of
       the Inupiat Eskimos" in IROMOTO (T.) and YAMADA (T.) Eds.
       Circumpolar Religion and Ecology (Tokyo: University of Tokyo
       Press), pp. 143-61
238   USHER (Jean) (1981) "Duncan of Metlakatla: the Victorian
       Origins of a Model Indian Community" in WARD (W. Peter) and
       McDONALD (R.) Eds. *British Columbia: Historical Readings*
       (Vancouver: Douglas & McIntyre), pp. 127-53
239   WEIL (Françoise) (1985) "Conversions et baptêmes en
       Nouvelle-France (XVIIᵉ-XVIIIᵉ siècles)" in BLANCKAERT (C.)
       Ed. *Naissance de l'ethnologie?* (Paris: Les Éditions du cerf,
       sciences humaines et religieuses, nouvelle série)
240   WHITEHEAD (Margaret) (1995) "'Let the Women Keep Silence':
       Women Missionaries and Preaching in British Columbia,
       1860s-1940s." In MUIR (Elizabeth) and WHITELEY (Marilyn)
       Eds. *Changing Roles of Women Within the Christian Church in
       Canada* (Toronto: U. of Toronto Press), pp. 116-35
241   WILSON (J.) (1986) "No Blanket to be Worn in School" in
       BARMAN (Jean) et al., Eds. *Indian Education in Canada*, vol. 1
       The Legacy (Vancouver:UBC Press), pp. 64-87 [first published in
       Histoire sociale/Social History vol. 7 (November 1974), pp.
       292-305]

Articles published in periodicals

300   "Amerindian Churches" (1989) "Pastoral and Theological
       Challenges" *Kerygma* (Ottawa) tome 23, pp. 121-230
301   "An Apology" (1992) "An Apology to the First Nations of Canada
       by the Oblate Conference of Canada" *Western Oblate
       Studies2/Études Oblates de l'Ouest 2*, pp. 259-62
302   ABEL (Kerry) (1986) "Prophets, Priests and Preachers: Dene
       Shamans and Christian Missions in the Nineteenth Century"
       Historical Papers of the CHA, pp. 211-24
303   ARCHER (John) (1988) "The Anglican Church and the Indian in
       the Northwest" *Journal of the Canadian Church Historical Society*
       vol. 28, no. 1, pp. 19-30
304   BADERTSCHER (John) (1982) "Irony and Liberation: A Study in
       Canadian History" *The Annual of the Society of Christian Ethics*,
       pp. 45-69 ["incisive analysis of early missions in Manitoba"]

305   BANKS (Joyce) (1984) "The Church Missionary Society Press at Moose Factory, 1853-1859" *Journal of the Canadian Church Historical Society* vol. 26, no. 2, pp. 69-80

306   BANKS (Joyce) (1983) "The Printing of the Cree Bible" *Papers of the Bibliographical Society of Canada* vol. 22, pp. 12-24

307   BEAUDRY (Nicole) (1991) "Rêves, chants et prières Dènès: une confluence de spiritualités" *Recherches amérindiennes au Québec* vol. 21, no. 4, pp. 21-36

308   BENOIT (Barbara) (1980) "The Mission at Île-à-la-Crosse" *The Beaver* (winter), pp. 40-50

309   BLANCHARD (David) (1982) "... To the Other Side of the Sky: Catholicism at Kahnawake, 1667-1700" *Anthropologica* (Ottawa) vol. 24, pp. 77-102

310   BOLT (Clarence) (1983) "The Conversion of the Port Simpson Tsimshian: Indian Control or Missionary Manipulation?" *BC Studies* vol. 57, pp. 38-56 [also publ. in FISHER (Robin) and COATES (Ken) Eds. (1988) *Out of the Background* (Toronto: Copp Clark), pp. 219-35 and in THORNER (Thomas) Ed. (1989) *Sa Ts'e: Historical Perspectives on Northern British Columbia* (Prince George, BC: College of New Caledonia Press), pp. 159-75]

311   BRANDSON (Lorraine) (1994) "Ataata Mary (Guy Mary-Rousselière, o.m.i. (1913-1994): In Memoriam" *Études/Inuit/Studies* vol. 18, nos. 1-2, pp. 270-2

312   BROOKS (William) (1970) "British Wesleyan Methodist Missionary Activities in the Hudson's Bay Company Territory, 1840-1854" *Study Sessions of the Canadian Catholic Historical Association/Sessions d'études de la Société canadienne d'histoire de l'Église catholique*, pp. 21-33

313   BROWN (Jennifer) (1987) "'I Wish to Be As I See You': An Ojibwa-Methodist Encounter in Fur Trade Country, Rainy Lake, 1854-1855" *Arctic Anthropology* vol. 24, pp. 19-31

314   BROWN (Jennifer) (1981) "Mission Indian Progress and Dependency: Ambiguous Images from Canadian Methodist Lantern Slides" *Arctic Anthropology* vol. 18, no. 2, pp. 17-27

315   BULIARD (Denis) (1984) "Nel Gran Nord Canadese" *Missioni OMI* (Rome) vol. 63, pp. 4-9

316   BURCH (Ernest) (1994) "The Iñupiat and the Christianization of Arctic Alaska" *Études/Inuit/Studies* vol. 18, nos. 1-2, pp. 81-107)

317   CARNEY (Robert) (1983) "The Canadian Inuit and Vocational Education" *Études/Inuit/Studies* vol. 7, no. 1, pp. 85-116

318   CARNEY (Robert) (1992) "Residential Schooling at Fort Chipewyan and Fort Resolution, 1874-1974" *Western Oblate Studies 2/Études oblates de l'Ouest 2*, pp. 115-38

319   CARRIÈRE (Gaston) (1972) "Contributions des missionnaires à la sauvegarde de la culture indienne" *Études Oblates* vol. 31 (juillet-septembre), pp. 165-204

320   CARRIÈRE (Gaston) (1979) "The Early Efforts of the Oblate Missionaries in Western Canada" *Prairie Forum* vol. 4, no. 1, pp. 1-26

321   CARRIÈRE (Gaston) (1971) "Fondation et développement des missions catholiques dans la Terre de Rupert et les Territoires du Nord-Ouest (1845-1861)" *Revue de l'Université d'Ottawa* vol. 41, no. 1, pp. 253-81; no. 2, pp. 397-427

322   CARRIÈRE (Gaston) (1978) "Letter from Bishop Alexandre Taché to his Mother Concerning his Life with the Chipewyan Nation [4 Jan. 1851]" *Prairie Forum* vol. 3, pp. 131-56

323   CARRIÈRE (Gaston) (1970) "The Oblates and the Northwest, 1845-61" *Study Sessions of the Canadian Catholic Historical Association/Sessions d'études de la Société canadienne d'histoire de l'Église catholique*, pp. 35-65

324   CARRIÈRE (Gaston) (1984) "Les soins médicaux apportés aux indiens par les Oblats" *Vie Oblate* vol. 43, pp. 123-57

325   CARTER (Sarah) (1984) "The Missionaries' Indian: The Publications of John McDougall, John Maclean and Egerton Ryerson Young" *Prairie Forum* vol. 9, no. 1, pp. 27-44

326   CHAMPAGNE (Claude) (1989) "La formation des Oblats, missionnaires dans le Nord-Ouest canadien" *Study Sessions of the Canadian Catholic Historical Association/Sessions d'études de la Société canadienne d'histoire de l'Église catholique* no. 56, pp. 21-33

327   CHOQUETTE (Leslie) (1992) "'Ces Amazones du Grand Dieu': Women and Mission in Seventeenth Century Canada" *French Historical Studies* vol. 17, no. 3, pp. 627-55

328   COATES (Ken) (1984-85) "'Betwixt and Between': The Anglican Church and the Children of Carcross (Chooutla) Residential School, 1911-1954" *BC Studies* vol. 64, pp. 27-47 [also in COATES (Ken) and MORRISON (W.) Eds. (1989) *Interpreting Canada's North: Selected Readings* (Toronto: Copp Clark Pitman), pp. 150-168]

329   COATES (Ken) (1986) "Send Only Those Who Rise a Peg: Anglican Clergy in the Yukon, 1859-1932" *Journal of the Canadian Church Historical Society* vol. 28, no. 1, pp. 1-18

330   COCCOLA (Nicolas) (1980) "Oblate Work in Southern British Columbia, 1891-1905" *Études Oblates* pp. 145-65

331   COCCOLA (Nicolas) (1976) "Pioneer Days in Okanagan and Kootenay: The "Memoirs" of Father Nicolas Coccola, o.m.i., 1883-1890" *Études Oblates* pp. 21-49

332   COLLINS (David) (1997) "Culture, Christianity and the Northern
       Peoples of Canada and Siberia" *Religion, State and Society* vol. 25,
       no. 4, pp. 381-92

333   COLLINS (David) (1999) "Christian Missions and the First
       Peoples: Fifty Years of the Northern Canada Evangelical Mission"
       British Journal of Canadian Studies vol. 13, no. 1, pp. 1-16

334   CONKLING (Robert) (1974) "Legitimacy and Conversion in
       Social Change: The Case of French Missionaries and the
       Northeastern Algonkian" *Ethnohistory* vol. 21, no. 1, pp. 1-24

335   CROSBY (Douglas) (1991) "An Apology to the First Nations of
       Canada on Behalf of the 1200 Missionary Oblates of Mary
       Immaculate Living and Ministering in Canada" *Kerygma* vol. 25,
       pp. 129-33

336   D'ANGLURE (Bernard) (1997) "Pour un nouveau regard
       ethnographique sur le chamanisme, la possession et la
       christianisation/A New Look on Shamanism, Possession and
       Christianization" *Études/Inuit/Studies* vol. 21, nos.1-2, pp. 5-36
       [English version on pp. 21-36]

337   DESLANDRES (Dominique) (1987) "L'éducation des
       Amérindiennes d'après Marie Guyart de l'Incarnation" *Studies in
       Religion/Sciences religieuses* vol. 16, no. 1, pp. 91-110

338   DESLANDRES (Dominique) (1983) "Marie de l'Incarnation et les
       Amérindiennes: un projet éducatif au XVIIe siècle" *Recherches
       Amérindiennes au Québec* vol. 13, no. 4, pp. 277-85

339   DESLANDRES (Dominique) (1989) "Séculiers, laïcs, jésuites:
       épistémés et projets d'évangélisation et d'acculturation en
       Nouvelle-France. Les premières tentatives, 1604-1613" *Mélanges
       de l'école française de Rome* vol. 101, pp. 751-88

340   DEVENS (Carol) (1992) "'If We Get the Girls, We Get the Race':
       Missionary Education of Native American Girls" *Journal of World
       History* vol. 3, no. 2, pp. 219-37

341   DEVENS (Carol) (1986) "Separate Confrontations: Gender as a
       Factor in Indian Adaptation to European Colonization in New
       France" *American Quarterly* vol. 3, fall, pp. 461-80

342   DOBBIN (Michael) (1990) "She Sailed into History" *Up-Here
       Magazine* Nov/Dec, pp. 38-9

343   "L'Église du Nord/The Church in the North" (1984) [whole issue]
       Kerygma tome 18, no. 42, pp. 1-124

344   ERNEREK (Peter) (1993) "Between God and the Devil: Telling
       the Truth about Chesterfield Inlet School" *Arctic Circle*, spring,
       pp. 6, 11

345   EVANS (Karen) (1984) "Edmund James Peck: His Contribution to
       Eskimo Literacy and Publishing" *Journal of the Canadian Church
       Historical Society* vol. 26, no. 2, pp. 58-68

346   FAST (Vera) (1991) "Holy Men of Different Orders: James Evans and William Mason" *Journal of the Canadian Church Historical Society* vol. 33, no. 1, pp. 95-106

347   FIENUP-RIORDAN (Ann) (1988) "The Martyrdom of Brother Hooker: Conflict and Conversion on the Kuskokwim" *Alaska History* vol. 3, no. 1, pp. 1-26

348   FLANDERS (Nicholas) (1984) 7 "Religious Conflict and Social Change: A Case from Western Alaska" *Études/Inuit/Studies* vol. 8, supplementary issue, pp. 141-157

349   FOSTER (John) (1990) *"Le missionnaire* and *le chef Métis" Western Oblate Studies 1/Études oblates de l'Ouest 1* pp. 117-27

350   FOSTER (John) (1972) "Missionaries, Mixed-Bloods and the Fur Trade: Four Letters of the Reverend William Cockran, Red River Settlement, 1830-1833" *Western Canadian Journal of Anthropology* vol. 3, no. 1, pp. 94-125

351   FOWLER (Rod) (1989) "The New Caledonia Mission: An Historical Sketch of the Oblates of Mary Immaculate in North Central British Columbia" in THORNER (Thomas) Ed. *Sa Ts'e: Historical Perspectives on Northern British Columbia* (Prince George, BC: College of New Caledonia Press) pp. 129-57

352   FROSTIN (C.) (1979) "Méthodologie missionnaire et sentiment religieux en Amérique française" *Cahiers d'histoire* vol. 24.

353   FUMOLEAU (René) (1982) "Missionary Among the Dene" *Kerygma* tome 15, no. 37, pp. 139-66, and the French translation by A. Moreau (1982) "Missionnaire chez les Dènès" *Interculture* vol. 15, no. 1, pp. 9-31

354   FURNISS (Elizabeth) (1995) "Resistance, Coercion, and Revitalization: the Shuswap Encounter with Roman Catholic Missionaries, 1860-1900" *Ethnohistory* vol. 42, no. 2, pp. 231-63

355   GEORGIA (1988) "Memories of Father Théophile Didier, o.m.i." *Polo* no. 2, pp. 49-53

356   GOLDRING (Philip) (1984) "Religion, Missions and Native Culture" *Journal of the Canadian Church Historical Society* vol. 26, pp. 133-55

357   GOUGH (Barry) (1982) "A Priest versus the Potlach: the Reverend Alfred James Hall and the Fort Rupert Kwakiutl, 1878-1880" *Journal of the Canadian Church Historical Society* vol. 24, no. 2, pp. 75-89

358   GOUGH (Barry) (1984) "Pioneer Missionaries to the Nishga: The Crosscurrents of Demon Rum and British Gunboats, 1860-71" *Journal of the Canadian Church Historical Society* vol. 26, no. 2, pp. 81-95

359   GOULET (Jean-Guy) (1981) "Être soi-même comme aborigène: quelques réflexions sur la vie au Centre Kisemanito" *Kerygma* tome 15, no. 37, pp. 123-37

360   GOULET (Jean-Guy) (1984) "Liberation Theology and Missions in Canada" *Église et Théologie* vol. 15, pp. 293-319

361   GOULET (Jean-Guy) (1982) "Religious Dualism among Athapaskan Catholics" *Canadian Journal of Anthropology* vol. 3, no. 1, pp. 1-18

362   GOULET (Jean-Guy) (1992) "Visions et conversions chez les Dènès Tha. Expériences religieuses chez un peuple autochtone converti" *Religiologique* (Montréal) no. 6, pp. 147-82

363   GOULET (Jean-Guy) and PEELMAN (Achiel) (1984) "Die indianische Wirklichkeit und die katolische Kirche von Kanada" *Pro Mundi Vita* (Brussels) no. 93, pp. 2-40

364   GOURDEAU (Claire) (1995) "Marie de l'Incarnation et la culture amérindienne, 1639-1672" *Studies in Religion/Sciences Religieuses* vol. 24, no. 2, pp. 249-60

365   GRANT (John) (1978) "Indian Missions as European Enclaves" *Studies in Religion/Sciences Religieuses* vol. 7, no. 3, pp. 263-75

366   GRANT (John) (1980) "Missionaries and Messiahs in the Northwest" *Studies in Religion/Sciences Religieuses* vol. 9, no. 2, pp. 54-63

367   GRANT (John) (1979) "Rendevous at Manitowaning" *The Bulletin*, vol. 28, pp. 22-34

368   GRANT (Shelagh) "Religious Fanaticism at Leaf River, Ungava, 1931" *Études/Inuit/Studies* vol. 21, nos. 1-2, pp. 159-88

369   GRESKO (Jacqueline) [formerly KENNEDY-GRESCO] (1973) "Missionary Acculturation Programs in British Columbia" *Études Oblates* vol. 32, no. 3, pp. 12-27

370   GRESKO (Jacqueline) (1982) "Roman Catholic Missions to the Indians of British Columbia: A Reappraisal of the Lemert Thesis" *Journal of the Canadian Church Historical Society* vol. 24, pp. 51-62

371   GUALTIERI (Antonio) (1980a) "Canadian Missionary Perceptions of Indian and Inuit Cultural and Religious Tradition" *Studies in Religion/Sciences Religieuses* vol. 9, no. 3, pp. 299-314

372   GUALTIERI (Antonio) (1980b) "Indigenization of Christianity among the Indians and Inuit of the Western Arctic" *Canadian Ethnic Studies* vol. 12, no. 1, pp. 47-57

373   HARROD (Howard) (1984) "Missionary Life-World and Native Response: Jesuits in New France" *Studies in Religion/Sciences Religieuses* vol. 13, no. 2, pp. 179-92

374   HÉBERT (Léo-Paul) (1988) "Le père Jean-Baptiste de la Brosse, professeur, linguiste et ethnographe chez les Montagnais du Saguenay (1766-1782)" *Study Sessions of the Canadian Catholic Historical Association/Sessions d'études de la Société canadienne d'histoire de l'Église catholique* no. 55, pp. 7-39

375   HENDERSON (John) (1974) "Missionary Influences on the Haida
       Settlement and Subsistence Patterns, 1876-1920" *Ethnohistory* vol.
       21, no. 4, pp. 303-16
376   "Henry Budd" (1991) "Henry Budd, 1840-1990" [special issue]
       Journal of the Canadian Church Historical Society vol. 33, no. 1,
       passim
377   HERNOU (Paul) (1987) "Missionary Among the Cree of Northern
       Alberta: The Challenge of Inculturation" *Kerygma* vol. 21, pp.
       233-44
378   HOLST (Wayne) (1998) "The Study of Missionary
       Marginalization: the Oblates and the Dene Nation of Western and
       Northern Canada since 1847" *Missiology* vol. 26, no. 1, pp. 37-53
379   HOUGH (Brenda) (1991) "Prelates and Pioneers: the Anglican
       Church in Rupert's Land and English Mission Policy around 1840"
       Journal of the Canadian Church Historical Society vol. 33, no. 1,
       pp. 51-64
380   HUEL (Raymond) (1984) "Early Oblate Missions in the Canadian
       Northwest: The Evolution of a Missionary Strategy" *Vie Oblate*
       (Ottawa) vol. 48, pp. 237-51
381   HUEL (Raymond) (1994) "The Life-Cycle of an early Oblate
       Establishment: St. Peter's Mission, Reindeer Lake" *Vie Oblate* vol.
       53, pp. 235-64
382   HULTKRANZ (Åke) (1980) "The Problem of Christian Influence
       on Northern Algonkian Eschatology" *Studies in Religion/Sciences
       Religieuses* vol. 9, no. 2, pp. 161-8
383   "Inuit of Baker Lake" (1980) "The Inuit of Baker Lake, Quebec.
       English Missionaries were Strong Influence" *Musk-Ox* no. 27, pp.
       88-90
384   JAENEN (Cornelius) (1985) "Amerindian Responses to French
       Missionary Intrusion, 1611-1760: A Categorization" [In
       Religion/Culture: Comparative Canadian Perspectives, ed. by
       William Westfall, a special issue of] *Canadian Issues/Thèmes
       canadiennes* vol. 7, pp. 182-97
385   JAENEN (Cornelius) (1974) "Amerindian Views of French
       Culture in the Seventeenth Century" *Canadian Historical Review*
       vol. 55, pp. 261-91
386   JENSEN (Philip) (1998) "The Sisters of St. Ann. The Pacific Coast
       Mission of Four Faithful Quebec Daughters" *Beaver* vol. 78, no. 4,
       pp. 29-34
387   JOHN PAUL II, Pope (1984) "Par vous, le Christ est Lui-Même
       Indien. Discours aux Indiens au sanctuaire des martyres de
       Huronie" *La Documentation Catholique* (Paris) vol. 66, pp. 968-70
388   JOHNS (Robert) (1973) "A History of St. Peter's Mission and of
       Education in Hay River, NWT, Prior to 1950" *Musk-Ox* no. 13, pp.
       22-32

389   JOHNSON (Jacques) (1981) "Kisemanito Centre Training Native
       Men for the Priesthood" *Kerygma*, tome 15, no. 37, pp. 111-22
390   JOLLES (Carol) (1989) "Salvation on St. Lawrence Island:
       Protestant Conversions Among the Sivuqaghhmiit" *Arctic
       Anthropology* vol. 26, no. 2, pp. 12-27
391   KOPPEDRAYER (K.) (1993) "The Making of the First Iroquois
       Virgin: Early Jesuit Biographies of the Blessed Kateri Tekakwitha"
       Ethnohistory vol. 4, pp. 277-306
392   KUGEL (Rebecca) (1994) "Of Missionaries and their Cattle:
       Ojibwa Perceptions of a Missionary as an Evil Shaman"
       Ethnohistory vol. 42, no. 2, pp. 227-44
393   KUGEL (Rebecca) (1990) "Religion Mixed with Politics: the 1836
       Conversion of Mang'osid of Fond du Lac" *Ethnohistory* vol. 37,
       no. 2, pp. 126-57
394   LACOMBE (Guy) (1994) "Les Oblats de Marie Immaculée et le
       Nord canadien il y a cent ans" *Vie Oblate* vol. 53, pp. 155-63
395   LAFLÈCHE (Guy) (1980) "La chamanisme des Amérindiens et
       des missionnaires de la Nouvelle-France" *Studies in
       Religion/Sciences Religieuses* vol. 9, no. 2, pp. 137-60
396   LAMIRANDE (Émilien) (1990) "Le père Honoré-Timothée
       Lempfrit: son ministère auprès des autochtones de l'Île de
       Vancouver (1849-1852)" *Western Oblate Studies 1/Études oblates
       de l'Ouest 1* pp. 53-70
397   LEACOCK (Eleanor) and GOODMAN (Jacqueline) (1976)
       "Montagnais Marriage and the Jesuits in the Seventeenth Century:
       Incidents from the Relations of Paul le Jeune" *Western Canadian
       Journal of Anthropology* vol. 6, no. 3, pp. 77-91
398   LEAHEY (M.) (1995) "'Comment peut un muet prescher
       l'évangile?' Jesuit Missionaries and the Native Languages of New
       France" *French Historical Studies* vol. 19, no. 1, pp. 105-31
399   LEIGHTON (Douglas) (1984) "The Ethnohistory of Missions in
       Southwestern Ontario" *Journal of the Canadian Church Historical
       Society* vol. 26, pp. 50-7
400   LEONARD (David) (1994) "Anglican and Oblate: The Quest for
       Souls in the Peace River Country, 1867-1900" *Western Oblate
       Studies 3/Études oblates de l'Ouest 3* pp. 119-38
401   LESAGE (Gilles) (1993) "L'Activité missionnaire dans la région
       du Lac des Bois au XVIIIᵉ et XIXᵉ siècles" *Vie Oblate* vol. 52, pp.
       139-62
402   LEVAQUE (Yvon) (1990) "The Oblates and Indian Residential
       Schools" *Western Oblate Studies 1/Études oblates de l'Ouest 1*
       pp. 181-91
403   LEVAQUE (Yvon) (1990) "Past and Future: the Oblates and
       Residential Schools" *Kerygma* tome 24, pp. 65-76

404   LONG (John) (1991) "Budd's Native Contemporaries in James Bay: Men of 'Refined Feelings', Representatives of the Whiteman's Civilization and 'Real Bush Indians'" *Journal of the Canadian Church Historical Society* vol. 33, no. 1, pp. 79-94

405   LONG (John) (1989) "The Cree Prophets: Oral and Documentary Accounts" *Journal of the Canadian Church Historical Society* vol. 31, no. 1, pp. 3-13

406   LONG (John) (1985) "John Horden, First Bishop of Moosonee: Diplomat and Man of Compromise" *Journal of the Canadian Church Historical Society* vol. 27, no. 2, pp. 86-97

407   LONG (John) (1986) "The Reverend George Barnley and the James Bay Cree" *Canadian Journal of Native Studies* vol. 6, no. 2, pp. 313-31

408   McCARTHY (Mary) (1990) "The Founding of Providence Mission" *Western Oblate Studies 1/Études oblates de l'Ouest 1* pp. 37-49

409   McLAREN (Darcee) (1996) "Living the Middle Ground: Two Dakota Missionaries, 1887-1912" *Ethnohistory* vol. 43, no. 2, pp. 277-305

410   McNALLY (Vincent) (1992) "A Lost Opportunity? A Study of Relations Between the Native People and the Diocese of Victoria" *Western Oblate Studies 2/Études oblates de l'Ouest 2* pp. 159-78

411   MARY-ROUSSELIÈRE (Guy) (1984) "Exploration and Evangelization of the Great Canadian North: Vikings, Coureurs des Bois, and Missionaries" *Arctic* vol. 37, no. 4, pp. 590-602

412   MARY-ROUSSELIÈRE (Guy) (1992) "Father André Pierre Steinmann, o.m.i., 1912-1991" *Eskimo* vol. 49 (NS vol. 43), pp. 3-13

413   MARY-ROUSSELIÈRE (Guy) (1971) "I Live with the Eskimos" *National Geographic* vol. 139, no. 2, pp. 188-217

414   MAURIER (H.) (1988) "Mission chrétienne et genres de vie: le cas de la mission jésuite chez les Hurons" *Mélanges de science religieuse* (Lille) vol. 45, no. 1(mars), pp. 5-24

415   MEEK (Donald) (1989) "Scottish Highlanders, North American Indians and the SSPCK: Some Cultural Perspectives" *Records of the Scottish Church History Society* (Edinburgh) vol. 23, pp. 78-96

416   MEEUS (Joseph) (1991) "Les familles de catéchistes dans l'Arctique" *Pôle et tropiques* (Lyon) nos. 11-12, pp. 19-24

417   MELANSON (Maurice) (1974) "Antoine Gagnon, prêtre, missionnaire et grand vicaire en Acadie, 1809-1849" *La Société historique acadienne*, cahier no. 44, pp. 161-77

418   MILLER (Elmer) (1978) "The Christian Missionary: Agent of Secularization" *Anthropological Quarterly* vol. 5, pp. 14-22

419   MILLER (James) (1987) "The Irony of Residential Schooling in Canada" *Canadian Journal of Native Education* vol. 14, pp. 3-14

420 MISHLER (Craig) (1990) "Missionaries in Collision: Anglicans and Oblates among the Gwich'in, 1861-1865" *Arctic* vol. 43, no. 2, pp. 121-6

421 MITCHAM (Allison) (1974) "Northern Mission, Priest, Parson and Prophet in the North: A Study in French and English Canadian Contemporary Fiction" *Laurentian University Review/Revue de l'Université Laurentienne* vol. 7, pp. 25-31

422 [Moravian Missions] (1988) [whole issue devoted to missions in North America, including USA] *Unitas Fratrum* (Hamburg), nos. 21-22

423 MORIN (Léopold) (1982) "Pour une église locale amérindienne" *Kerygma* tome 16, no. 38, pp. 1-16

424 MORRISON (Kenneth) (1990) "Baptism and Alliance: The Symbolic Mediations of Religious Syncretism" *Ethnohistory* vol. 37, no. 4, pp. 416-37

425 MORRISON (Kenneth) (1986) "Montagnais Missionization in Early New France: The Syncretic Imperative" *American Indian Culture and Research Journal* vol. 10, pp. 1-24

426 NADEAU (Francesco) (1986) "40 anni tra gli Inuit del Labrador" *Missioni OMI* vol. 65, pp. 223-6

427 "Native American Women's Responses to Christianity" (1996) [special issue] *Ethnohistory* vol. 43, no. 4

428 NAZAR (David) (1991) "Anishinabe and Jesuit, 1840-1880: Nineteenth Century Missiology" *Église et théologie* vol. 22, no. 2, pp. 157-76

429 NIEZEN (Ronald) (1997) "Healing and Conversion: Medical Evangelism in James Bay Cree Society" *Ethnohistory* vol. 44, no. 3, pp. 463-91

430 NOCK (David) (1973) "E. F. Wilson: Early Years as Missionary in Huron and Algoma" *Journal of the Canadian Church Historical Society* vol. 15, no. 4, pp. 78-96

431 NOCK (David) (1980) "The Failure of the C.M.S. Native Church Policy in Southwestern Ontario and Algoma" *Studies in Religion/ Sciences religieuses* vol. 9, no. 3, pp. 269-85

432 NORWOOD (Frederick) (1984) "Caught Between Two Missions" *Drew Gateway* vol. 54, nos. 2-3, pp. 76-84

433 O'HARA (William) (1992) "A Permanent Mission at Stuart Lake: French Oblates Bring the Word to New Caledonia, 1873" *Beaver* vol. 72, no. 2, pp. 37-42

434 OKITE (Odhiambo) (1974) "Talk with Chief John Snow" *International Review of Mission* vol. 63, April, pp. 180-2

435 O'NEILL (Sean) (1989) "French Jesuits' Motives for Baptizing Indians on the Frontier of New France" *Mid-America* (Chicago) vol. 71, pp. 123-36

436   PANNEKOEK (Frits) (1972) "Protestant Agricultural Zions for the Western Indian" *Journal of the Canadian Church Historical Society* vol. 14, no. 3

437   PAQUIN (Yvette) (1988-89) "A Pioneer in Service of the Inuit: Sister Yvonne Désilets, s.g.m., 1906- 1987" *Eskimo* NS vol. 36, pp. 9-14

438   PATTERSON (E.) (1981) "Nishga Initiative and Missionary Response: Robert Doolan at Quinwoch, BC" *Missiology* vol. 9, pp. 337-44

439   PEAKE (Frank) (1977) "The Achievements and Frustration of James Hunter" *Journal of the CanadianChurch Historical Society* vol. 19, nos. 3-4, pp. 138-65

440   PEAKE (Frank) (1988) "Church Missionary Society Personnel and Policy in Rupert's Land" *Journal of the Canadian Church Historical Society* vol. 30, no. 2, pp. 59-74

441   PEAKE (Frank) (1982) "David Anderson" *Journal of the Canadian Church Historical Society* vol. 24, April, pp. 3-46

442   PEAKE (Frank) (1989) "From the Red River to the Arctic: Essays on Anglican Missionary Expansion in the Nineteenth Century" [special issue] *Journal of the Canadian Church Historical Society* vol. 31, no. 2, pp. 1-169

443   PEAKE (Frank) (1977) "Fur Traders and Missionaries: Some Reflections of the Attitudes of the Hudson's Bay Company Towards Missionary Work Among the Indians" *Western Canadian Journal of Anthropology* vol. 3, no. 1, pp. 72-93

444   PEAKE (Frank) (1984) "John Booth Good in British Columbia: the Trials and Tribulations of the Church, 1861-1899" *Pacific Northwest Quarterly* vol. 75, no. 2, pp. 70-8

445   PEAKE (Frank) (1975) "Robert McDonald (1829-1913): The Great Unknown Missionary of the Northwest" *Journal of the Canadian Church Historical Society* vol. 17, September, pp. 54-72

446   PEELMAN (Achiel) (1982) "L'Émergence de l'Église aborigène au Canada: Un fait socio-culturel dans la société canadienne" *Kerygma* tome16, no. 38, pp. 17-33

447   PEELMAN (Achiel) (1984) "The Mission of the Church after Vatican II and the Native Peoples of Canada" *Kerygma* tome 18, pp. 1-9

448   PELLY (David) (1992) "Living History at Chesterfield Inlet" *Up Here Magazine* August-September, pp. 20-24

449   PERILLO (M.) (1996) "The Lily of the Mohawks, Kateri Tekakwitha" *Christ to the World* (Rome) vol. 41, pp. 323-8

450   PHILLIPS (Todd) (1993) "A Wounded Generation Begins to Heal" *Arctic Circle*, fall/winter, pp. 21-29

451   PIROTTE (Jean) (1996) "Les Stratégies missionnaires du XIXᵉ au début du XXᵉ siècle. Une mise en perspective générale de l'intérêt

pour les missions du Grand Nord canadien" *Études d'Histoire religieuse* (Ottawa) vol. 62, pp. 9-41

452   POMEDLI (Michael) (1991) "Cultural Diversity Enriching Christian Experience" *Studies in Religion/Sciences Religieuses* vol. 20, no. 1, pp. 39-49. [Jesuits in New France]

453   POULIOT (Léon) (1970) "Mgr Ignace Bourget et la mission de la Rivière Rouge" *Study Sessions of the Canadian Catholic Historical Association/Sessions d'études de la Société canadienne d'histoire de l'Église catholique* no. 37, pp. 17-30

454   POWER (Michael) (1984) "Father Edmund Burke: Along the Detroit River Frontier, 1794-1797" *Study Sessions of the Canadian Catholic Historical Association/Sessions d'études de la Société canadienne d'histoire de l'Église catholique* pp. 29-46

455   PRITCHARD (James) (1973) "For the Glory of God: The Quinte Mission, 1660-1680" *Ontario History* vol. 65, no. 3, pp. 133-48

456   RAIBMAN (Paige) (1996) "'In Loco Parentis': G. H. Raley and a Residential School Philosophy" *Journal of the Canadian Church Historical Society* vol. 38, pp. 29-52

457   REMIE (Cornelius) (1983) "Culture Change and Religious Continuity among the Arviligdjuarmiut of Pelly Bay, N.W.T., 1935-1963" *Études/Inuit/Studies* vol. 7, no. 2, pp. 53-77

458   RICHTER (Daniel) (1985) "Iroquois versus Iroquois: Jesuit Missions and Christianity in Village Politics, 1642-1686" *Ethnohistory* vol. 32, no. 1, pp. 1-16

459   RIDINGTON (Robin) (1987) "From Hunt Chief to Prophet: Beaver Indian Dreamers and Christianity" *Arctic Anthropology* vol. 24, no. 1, pp. 8-18

460   RIPMEESTER (Michael) (1995) "'It is Scarceley to be Believed': The Mississauga Indians and the Grape Island Mission, 1826-18367" *Canadian Geographer* vol. 39, no. 2, pp. 157-68

461   ROLLMANN (Hans) (1984) "Inuit Shamanism and the Moravian Missionaries of Labrador: A Textual Agenda for the Study of Native Inuit Religion" *Études/Inuit/Studies* vol. 8, no. 2, pp. 131-8

462   RONDA (James) (1972) "The European Indian: Jesuit Civilization Planning in New France" *Church History* vol. 41, no. 3, pp. 385-95

463   RONDA (James) (1979) "The Sillery Experiment: A Jesuit-Indian Village in New France, 1637-1663" *American Indian Culture and Research Journal* vol. 3, no. 1, pp. 1-18

464   RONDA (James) (1977) "'We Are Well As We Are': An Indian Critique of Seventeenth Century Christian Missions" *William and Mary Quarterly* vol. 34, no. 1, pp. 66-82

465   RUGGLE (Richard) (1978) "A House Divided against Itself: The Denominational Antagonisms of the Grand River Mission" *Papers of the Canadian Society of Church History* no. 1

466   RUTHERDALE (Myra) (1994-5) "Revisiting Colonization
       Through Gender: Anglican Missionary Women in the Pacific
       Northwest and the Arctic, 1860-1945" *BC Studies*, special issue
       no. 104, pp. 3-23

467   SAMPATH (H.) (1988) "Missionaries, Medicine and Shamanism
       in the Canadian Eastern Arctic" *Arctic Medical Research* vol. 47,
       suppl. 1, pp. 303-07

468   SCOTT (Jamie) (1997) "Colonial, Neo-Colonial, Post-Colonial:
       Images of Christian Mission in Hiram A. Cody's *The
       Frontiersman*, Rudy Wiebe's *First and Vital Candle* and Basil
       Johnston's *Indian School Days"Journal of Canadian Studies* vol.
       32, no. 3, pp. 140-161

469   SIMONSON (Gayle) (1988) "The Prayer Man: Ojibwa Henry Bird
       Steinhauer Brought Religion to the Cree" *The Beaver* October-
       November, pp. 28-33

470   SMILEY (William) (1994) "'The Most Good to the Indians': The
       Reverend James Nesbit and the Prince Albert Mission"
       Saskatchewan History vol. 46, no. 2, pp. 34-51

471   SMITH (Philip) (1986) "Beothuks and Methodists" *Acadiensis* vol.
       16, no. 1, pp. 118-35

472   STACKHOUSE (John) (1988) "Pioneers and Revisionists: Recent
       Books on Canadian Religious History" *Fides et Historia* vol. 20,
       pp. 67-73

473   STARKLOFF (Carl) (1985) "Religious Renewal in Native North
       America: The Contemporary Call to Mission" *Missiology* vol. 13,
       no. 1, pp. 81-101

474   STEVENSON (Winona) (1991) "'Our Man in the Field': Charles
       Pratt, a CMS Native Catechist in Rupert's Land" *Journal of the
       Canadian Church Historical Society* vol. 33, no. 1, pp. 65-78

475   STONE (Thomas) (1981) "Whalers and Missionaries at Herschel
       Island" *Ethnohistory* vol. 28, no. 2, pp. 101-24

476   TALJIT (Gary) (1992) "Good Intentions, Debateable Results:
       Catholic Missionaries and Indian Schooling in Hobbema,
       1891-1914 " *Past Imperfect* vol. 1, pp. 133-54

477   TEMME (Jon) (1988) "Jesus in the 'New World'. North American
       Native Responses to the European Christ" *International Review of
       Mission* vol. 77, pp. 59-66

478   THOMPSON (Arthur) (1973) "The Wife of the Missionary"
       Journal of the Canadian Church Historical Society vol. 15, pp.
       35-44

480   TROTT (Christopher) (1998) "Mission and Opposition in North
       Baffin Island" *Journal of the Canadian Church Historical Society*
       vol. 40, pp. 31-55

481   TROTT (Christopher) (1997) "The Rapture and the Rupture:
       Religious Change Amongst the Inuit of North Baffin Land"
       Études/Inuit/Studies vol. 21, nos.1-2, pp. 209-28

482   TRUDEL (François) (1990) "Peter Okakterook: un Inuk au service
       de la Compagnie de la Baie d'Hudson et de la Church Missionary
       Society (1848?-1858)" *Recherches amérindiennes au Québec* vol.
       20, nos. 3-4, pp. 19-29

483   USHER (Jean) (1971) "Apostles and Aborigines: The Social
       Theory of the Church Missionary Society" *Social History* vol. 7,
       pp. 28-52

484   VANAST (Walter) (1991) "The Death of Jennie Kanajuq:
       Tuberculosis, Religious Competition and Cultural Conflict in
       Coppermine, 1929-31" *Études/Inuit/Studies* vol. 15, no. 1, pp.
       75-104

485   VOISINE (Nive) (1970) "L'Abbé Louis-François Laflèche,
       missionnaire dans l'Ouest" *Study Sessions of the Canadian
       Catholic Historical Association/Sessions d'études de la Société
       canadienne d'histoire de l'Église catholique* no. 36, pp. 61-69

486   WEIL (François) (1988) "La christianisation des Indiens de la
       Nouvelle France, XVIIe-XVIIIe siècles" *Hispania Sacra* vol. 40,
       no. 82, pp. 747-61

487   WHITAKER (Ian) (1971) "A. C. Garrioch and Early Pioneering
       Life in the North West" *Journal of the Canadian Church
       Historical Society* vol. 13, no. 1, pp. 4-14

488   WHITE (Gavin) (1975) "Missionaries and Traders in Baffin
       Island, 1894-1913" *Journal of the Canadian Church Historical
       Society* vol. 17, no. 1, pp. 2-10

489   WHITE (Howard) (1974) "Metlakatla: Bringing the Indians to
       their Knees: The West Coast's First Christian Mission" *Raincoast
       Chronicles* vol. 1, no. 4, pp. 24-37

490   WHITEHEAD (Margaret) (1992-3) "'A Useful Christian Woman':
       First Nations" Women and Protestant Missionary Work in British
       Columbia" *Atlantis* vol. 18, nos. 1-2, pp. 142-66

491   WHITEHEAD (Margaret) (1981) "Christianity: A Matter of
       Choice: The Historic Role of Indian Catechists in Oregon Territory
       and British Columbia" *Pacific Northwest Quarterly* vol. 72, no. 3
       (July) pp. 98-106

492   WILLIAMSON (Norman) (1980) "Abishabis the Cree" *Studies in
       Religion/Sciences Religieuses* vol. 9, no. 2, pp. 217-45

493   WILSON (J.) (1974) "A Note on the Shingwauk Industrial Home
       for Indians" *Journal of the Canadian Church Historical Society*
       vol. 16, no. 4, pp. 66-71

494   ZIMMER (Ronald) (1973) "Early Oblate Attempts for Indian and
       Métis Priests in Canada" *Études Oblates* vol. 32, pp. 276-91

Unpublished masters' and doctoral theses

500   CHILTON (Roger) (1998) *Euthanasia of a Mission: The Work of the Church Missionary Society in Western Canada, Leading to the Society's Withdrawal in 1920 and the Consequences for the Canadian Church* Ph.D., Oxford University

501   FISKE (Jo-Anne) (1981*) And Then We Prayed Again: Carrier Women, Colonialism, and Mission Schools* MA, University of British Columbia

502   GETTY (Ian) (1971) *The Church Missionary Society among the Blackfeet Indians of Southern Alberta, 1880-1895* MA, University of Calgary

503   GOOSSEN (Norma) (1975) *The Relationship between the Church Missionary Society and the Hudson's Bay Company in Rupert's Land, 1821 to 1860, with a Case Study of the Stanley Mission under the Direction of the Rev. Robert Hunt* M.A., University of Manitoba

504   KENNEDY (Judith) (1970) *Qu'Appelle Industrial School: "White Rites" for the Indians of the Old North-West* MA, Carleton University

505   LASCELLES (Thomas) (1987) *Leon Fouquet and the Kootenay Indians, 1874-1887* MA, Simon Fraser University

506   MACLEAN (H.) (1978) *The Hidden Agenda: Methodist Attitudes to the Ojibwa and the Development of Indian Schooling in Upper Canada, 1821-1860* M.A., University of Toronto

507   MAKINDISA (Isaac) (1984) *The Praying Man: The Life and Times of Henry Bird Steinhauer* PhD., University of Alberta

508   NIX (J.) (1977) *John Maclean's Mission to the Blood Indians, 1880-1889* MA, McGill University

509   PETTIPAS (Katherine) (1972) *A History of the Work of the Reverend Henry Budd Conducted under the Auspices of the Church Missionary Society, 1840-1875* MA, University of Manitoba

510   ROBIN (Peter) (1991) *Beyond the Bounds of the West: The Life of John Booth Good, 1833-1916* MA, University of Victoria

511   RUMLEY (Hilary) (1973) *Reactions to Contact and Colonization: An Interpretation of Religious and Social Change among the Indians of British Columbia* MA, University of British Columbia

Appendix (supplementary material in all categories)

520   ALLARD (Claude) (1982) "Les pères Capucins et les Micmacs de Restigouche" *Gaspésie* vol. 21, no. 1 (janvier-mars), pp. 26-7

521   ANGEL (Michel) (1986) *The Ojibwa-Missionary Encounter at Rainy Lake Mission, 1837-1857* MA, University of Manitoba

522   AXTELL (James) (1991) "Preachers, Priests and Pagans: Catholic and Protestant Missions in Colonial North America" in GOUGH (Barry) Ed. *New Dimensions in Ethnohistory* (Hull: Canadian Museum of Civilization), pp. 65-78

523   BARKER (John) (1988) "Bibliography of Missionary Activities and Religious Change in the Northwest Coast Societies" *Northwest Anthropological Research Notes* vol. 22, no. 1, pp. 13-58

524   BARKER (John) (1998) "Tangled Reconciliations: The Anglican Church and the Nisga'a of British Columbia" *American Ethnologist* vol. 25, no. 3, pp. 433-51

525   BARRON (F. Laurie) (1983) "Alcoholism, Indians and the Anti-Drink Cause in the Protestant Indian Missions of Upper Canada, 1822-1850" in GETTY (Ian) and LUSSIER (Antoine) Eds. *As Long as the Sun Shines and the Water Flows. A Reader in Canadian Native Studies* (Vancouver: UBC Press), pp. 191-202

526   BEAULIEU (Alain) (1990) *Convertissez les fils de Caïn: Jésuites et Amérindiens nomades en Nouvelle-France, 1632-1642* (Québec: Nuit Blanche)

527   BECKER (A.) (1976) "The Lake Geneva Mission, Wakaw" *Saskatchewan History* vol. 29, no. 2 (spring), pp. 51-64

528   BERTHIAUME (Pierre) (1998) "Paul Lejeune, ou le missionnaire possédé" *Voix et images* vol. 23, no. 3 (printemps), pp. 529-43

529   BIBEAU (Véronique) (1998) "La prière comme signe de la conversion" *Cahiers d'histoire*, vol. 18, no. 2, pp. 119-44

530   BITTERLI (Urs) (1989) *Cultures in Conflict: Encounters between European and Non-European Cultures, 1492-1800* (Stanford: Stanford U. Press). Ch.4 is entitled "Missionary Work as a Cultural Relationship: The French in Canada"

531   BONVILLAIN (Nancy) (1986) "The Iroquois and the Jesuits: Strategies of Influence and Resistance" *American Indian Culture and Research Journal* vol. 10, no. 1, pp. 29-42

532   BOUDREAU (Ephrem) (1971) "L'Abbé Maillard, apôtre des Micmacs" *La Société historique acadienne* vol. 4, no. 5 (avril-juin), pp. 177-99

533   BREDIN (Thomas) (1981) "The Reverend David Jones, Missionary at Red River, 1823-28" *Beaver* outfit 312 (2), pp. 47-52

534   BRICE-BENNETT (CAROL) (1990) "Missionaries as Traders: Moravians and Labrador Inuit, 1771-1860" in OMMER (Rosemary) Ed. *Merchant Credit and Labrador Strategies in Historical Perspective* (Fredericton, NB: Acadiensis Press), pp. 223-46

535   BRICE-BENNETT (CAROL) (1985) *Two Opinions: Inuit and Moravian Missionaries in Labrador, 1804-1860* MA, Memorial University

536   BROWN (Bern Will) (1999-2000) *Arctic Journal, 2 vols* (Toronto: Novalis)

537   BROWN (Violet) (1985) "Over the Red Deer: Life of a Homestead Missionary" *Alberta History* vol. 33, no. 3, pp. 9-18

538   CARON (Adrien) (1977) *La Mission du Père Paul le Jeune sur la Côte-du-Sud, 1633-1634* (La Pocatière: Société historique de la Côte-du-Sud) Collection "Cahier d'histoire" no. 1

539   CARRIÈRE (Gaston) (1982) "L'expansion missionnaire en Amérique du Nord" in *l'Église catholique et la Société du Québec: le grand héritage* (Québec: Musée du Québec), pp. 1-18

540   CAYEN (Daniel) (1981) "Les missions catholiques du nord-est ontarien au XIXᵉ siècle" *Aspects du Nouvel-Ontario* vol. 1 (Sudbury), pp. 23-39

541   CHALMERS (John) (1983) "Missions and Schools in the Athabasca" *Alberta History* vol. 31, no. 1, pp. 24-29

542   CHERRINGTON (John) (1974) *Mission on the Fraser* (Vancouver: Mitchell Press)

543   CHOQUE (Charles) (1987) *Joseph Buliard, Fisher of Men: From Franche-Comté to the Canadian North. Joseph Buliard, Missionary Oblate of Mary Immaculate, Apostle of the Inuit, 1914-1956* (Churchill: Roman Catholic Episcopal Corporation)

544   CODIGNOLA (Luca) "The Battle is Over: Campeau's Monumenta vs. Thwaites" Jesuit Relations, 1602-1650" *European Review of Native American Studies* vol. 10, no. 2, pp. 3-10

545   COOPER (Carol) (1986) *Anglican Missions and the Subarctic Fur Trade: A Study of the Rt. Reverend John Horden and the Native Peoples of Moosonee, 1851-1893* MA. Waterloo University

546   CROIX (Alain) (1988) "Missions, Hurons et Bas-Bretons au XVIIᵉ siècle" in *Les dynamismes culturels en France et au Québec. Colloque France-Québec, Rennes 2 et 3 juin 1988, Annales de Bretagne et des pays de l'Ouest* vol. 95, no. 4, pp. 487-98

547   DELÂGE (Denys) (1991) "Les Iroquois chrétiens des 'réductions' 1667-1770" *Recherches amérindiennes au Québec* vol. 21, nos. 1-2 (printemps), pp. 59-70; no. 3 (automne), pp. 39-50

548   DESLANDRES (Monique) (1985) *Attitude de Marie de l'Incarnation à l'égard des Amérindiens* MA, McGill University

549   DESLANDRES (Dominique) (1991) "Les laïcs et la conversion en Acadie" *Annales de Bretagne et des pays de l'Ouest* (Rennes) vol. 98, pp. 221-30

550   DIETER (Constance) (1998) *From our Mother's Arms: The Integrational Impact of Residential Schools in Saskatchewan* (Toronto: United Church Publishing)

551   DOUGLAS (Gilean) (1983) "The Bible Barge to Kingdom Come" *Raincoast Chronicles* no. 10, pp. 4-10

552   DUBÉ (Pauline) (1991) *Édition critique et annotée du Mémoire instructif contenant la conduite des pères Récollets de Paris en leur mission de Canada depuis l'année 1615 jusques en la présente, 1684* Mémoire de maîtrise (littérature québécoise), Université Laval

553   DUBOIS (Paul-André) (1997) *De l'oreille au coeur: naissance du chant religieux en langues amérindiennes dans les missions de Nouvelle-France, 1600-1650* (Sillery, Sainte-Foy: Septentrion/ CELAT) Collection "Nouveaux cahiers du CELAT" no. 19

554   FAST (Vera) (1984) *The Protestant Missionary and Fur Trade Society: Initial Contact in the Hudson's Bay Territory, 1820-1850* PhD, University of Manitoba

555   FINGARD (Judith) (1972) "The New England Company and the New Brunswick Indians, 1786-1826: A Comment on the Colonial Perversion of British Benevolence" *Acadiensis* vol. 1, no. 2, pp. 29-42

556   FOWLER (Rodney) (1990) "The Lemert Thesis and the Sechelt Mission" *Historical Studies [of] the Canadian Catholic Historical Association* vol. 57, pp. 51-64

557   FURNISS (Elizabeth) (1995) *Victims of Benevolence: The Dark Legacy of the Williams Lake Residential School* (Vancouver: Arsenal Pulp Press)

558   GOSSELIN (Ronald) (1984) "La christianisation de la forêt boréale" in *L'Église catholique et la société du Québec: le grand héritage* (Québec: Musée du Québec), pp. 31-61

559   GRÉGOIRE (Vincent) (1997) "Les 'reductions' de Nouvelle-France: une illustration de la pratique Jésuite" *Dix-septième siècle* vol. 49, no. 3, pp. 519-29

560   HARPER (Ken) (1981) "The Moravian Mission at Cumberland Sound" *Beaver* outfit 312 (2), pp. 53-59

561   HATFIELD (Leonard) (1987) *Simon Gibbons, First Eskimo Priest: The Life of a Unique Clergyman and Church Builder* (Hantsport: Lancelot Press)

562   HILLER (James) (1988) "Early Patrons of the Labrador Eskimos: The Moravian Mission in Labrador, 1764-1805" in PAINE (Robert) Ed. *Patrons and Brokers in the East Arctic* (St. John's, NF: Institute of Social and Economic Research, Memorial University), pp. 47-97

563   HUEL (Raymond) ed. (1990) *Actes du premier colloque sur l'histoire des Oblats dans l'Ouest et le Nord canadien/Proceedings of the First Symposium on the History of the Oblates...* (Edmonton: Western Canadian Publishers) contains half a dozen relevant papers

564   HURTIBISE (Pierre) "Les mythes mobilisateurs de l'entreprise missionnaire et coloniale en Nouvelle-France" in CODIGNOLA (Luca) and LURAGHI (Raimondo) Eds. (1986) *Canada ieri e oggi. Atti del 6e convegnon internazzionale di studi canadense* (Fasano: Schena editore), Collection "Cultura straniera" pp. 43-57

565   HUTCHINSON (Gerald) (1990) *The Meeting Place: Rundle's Mission at Pigeon Lake* (Edmonton: Rundle's Mission Conference Centre)

566   JACQUIN (Philippe) (1989) "Le combat des esprits: le missionnaire et le shaman chez les Iroquois au XVIIIe siècle" in *Populations et cultures: études réunies en l'honneur de François Lebrun* (Rennes: Université de Rennes II)

567   JAENEN (Cornelius) (1977) "Missionary Approaches to Native Peoples" in MUISE (D.) Ed. *Approaches to Native History in Canada: Papers of a Conference held at the National Museum of Man* (Ottawa: National Museums of Canada), pp. 5-15

568   JOUVE (Odoric-Marie) et al. (1996) *Dictionnaire biographique des Récollets missionnaires en Nouvelle-France, 1615-1645, 1670-1849* (Montréal: Bellarmin)

569   KORP (Maureen) (1995) "Problems of Prejudice in Thwaites" Edition of the Jesuit Relations' *Historical Reflections/Réflexions historiques* (Alfred, NY) vol. 21, no. 2, pp. 261-76

570   LATOURELLE (René) (1993) *Jean de Brébeuf* (Montréal: Bellarmin)

571   LATOURELLE (René) (1999) *François-Joseph Bressani: missionnaire et humaniste* (Saint-Laurent: Bellarmin)

572   LEMAY (Diane) (1992) *La perception de la femme amérindienne par les missionnaires de la Nouvelle-France* Mémoire de maîtrise, Université d'Ottawa

573   LE TRESTE (Joseph) (1997) *Souvenirs d'un missionnaire breton dans le Nord-Ouest canadien.* Texte établi et commenté par Juliette Champagne (Sillery: Septentrion; Rennes: Apogée)

574   LONG (John) (1986) *"Shaganash": Early Protestant Missionaries and the Adoption of Christianity by the Western James Bay Cree, 1840-1893* Ph.D., University of Toronto

575   LONSDALE (Richard) (1973) *A History of the Columbia Coast Mission* MA, University of Victoria

576   MALI (Anya) (1996) "Strange Encounters: Missionary Activity and Mystical Thought in Seventeenth Century New France" *History of European Ideas* vol. 22, no. 2, pp. 67-92

577   McNALLY (Vincent) (2000) *The Lord's Distant Vineyard: A History of the Oblates and the Catholic Community in British Columbia* (Edmonton: U. of Alberta Press/Western Canadian Publishers)

578   MÉNARD (Chantal) (1997) *Missions de Sept-Îles et de Mingon au XIXe siècle: Oblats de Marie Immaculeé et Innus-Montagnais de 1844 à 1911* Mémoire de maîtrise (histoire), Université de Montréal

579   MILLOY (Peter) (1998) "Converting the Savage: Jesuit and Montagnais in Seventeenth Century New France" *Catholic Historical Review* vol. 84, no. 2, pp. 219-39

580   NOCK (David) (1982) "A Chapter in the Amateur Period of Canadian Anthropology: A Missionary Case Study" *Canadian Journal of Native Studies* vol. 2, no. 2, pp. 249-68

581   NOCK (David) (1978) "The Social Effects of Missionary Education: A Victorian Case Study" in NELSON (R.) and NOCK (David) Eds. *Reading, Writing and Riches: Education and the Socio-Economic Order in North America* (Kitchener: Between the Lines), pp. 233-50 (a critical analysis of the Shingwauk Home)

582   O'BOMSAWIN (Jean-Louis) (1986) "Joseph de Cozangue, un missionnaire Abenaki à Odanak" *Les Cahiers nicolétains* vol. 8, no. 1 (mars), pp. 3-22

583   O'DONNELL (Kathleen) (1972) "Brébeuf's Spiritual Journal" *Canadian Literature* no. 53 (summer), pp. 42-50

584   OLIVIER (Réjean) (1983) *Le père Albert Lacombe, o.m.i (1827-1916)...Bibliographie...de ses écrits...suivi de données biographiques, dont celles du Père Gaston Carrière* (L'Assomption: Collège de l'Assomption, Bibliothèque)

585   OURY (Guy-Marie) (1991) *Jérôme le Royer, Sieur de La Dauversière, l'homme qui a conçu Montréal: étude d'une spiritualité* (Montréal: Éditions du Méridien)

586   OURY (Guy-Marie) (1993) "Le projet missionnaire de M. de La Dauversière (1597-1659), premier seigneur de Montréal" *Études d'histoire religieuses* vol. 59, pp. 5-23

587   OURY (Guy-Marie) (1993) "Montréal: le projet de Jérôme de la Dauversière. Un missionnaire laïque à Montréal" *La Province de Maine* vol. 95, no. 26, pp. 185-95; no. 27, pp. 263-71

588   PATTERSON (Edward) (1982) *Mission on the Nass: The Evangelization of the Nishga (1860-1890)* (Waterloo, ON: Eulachon Press)

589   PAYNTER (Margaret) (1978) *Miracle at Metlakatla: The Inspiring Story of William Duncan, a Missionary* (St. Louis, MO: Concordia Publishing House)

590   PEEL (Bruce) (1974) *Rossville Mission Press: The Invention of the Cree Syllabic Characters and the First Printing in Rupert's Land* (Montreal: Osiris)

591   PRESTON (Richard) (1987) "Catholicism at Attawapiskat: A Case of Cultural Change" in COWAN (William) Ed. *Papers of the*

Eighteenth Algonquian Conference (Ottawa: Carleton University Press), pp. 271-86

592   PRUCHA (Francis) (1988) "Two Roads of Conversion. Protestant and Catholic Missionaries in the Pacific Northwest" *Pacific Northwest Quarterly* vol. 79, no. 5 (October), pp. 130-8

593   RIO (Marcel) and AUBIN (Hervé) (1995) *Un vrai Inuk: Marcel Rio, itinéraire d'un homme de foi* [textes et souvenirs rassemblés par Hervé Aubin] (Outremont: Novalis)

594   ROBERT (Isabelle) (1990) *Étude des vestiges archéologiques de la mission des Jésuites à Sillery* Mémoire de Maîtrise (arts et traditions populaires), Université Laval

595   SAINT-GEORGES (Luce) (1984) *L'Enseignement catéchétique des Jésuites au XVIIe siècle: l'exemple montagnais* Ph.D., Columbia University

596   SAVOIE (Donat) (1971) "Bibliographie d'Émile Petitot, missionnaire dans le Nord-Ouest canadien" *Anthropologica* vol. 13, no. 1-2, pp. 1959-68

597   SCOTT-BROWN (Joan) (1987) "Calgary Indian Industrial School, 1896-1907" *Canadian Journal of Native Education* vol. 14, no. 1 (1987), pp. 41-9

598   STEVENSON (Winona) (1988) *The Church Missionary Society Red River Mission and the Emergence of a Native Ministry, 1820-1860; with a Case Study of Charles Pratt of Touchwood Hills* MA, University of British Columbia

599   STEVENSON (Winona) (1988) "The Red River Mission School and John West's 'Little Charges'" *Native Studies Review* vol. 4, no. 1-2

600   TAYLOR (J. Garth) (1977) "Moravian Mission Influence on Labrador Inuit Subsistence" in MUISE (D.) Ed. *Approaches to Native History in Canada: Papers of a Conference held at the National Museum of Man* (Ottawa: National Museums of Canada), pp. 16-29

601   TAYLOR (Monique) (1998) "'This is our Dwelling': The Landscape Experience of the Jesuit Missionaries to the Huron, 1626-1650" *Revue d'études canadiennes/Journal of Canadian Studies* vol. 33, no. 2 (summer), pp. 85-96

602   THOMSON (Duane) (1990) "The Missionaries" in WEBBER (Jean) Ed. *Okanagan Sources* (Penticton, BC: Theytus Books), pp. 118-41

603   TREVITHICK (Scott) (1998) "Native Residential Schooling in Canada: A Review of Literature" *Canadian Journal of Native Studies/La revue canadienne des études autochtones* vol. 18, no. 1, pp. 49-86

604   TRIGGER (Bruce) (1983) "The Deadly Harvest: Jesuit Missions among the Huron" in CROSS (Michael) and KEALEY (Gregory)

Eds. *Economy and Society during the French Regime to 1759* (Toronto: McClelland & Stewart), pp. 154-82

605 USHER (Jean) (1971) "The Long Slumbering Offspring of Adam: The Evangelical Approach to the Tsimshian" *Anthropologica* vol. 13, no. 1-2, pp. 37-61

606 WAKELY (Francis) (1976) "Missionary Activity among the Iroquois, 1642-1718" *Rochester History* vol. 38, no. 4 (December), pp. 1-24

607 WASYLOW (Walter) (1972) *History of Battleford Industrial School for Indians* Med, University of Saskatchewan

608 WESTMEIER (Karl-Wilhelm) (1995) *The Evacuation of Skekomeko and the Early Moravian Missions to Native North America* (Lewiston: Edward Mellen Press)

609 WHITEHEAD (Margaret) (1981) *Now You Are My Brother: Missionaries in British Columbia* (Victoria, BC: Sound and Moving Image Division, Provincial Archives)

610 WILSON (Keith) (1988) *William Carpenter Bompas* (Winnipeg: Faculty of Education, University of Manitoba)

611 WOLFART (H. Christoph) (1984) "Notes of the Cree Texts in Petitot's *Traditions indiennes du Canada nord-ouest*" in WOLFART (H. C.) Ed. *Essays in Algonquian Bibliography in Honour of V.M. Dechene* (Winnipeg: Algonquian and Iroquoian Linguistics), pp. 47-78

612 ZAROWNY (Marie) (1995) "Proclaiming the Good News with a People that has been Culturally Oppressed: A Beginning Dialogue" *Mission* vol. 2, no. 2, pp. 193-206

Chapter 4

Aboriginal People in the City

Roy Todd

*Many Canadians think of Aboriginal people as living on
reserves or at least in rural areas. This perception is
deeply rooted and persistently reinforced. Yet almost half
of Aboriginal people in Canada live in cities and towns
(RCAP, 1996c, p. 519).*

Introduction

There is an apparent emphasis upon Aboriginal People on reserves in
public discussion in Canada, in the volumes of the Royal Commission
on Aboriginal Peoples, and in the academic literature. The most
common topics of discussion, including land claims, treaty rights,
disputes about clear-cut logging and conflict over hydro-electric
schemes, are matters which primarily affect First Nations in territory
which is away from the cities. News reporting, with an emphasis upon
incidents and conflict, provides a similar shape to Aboriginal matters.
Throughout the 1990s incidents and confrontations such as that at Oka
and blockades of access roads give an emphasis to the struggle for
Native Peoples' rights away from the cities.

While these struggles and negotiations have been going on there
has been a quiet and gradual re-location of Aboriginal people through
migration to urban areas. This chapter is concerned with these
Aboriginal city dwellers and their relations with other Canadians.
There are three main sections. First, there is a discussion of the
migration of Aboriginal people to the cities. This includes information
about their demographic and socio-economic profiles, work and

education and explores aspects of social inequalities within the urban Aboriginal population. Second, there is an overview of the ways in which Aboriginal people have encountered the criminal justice system. Finally, there is an outline of material gathered from two Canadian cities, analysing the ways in which Aboriginal people are negotiating relationships with police services to provide support for their urban communities. Here the main focus is upon the reshaping of relations between the police and Aboriginal people and the construction of Aboriginal identity in this context. The Aboriginal organisations studied form a hub for the provision of a wide range of social, health and educational services to the Aboriginal people in the cities. Therefore, the questions which emerge from this analysis relate to the possibilities of Aboriginal people in urban areas gaining equitable access to a range of services as well as achieving the benefits of fair treatment with regard to criminal justice. The case studies can be broadly conceived as related to the negotiation of social inclusion and citizenship rights for urban Aboriginal people: integration by contrast with a potential destiny of social exclusion and marginality.

Aboriginal People in Urban Areas

The Social and Demographic Characteristics of Urban Aboriginal People

What is the magnitude of the population with which we are concerned? In the 1996 census, just over a million people (1,101,960) reported Aboriginal ancestry. The balance between single and multiple ancestry favoured the latter: 477,630 claimed Aboriginal ancestry only, whereas 624,330 claimed Aboriginal ancestry as part of a multiple response. The figures for identity are lower: 867,225 reported North-American Indian ancestry, while 535,075 reported North-American Indian identity (*Statistics Canada*, 1998).

These figures can only be taken to be approximate for under-counting in the census is acknowledged as a problem because of lack of access to Aboriginal communities. It is possible that under-numeration is particularly significant in cities with a transient population including homeless people lacking hostel accommodation. Consequently, population estimates by those who work amongst urban Aboriginal people are often significantly higher than those derived from census data.

The trend towards urbanisation of the Canadian population as a whole is being mirrored by the Aboriginal population. Just over three-quarters (77% in 1991) of Canada's population lives in urban areas (*Canada Year Book*, 1997) and although the Aboriginal population is less urbanised than the non-Aboriginal population, the trend towards greater urbanisation has been continuing, with a particularly large increase in the 1960s. The growth of Aboriginal populations has occurred at the same time as the major Canadian cities are becoming more global in their profiles. Social and political institutions are adapting to these changes and questions can be raised about the extent to which local government, educational, social and police services are responding to the Aboriginal people in their midst.

Table 1:   **Percentage of Urban Aboriginal Peoples, 1871-1991**

1871	1881	1901	1911	1921	1931	1941	1951	1961	1971	1981	1991
1.7	0.6	5.1	3.7	3.7	3.9	3.6	6.7	12.9	30.1	36.4	42.3

Source: Driedger, 1996.

The Royal Commission on Aboriginal Peoples, using census and survey data, confirmed that a substantial number of Aboriginal people live in urban areas. It also identified a trend towards a growing population:

Aboriginal people living in urban areas number about 320,000 or 45 per cent of the total Aboriginal population. By the year 2016, they will number about 455,000 (RCAP, 1996c, p. 520).

Census data on comparative numbers of Aboriginal people in urban and rural areas, in metropolitan areas, on reserves and off reserves, point to the relative isolation of some Aboriginal people compared to others. Statistics Canada summarises the general distribution of the population as follows:

About three of every 10 Aboriginal people lived on rural reserves, and another three in 10 lived in census metropolitan areas. One-quarter lived in urban areas other than census metropolitan areas, and one-fifth in rural areas other than reserves, often isolated in northern communities (*Statistics Canada*, *The Daily*, 13 January, 1998, p. 5).

This rural isolation contrasts with the patterns of urban distribution, evident from consideration of metropolitan areas. The urban Aboriginal population is concentrated in particular cities. About one-fifth of Aboriginal people (171,000) lived in 7 metropolitan areas (Winnipeg, Edmonton, Vancouver, Saskatoon, Toronto, Calgary and Regina).

Table 2:   **Aboriginal Population in Selected Metropolitan Areas (1996 census)**

	Total population	Aboriginal population	Aboriginal pop. as percentage of total population
Toronto	4,232,905	16,100	0.4
Winnipeg	660,055	45,750	6.9
Regina	191,480	13,605	7.1
Saskatoon	216,445	16,160	7.5
Calgary	815,985	15,200	1.9
Edmonton	854,230	32,825	3.8
Vancouver	1,813,935	31,140	1.7

Source: *Statistics Canada*, 1998.

Why are Aboriginal people leaving reserves and other rural locations and moving to the cities? Reasons for migration from reserve locations were classified for a research study for the RCAP (Clatworthy, summarised in RCAP, 1996c, p. 574). In approximate descending order, these reasons are categorised as: family related, housing, access to employment, community factors, access to school, forced to move, and health related. The first three categories cumulatively account for the migration of 77% of men and 69% of women. As mentioned above, the majority of Aboriginal migrants to the cities are women. Their reasons for moving to the cities include: to escape physical and sexual abuse, to move away from a situation where they were oppressed and lacking control, to move away because they lost Status (through marrying a non-Indian).

Although there are no aggregate sources of data which indicate real or relative numbers involved, there have also been state led initiatives to foster re-location from reserves to urban areas, including support for Aboriginal people through the funding of centres in some cities (Satzewich and Wotherspoon, 1993).

As mentioned above, this urbanisation trend follows a general trend in Canada, and suggests that the urban/rural balance is approaching even weighting in broad terms. It is clear, nevertheless, that moves to the city are not made by a representative sub-group of the Aboriginal population. Some significant differences exist between the urban population and the population as a whole. The Royal Commission on Aboriginal Peoples identified 5 features of the urban Aboriginal population based upon the 1991 census which show relative differences between Aboriginal and non-Aboriginal city dwellers:

- a high proportion of women
- younger than the general population
- less well educated
- economically disadvantaged
- a high incidence of poverty

The urban Aboriginal population in 1996 was 10 years younger on average than the general population (25.5 years against 35.4 years). Children under 15 accounted for 35% of all Aboriginal people, compared with only 20% of the total population. The proportion in urban areas is slightly lower at 32%. There were significantly higher proportions of children in the urban areas. Aboriginal children under 15 were 12% of young people in this age group in Winnipeg, with 13% in Regina and 13% in Saskatoon.

Family composition is another feature relevant to understanding circumstances of the urban Aboriginal population. About one-third (32%) of Aboriginal children under the age of 15 lived in a lone-parent family (twice the rate for the general population). About 11% did not live with their parents. The rate is significantly higher in metropolitan areas. In Winnipeg, Regina and Saskatoon about one-half lived with a single parent. Across the country, about 46% of Aboriginal children under 15, living in a family in the cities were from lone parent families (1996 census data, *Statistics Canada, The Daily*, 1998).

The educational profile, including knowledge of Aboriginal languages, is a significant dimension of cultural capital for structuring relations within and between non-Aboriginal and Aboriginal communities. Knowledge of an Aboriginal language was lowest in urban areas (11% in census metropolitan areas, 18% in other urban areas, and 56% on reserves and settlements). For some, the educational experience of residential schools is linked with loss of knowledge, or failure to develop knowledge, of an Aboriginal language. The impact of residential schools, educationally, socially and personally, for urban Aboriginal people remains significant:

> In retrospect, the legacy of the residential schools can be seen on every street corner in Canada. There are thousands of once-proud native people who have been reduced to drunken shells by their experiences in those institutions (Dickson, 1993; quoted in Miller, 1996, p. 439).

Lower levels of education in comparison with non-Aboriginal people, irrespective of age group, have been obtained by Aboriginal people. At least high school diplomas had been obtained by 65% of the non-Aboriginal population but less than half of the Aboriginal population (46%) have attained that level. Whereas 16% of the non-Aboriginal population are university graduates, only 4.5% of the Aboriginal population have university degrees or certificates. Although educational levels have been improving in the Aboriginal population, there are still marked differentials in the education of young adults in comparison with their counterparts in the non-Aboriginal population.

Diversity Amongst Aboriginal People

The data summarised so far draws attention to the direction of differences, tending to focus upon averages, comparing aggregate data on the Aboriginal and non-Aboriginal population. In some cases it reveals aspects of the statistical relationship between data on urban Aboriginal people and those not in urban areas. However, it is also relevant to ask about differences within the Aboriginal populations and in particular, for the purposes of this chapter, material differences amongst urban Aboriginal people, for within this population there is an unevenness of experience. The intersection of these facets of experience produces particular difficulties for women and children:

> In Winnipeg, Regina and Saskatoon, the 1991 census found that more than 60 per cent of Aboriginal households were below the low income cut-off—the poverty line defined by Statistics Canada. For single parent households headed by women, the situation was disastrous—between 80 and 90 per cent were below the line. Moreover, the situation was almost as bad in nearly every major city in Canada (RCAP, 1996c, p. 521).

The diversity of the urban Aboriginal population in terms of band membership or affiliation in some of the major cities is striking but in others there is a concentration of people from particular nations. In Winnipeg, 70% of Aboriginal residents are Ojibwa as are 81% of those in Thunder Bay. In Halifax, 79% of Aboriginal residents are Mi'kmaq. In Edmonton, 63% are Cree. By contrast, Vancouver has an Aboriginal population from at least 35 nations (RCAP, 1996c).

The major forms of structured social inequality in Canada associated with inter-related problems such as poverty, housing and worklessness can also be found in the urban Aboriginal population. Summarising research from the 1970s and 1980s of Aboriginal people living off-reserve (of whom the majority would be in urban areas), Satzewich and Wotherspoon (1993) write:

> Most studies of off-reserve natives have focused upon the disadvantages experienced by native peoples relative to other groups and the related problems of adjustment and social disorganization....As with reserve life, a chronicle of unemployment or sporadic employment, poor housing conditions and overcrowded dwellings, lack of basic services, alcoholism, and ill health runs throughout portrayals of native life off the reserve. In addition, several problems such as high mobility, high crime and arrest rates, prostitution, lack of family or community support, and overt racism in employ-

ment, housing, and general social circumstances are often more pronounced for native persons who do not live on reserves (p. 98).

Table 3: **Aboriginal Population of Vancouver by Nation of Origin, Larger Groups (1991)**

	Number	Percentage
Carrier	340	3.2
Coast Tsimshian	400	3.8
Cree	1050	9.8
Gitxsan	440	4.1
Heilshuk	420	3.9
Haida	435	4.1
Halkomelem	1465	13.7
Kwakwa ka'wakw	610	5.7
Nisga'a	420	3.9
Ojibwa	900	8.4
Squamish	1300	12.2

Source: RCAP, 1996c, pp. 595-7.

For McMillan (1988) urbanisation is likely to result in unemployment and to be a source of social problems:

> For many, lacking education or specialised job training, the search for employment is in vain. The "good life" visualised when they left the reserve remains elusive, and their poverty restricts their opportunities. Alcohol abuse is a problem for many, often leading to clashes with the law (McMillan, 1988, p. 301).

Nevertheless, urban Aboriginal people do find work, sometimes creating specialist areas of work for themselves, sometimes living relatively invisibly in working class and other occupations. One exception to the profile of worklessness suggested for urban Aboriginals is that of the Mi'kmaq, who have achieved a degree of specialisation in employment. Here there may be similarity to the creation of niche opportunities by minority ethnic groups:

> Like the Mohawk before them, the Mi'kmaq discovered in "high steel" construction work an occupation that was well paying and psychologically satisfying. While some moved permanently to the city, many remain transients, returning to the reserve at frequent intervals (*ibid.*, pp. 52-53).

Here it can be noted that some authors show a reluctance to accept similarities between urban Aboriginals and other migrants. Satzewich and Wotherspoon (1993) refer critically to the argument that Native peoples in the city face circumstances similar to "newcomers" from any background.

A further dimension of urban Aboriginal life is residential density, which carries connotations of ghetto life. Driedger (1996) summarises studies of ethnic concentration in 14 Canadian cities which indicate high levels of clustering of Aboriginal people and offers an explanation:

> Aboriginals in Canadian cities are forced to live in the inner cities because of unemployment, low incomes, and often discrimination (p. 219).

While the authors referred to above emphasise low incomes, unemployment and low status occupations, there are also examples, albeit relatively few in number, of contrasting experiences in the labour market following educational experiences which contrast with those referred to above. A study of the early labour market experiences of graduates from Canadian universities and community colleges in 1990, based upon a sample survey, found differences between the Aboriginal population and the general population as well as differences within the Aboriginal population (Wannell and Caron, 1994). These data are presented with a warning that they are based upon small numbers and that sub-divisions within each area discussed are therefore not reliable. Figures for Aboriginal participation in post-secondary education are lower, at 1.2 percent of university graduates and 2.8 percent of community college graduates, than might be predicted from their numbers as a proportion of the total population (3.8 percent) or of the workforce population (3%). Only half of one percent of advanced degree holders is identified as of Aboriginal origin.

Once in work, the average annual earnings of Aboriginal university graduates (in 1992) were about the same as that of other graduates (slightly higher at $36,100 for the Aboriginal sample, compared with $35,200 for those who were not Aboriginal (Wannell and Caron,1994). The average annual earnings of community college graduates was the same for Aboriginal as non-Aboriginal people at $26,600. Almost two thirds (63%) of university graduates who are Aboriginal work in the public sector, compared with just over half of other university graduates (52%) and community college graduates (55%). These figures on earnings and employment are tempered by the figures on participation in the labour force (Wannell and Caron, 1994).

There are disparities between the unemployment rates for Aboriginal graduates, particularly in the Atlantic provinces and Saskatchewan. Among university graduates, the unemployment rates are slightly higher for Aboriginal peoples than those who are not Aboriginal. Data from community college graduates show greater discrepancies between the Aboriginal population and others, with an unemployment rate of 22.2% compared with 12.7% for those who are not Aboriginal. There is a greater proportion of Aboriginal graduates who are listed as "not in Labour Force" amongst women community college graduates: 87% of Aboriginal women are recorded as participating in the labour market, compared with 94% of other female community college graduates (Wannell and Caron, 1994).

The data from this survey show a higher proportion of Aboriginal community college graduates following trade and vocational courses than college Certificate or Diploma courses. The most common fields of study are classified as Social Sciences and Services, Natural Sciences and Primary Industries, and Mechanical and Structural Engineering. The interaction between qualifications and location might contribute to the relatively low labour force participation rates. These data show patterns of inequality in participation which are in the same direction as but show smaller differentials than data for the Aboriginal population as a whole. Bernier (1997) summarises a number of studies which reinforce the picture of significantly lower participation in the labour force, higher unemployment rates, and lower earnings for the Aboriginal population in comparison with those of non-Aboriginal origins.

The discussion above, which indicates a lack of difference between one Aboriginal group (University graduates) and the non-Aboriginal population in earnings, also draws attention to disparities within the Aboriginal population. It should be noted that Aboriginal university graduates appear to be exceptional in comparison with other groups of Aboriginal people. Moreover, the differentials between groups of Aboriginal people with relation to earnings are marked. These comparative data are recent and as Bernier (1997) notes, are almost all based upon data from the 1991 census. Having referred to a study by Clatworthy et al. (1995) reporting substantial differences in earnings among Aboriginal people (e.g., non-registered Indians, $21,035; Métis, $18,467; registered Indians, $15,791; Inuit, $15,690), Bernier (1997) goes on to report other data on wage inequality.

The main findings relating to earnings differences in 1991 are:

- Canadian workers of Aboriginal origin earned $6,500 less than Canadian workers as a whole
- Canadian workers who reported Aboriginal identity earned $9,400 less than Canadian workers as a whole

The data also reveal greater inequality and polarisation in income for those of Aboriginal origin than among the general population. This may partly be accounted for by demographic factors (the youth of the Aboriginal population being particularly significant). Bernier concludes:

> This study confirms the findings of earlier studies and the general belief that, on average, Aboriginal peoples earn less than Canadians as a whole...there is greater inequality in the distribution of wages for Aboriginal workers than for Canadian workers as a whole, even after allowing for demographic differences. Not only do Aboriginals earn lower wages than Canadians as a whole (for comparable work)—inter-group inequality—but they also experience a more unequal wage distribution—intra-group inequality (1997, p. 15).

There are differences in the occupational distribution which contribute to these differences with fewer professionals, managers and technicians among Aboriginal workers and slightly more workers in the services and blue collar sectors (Bernier, 1997).

The aggregate data presented so far provides us with statistical evidence of difference but only hint at what these data might mean for the qualitative dimensions of life in the cities. LaPrairie (1994) undertook a study of inner city Aboriginal people which is based upon a survey of Aboriginal people living in Edmonton, Regina, Toronto and Montreal. The sampling rationale led to a focus on those at the lowest end of the social scale, the most marginalised (from Aboriginal and non-Aboriginal communities), with lives characterised by violence and frequent encounters with the criminal justice system. The analysis of the survey responses revealed differentiation, which included signs of solidarity, of differential concerns with racism ("The concentration on racial differences is, in some sense, a privilege of those 'better off'." p. 86) and different perceptions of victimisation. LaPrairie's conclusion draws attention to differences between groups in her sample and identifies the most disadvantaged:

As revealed in the inner-city sample, there is neither equality of victimization (as reflected in people's backgrounds, experiences, life chances, socio-economic levels, etc.), nor equality of need. Nor is there the same ability of people to explore and use services and opportunities. There are differences in reasons for coming to cities and in the "tools" people bring with them. The most disadvantaged people are street level males and, to a lesser, extent females, who are marginalized in both native and non-native society. But the other groups are also marginalized, particularly in relation to non-aboriginal and aboriginal society (1994, p. 84).

The potential political consequences of the situation of urban Aboriginal people have been considered by some authors. Satzewich and Wotherspoon (1993) argue that there were fears in the 1980s that high unemployment and poverty might lead to unrest in the cities, particularly those with a concentration of young unemployed Aboriginals. However, the experiences described by La Prairie suggest that for many in the cities, social isolation, solitude and individual powerlessness follow from migration rather than social organisation, collective action and the emergence of radicalised forms of group empowerment.

To summarise the argument so far: there has been a strong trend towards urbanisation of the Aboriginal population. A general summary of the characteristics of the urban Aboriginal population suggests a complex profile with tendencies towards low levels of education and high incidences of poverty and worklessness, a high level of single-parent families, and a relatively high proportion of women and young people. Nevertheless there is also evidence of diversity of education, income and employment in the population.

Urbanisation and Identity

Before turning to case studies, with an examination of some of the collective responses of Aboriginal people and their organisations in the cities, we can raise a set of questions about the consequences of urbanisation for Aboriginal identity. To what extent does the urban Aboriginal experience a loss of Aboriginal identity? Does urbanisation promote further invisibility of the Aboriginal population and result in assimilation? What qualitative changes might occur in Aboriginal identity in urban contexts? Is it diminished, dissolved, lost from collective experience? Or are there new formulations where tradition is being remade and where Aboriginal culture serves to reinforce Aboriginal networks?

The picture which emerges from the aggregate and survey data summarised above does not suggest a strong urban, Aboriginal identity. Census data does not indicate a growing trend in the numbers of those who assert Aboriginal identity. Studies of the origins and affiliations of Aboriginal people by band in many cities suggest the possibility of fragmentation rather than pan-Aboriginal organisation.

The issue of contemporary change in Aboriginal identity is addressed by the Royal Commission on Aboriginal Peoples. In one paragraph, the RCAP offers several models of cultural identity in the city. First, it gives a uni-dimensional account, with Aboriginal identity maintenance at one end of a continuum and identity dissolution, with complete assimilation at the other end:

The requirements of survival in the city frequently force Aboriginal people to change their way of life and reshape the way they express their beliefs and values. The resulting adaptations run a complete range, from maintenance of a strong Aboriginal identity based on traditional Aboriginal culture to assimilation into the pervasive non-Aboriginal culture (*RCAP*, 1996c, p. 522).

Then there is a model of cultures as bounded territories, with a void between them that is essentially an anomic space:

Some remain trapped between worlds, unable to find their place in either culture; this often creates tension, alienation and identity confusion (*ibid.*).

Finally, there is a constructionist model, where culture grows from the identities and meanings derived from taking new initiatives:

Others successfully adapt to urban life by blending aspects of both cultures and becoming bicultural; they maintain a strong Aboriginal identity into which they integrate elements of non-Aboriginal culture. A small but growing number of Aboriginal people have created positive new identities in response to the challenges and opportunities of urban life (*ibid.*).

The actions taken, institutions created, dialogues begun and negotiations made in the lives described in this last quotation also change non-Aboriginal people. In living from day to day as Aboriginal people with a new identity that engages with non-Aboriginal people, Aboriginal people in the city are doing no more than many migrants to the city. They are also re-shaping the city.

In arguing that migrant Aboriginal people living off-reserve do not necessarily succumb to the pressures from the dominant culture around them, the notion of being trapped between two sets of cultural forces is rejected. Here there are some possible parallels with studies of Indian (Asian) families in which there is inter-marriage. The concept of being positioned between two static sets of identities is forcefully opposed by some authors, for example:

...the "between two worlds" metaphor of the multicultural literature is outmoded and condescending (Luke and Luke, 1998, p. 750).

The situation of those who establish marriages with members of other cultures might be seen as an important test case of the ways in which people in new and unfamiliar circumstances can construct new ways, new practical models, new vocabularies of action and new identities. Luke and Luke (1998) argue that:

> Interracial families are a focal site for the construction of identities and practices of "new ethnicities" (*ibid.*, p. 748).

The most salient dimensions of experience and identity in these contexts may be refashioned, challenging traditional relationships with new relationships:

> ...opening an array of possibilites for transformed and hybridized cultural, religious and gendered practices and reconfigured power relations (*ibid.*, p. 749).

Luke and Luke consider these newly negotiated relations to have unexpected outcomes and to have, through the institutional contexts in which they are negotiated, a broader impact than might be assumed from the intimate and personal nature of their origin, leading to:

> ...local moments of the politics of identity in new times where relations of power, cultural practices and intergenerational continuities are reshaped in new and often not fully predictable ways (*ibid.*, p. 750).

It can be argued, as the case studies below make clear, that in urban environments, Aboriginal people are constructing new identities. The terrain in which they are negotiating these new identities and to some extent shaping new relations is clearly harsh. One of the harshest contexts is that in which Aboriginal people encounter criminal justice and to summarise this aspect of Aboriginal experience puts the achievements of some urban Aboriginal organisations in a clear light.

Aboriginal People and Criminal Justice

Here we turn to a particularly critical issue for Aboriginal people in cities: their relationships with the police. This takes the discussion towards consideration of distinctive issues related to the conjunction of Aboriginal traditions and an established institution which has a historical, colonial relationship with Aboriginal people commonly evaluated as oppressive. Placing police-Aboriginal relationships within in the wider context of Aboriginal experience in the criminal justice system underscores the significance of the police-Aboriginal relationships noted in the case studies below. It is also possible to expose disparities in the underlying conceptions of justice (see Chapter 6 by David Wall for a further discussion of this theme) and to recognise the mutual adaptations possible among Aboriginal people and police services. Finally, the discussion below also clarifies some aspects of Aboriginal migration to the cities, particularly among women, which has been mentioned above.

The discussion in this section includes some material covered in Chapter 4 by Todd and Todd, (1997) "Police Community Partnerships in Canada: Bridging Solitudes." Aboriginal police services have been established in a number of areas and have different degrees of independence from the RCMP and local, non-Aboriginal police forces. These initiatives, with new developments of traditional roles such as watchmen, are evolving in recent policing arrangements for on-reserve Aboriginal people. An example is the Stl'atl'imx Nation Tribal Police, which is described as having the intent "to provide an improved quality of policing service" (Stl'atl'mix Nation Tribal Police and Stl'atl'imx Tribal Police Board, 1995, p. 3). However, within the cities, Aboriginal people live inescapably within the domain of the non-Aboriginal justice system. As a consequence, liaison between Aboriginal people and the police in urban areas may be seen as a test of the capacity for reflexivity and adjustment within both police services and amongst the Aboriginal communities in the cities, as can be evaluated in the case studies which follow.

The first paragraph of the Introduction to the *Royal Commission on Aboriginal People* on "Aboriginal People and Criminal Justice" states:

The first challenge in writing a report on justice is that "the overall perspective of an Aboriginal person towards Canadian legal institutions is one of being surrounded by injustice without knowing where justice lies, without knowing whether justice is possible," (*RCAP*, 1996, p. 1; with quotation taken from P.A. Monture-Okanee and M.E. Turpel, 1992, p. 249).

Within this context, the development of liaison between police and Aboriginal people in the cities is clearly a considerable challenge to Aboriginal people and to police officers. The generalisation above by the Royal Commission, which leaves no possibility of exceptions, is based upon an extensive review of investigations and inquiries from coast to coast. A summary of reports to the Royal Commission from the Aboriginal people of Manitoba, which condemns all parts of the criminal justice system equally, may be taken as broadly representative:

They spoke of policing that is at times unresponsive and at times over-zealous, usually insensitive and often abusive, They spoke of a system of laws and courts that ignores significant cultural factors and subjects them to incomprehensible proceedings and inordinate delays in the disposition of their cases. They spoke of a penal system that is harsh and unproductive. They spoke of parole procedures that delay their release from the penal system. They spoke of child welfare and youth justice systems that isolate young people from their families and their communities. They spoke too of historical wrongs, of betrayals and injustice, and of a vision for restoring social harmony to their communities (*RCAP*, 1996, p. 1).

A distillation of the statistics on Native involvement with the criminal justice system demonstrates with great clarity some of the reasons for the nature and extent of concerns about justice and First Nations people. The Royal Commission on Aboriginal Peoples summarises data from the conclusions of the Indian Policing Policy Review:

...crime rates for on-reserve Indians are significantly higher than for off-reserve Indians and than the overall national crime rate...the rate of on-reserve violent crimes per 1,000 is six times the national average, for property crimes the rate is two times the national average, and for other criminal code offences the rate is four times the national average (*RCAP*, 1996a, p. 34, citing the Indian Policing Policy Review, 1990, p. 3).

The Aboriginal Justice Inquiry of Manitoba reported higher crime rates on Indian reserves than in non-reserve areas, using data from 1989-90. A study conducted for the Grand Council of the Cree in 1991 reported a significantly higher crime rate in a sample of Cree communities compared to rates for Quebec and the overall Canadian rate. These data included an assault rate of more than five times the Quebec average and more than three times the national average (Royal Commission on Aboriginal Peoples, 1996a).

At the end of the criminal justice chain, Native people are especially over-represented. The figures on incarceration show differential treatment in a particularly stark light. A report of the Canadian Bar Association (1988) is cited by the Royal Commission:

> Government figures which reflect different definitions of "Native" and which probably underestimate the number of prisoners who consider themselves Native show that almost 10 per cent of the federal penitentiary population is Native (including about 13 per cent of the federal women's prisoner population) compared to about 2 per cent of the population nationally. In the west and northern parts of Canada where there are relatively high concentrations of Native communities, the over-representation is more dramatic. In the Prairie region, Natives make up about 5 per cent of the total population but 32 per cent of the penitentiary population and in the Pacific region Native prisoners constitute about 12 per cent of the penitentiary population while less than 5 per cent of the region's general population is of Native ancestry. Even more disturbing, the disproportionality is growing (Jackson, 1988; reprinted in 1989, p. 220, and cited in *RCAP*, 1996a).

Recognition of the unequal treatment of Aboriginal people within the criminal justice system has led to recommendations that alternatives be devised based upon traditional Aboriginal justice systems. A preliminary report of The Royal Commission on Aboriginal Peoples includes a comment that:

It is the view of this Commission that recognizing the right of Aboriginal peoples to re-establish their own justice systems and providing the resources to exercise that right is a necessary part of the new relationship we have proposed (*RCAP*, 1995a, p. 76).

The alternative of Aboriginal justice has been typified in a number of ways (see for example: LaPrairie, 1994; LaRocque, 1997, Royal Commission on Aboriginal Justice, 1995a). Yet common elements of these comparisons appear to include rejection of some features of non-Aboriginal systems and proposals that positive elements of Aboriginal systems include a degree of mediation, or restoring harmony to the situation, or different treatment for the offender. One of the two commissioners in the Aboriginal Justice Inquiry of Manitoba, Judge Murray Sinclair, is cited at length by the Royal Commission (1995a, pp. 59-64) in analysing some of the differences between Aboriginal and non-Aboriginal understandings of justice. This account stresses that the main purpose of justice in an Aboriginal context is "restoring peace and equilibrium to the community" (p. 59) which compels the accused to come to terms with his or her conscience and reconcile with his or her community. There are other characteristics related to this, with distinctive approaches to punishment, imprisonment and truth.

Calls for the implementation of Aboriginal justice have triggered cautious and challenging reactions. Of particular relevance to this project are concerns about the treatment, or neglect, of victims of crime if some typologies of traditional models were to be implemented. LaRocque (1997) raises this issue as follows:

Aboriginal mediation programs generally operate in the following way: the "offender" is also seen as a "victim" and his "needs" must also be met for "healing" to occur. To achieve this, both victim and abuser are brought together to share their "pain." Often, the focus is on the "pain" of the attacker. The basis for this process is the "restoration of harmony" in the community, and it is the community that determines the "punishment" for the offender. However, punishment has meant virtually nothing, particularly in cases of sexual assault (LaRocque, 1997, p. 80).

There is thus some concern about the effects upon victims of violence, and LaRocque sounds a cautionary note about "traditional" forms of justice, calling for critique and careful evaluation:

Because these "traditional" perspectives on "culturally appropriate" justice models as practised on victims of violence may be having drastic effects on the victims and therefore on the Native community, they must be questioned and re-evaluated (*ibid.*, p. 76).

An important dimension of this challenge is that of gender. It has been argued that the rights of women in particular have been neglected or not fully recognised in some calls for change and that these rights might not be recognised in decisions in Aboriginal jurisdictions. LaRocque establishes a requirement that women's perspectives should be taken into account in the construction of justice systems for Aboriginal communities:

In order to redress the wrongs of an ineffective, racist, dominant system, Aboriginal communities should not feel compelled to replace them with disregard for innocent people's rights. Nor should Aboriginal communities disregard women's perspectives...(*ibid.*, p. 96).

Jackson (1994) has also recognised the anxiety that trends towards Aboriginal self-government may lead to loss of some of the democratic protections for women's rights:

There is, for many Aboriginal people, the hope that a fading cultural identity can be recovered and that a strong desire for self-government and autonomy can be achieved. At the same time, for many Aboriginal women, there is an interest in preserving and extending gender equality. Thus, a central issue for Aboriginal women concerns what a return to traditional customs would involve. Would it involve a return to the historical subservience of Aboriginal women to Aboriginal men, or would it involve the equality of power between Aboriginal men and women that existed earlier but was distorted by the imposition of European patriarchal law and practices? (Jackson, 1994, p. 193).

Both LaPrairie (1994) and Jackson lead us towards conceptions of partnership between Aboriginal and non-Aboriginal representatives with development of an integrated system. In her conclusion, Jackson draws upon traditional Aboriginal imagery:

The metaphor of the eagle flying should be kept in mind, not only for a vision of how Aboriginal men and women can work together, but also for a vision of how Aboriginal and non-Aboriginal peoples can work together. The eagle cannot fly with only one wing beating (*ibid.*, p. 195).

Within the cities used as the location for fieldwork in this study, the predicament of the large but frequently isolated and often transient population of Aboriginal people, away from the potential support of their communities, has been the focus of study. Here, policy responses have included the objective of assisting Aboriginal victims of crime, particularly Aboriginal women. To promote justice, forms of policing are required in these urban settings which, like their rural counterparts, combine the resources of mainstream Canadian justice and Aboriginal traditional approaches.

Some parallels exist between the experiences of policing Aboriginal people and other visible minorities. A contentious issue of policing with reference to minority ethnic groups and especially black people is the level of policing. Criticisms of police action by visible minorities, for example, arise from complaints of under-policing and over-policing. The underlying concept of a norm of levels of policing which if broken by under- or over-action of some sort is also raised in regard to Aboriginal people. While we might ask whether there are unacknowledged issues here, related to methodology and racialisation, the nature of the critique of police services that comes from suggestions about over-policing and under-policing deserves consideration.

The Aboriginal Justice Inquiry of Manitoba and the Cawsey task force in Alberta drew attention to over-policing as an aspect of systemic discrimination in the criminal justice system (Royal Commission on Aboriginal Peoples, 1996a). This can be illustrated by Quigley's argument, cited at length by the Royal Commission, connecting policing decisions with a chain of events leading to imprisonment, as follows:

Police use race as an indicator for patrols, for arrests, detentions...For instance, police in cities tend to patrol bars and streets where Aboriginal people congregate, rather than the private clubs frequented by white business people...The police rarely arrest whites for being intoxicated in public. No wonder there is resentment on the part of Aboriginal people arrested simply for being intoxicated. This situation very often results in an Aboriginal person being charged with obstruction, resisting arrest or assaulting a peace officer. An almost inevitable consequence is incarceration...Yet the whole sequence of events is, at least to some extent, a product of policing criteria that include race as a factor and selective enforcement of the law (Quigley, 1994, pp. 273-274).

The other part of this concern with levels of policing leads to consideration of under-policing. Here the concern is with lack of protection of Aboriginal people, especially from serious offences and especially with reference to vulnerable groups such as women and children within Aboriginal communities. For example, issues of under-policing have been identified by Pauktuutit, the Inuit Women's Association of Canada, whose report "Inuit Women and Justice" is cited by the Royal Commission on Aboriginal Peoples (RCAP, 1996a). Whereas over-policing creates victims within the criminal justice system, under-policing ignores victims. Just as the argument about over-policing compared the policing Aboriginals with policing of other Canadians, the argument about under-policing also brings us to a comparative point:

Until we have the necessary resources in our communities to provide for protection to women on a permanent basis (for example, police based in the community) and to provide a safe place where women can receive counselling, support and protection, many women will not leave and can't leave the violent home...

While we recognize that the realities of violence in the family translate into the need for added resources, it is not acceptable on the one hand, to tell us that this is a funding problem and that there is not enough money provided by the province to provide adequate policing. Yet on the other hand, the federal government provides enough funds to hire two police officers for Labrador and eight in Newfoundland to respond to cigarette smuggling. The communities of Postville, Rigolet, and Makkovik, like other communities on the coast, require police based in the community. Women in these communities are in a dangerous position (Pauktuutit, Inuit Women's Association of Canada, 1995, *Inuit Women and Justice: Progress Report No. 1*, pp. 16-17, cited in *RCAP*, 1996a, p. 38).

To summarise the discussions above, a continuing crisis of relations clearly exists between Aboriginal people and the criminal justice system. This has resulted in systematic over-representation in the statistics on criminal behaviour, and in imprisonment. It has also led to the neglect of concern for the victims of crime. The qualities of policing, arising from the use of stereotypes, and policing strategies which lead to over-policing and under-policing have been components of this systemic injustice. This context of criminal justice, or the absence thereof for Aboriginal people, is a highly significant part of the urban experience among Aboriginals. Many urban Aboriginal people experience forms of policing which leave them without confidence in police services. Aboriginal people who are victims of crime commonly lack support from police. Many urban Aboriginal people are aware of the realities of the culture of policing in rural areas, which has led to the crises of confidence referred to above.

So far, the two main sections of this chapter have drawn from existing evidence—particularly that derived from survey and census data and official reports—to outline the profiles of Aboriginal people in the cities and to consider the contextual background to the relation of Aboriginal people to the criminal justice system. In the final section of the chapter, evidence from field work in two Canadian cities is used to illustrate how some Aboriginal people are working to prevent victimisation, to provide resources and to re-shape the structures of relations between themselves and the institutions of the city.

Case Studies of Negotiation, Adaptation and Change

There are three parts to the following section. In each case, the data are derived from interviews, observations and the analysis of documents in two Canadian cities, Toronto and Vancouver. The first part examines the construction and development of the Metropolitan

Toronto Police Aboriginal Peacekeeping Unit and serves as an example of adaptation and change in a large urban police force. The second case examines the work of the Native Women's Resource Centre in Toronto, illustrating the ways in which resources from Aboriginal and non-Aboriginal cultures are deployed in mediating between urban conditions and Aboriginal people in the city. The third case outlines the work of the Vancouver Police and Native Liaison Society, an organisation working in a setting where the conditions of urban Aboriginal people are exceptionally harsh. Each one of these cases contains examples of urban Aboriginal people acting collectively and resourcefully to develop projects and programmes which serve their communities, bridging gaps between the social inequalities within the Aboriginal populations of the cities and leading to a degree of change in non-Aboriginal institutions.

Metropolitan Toronto Police Aboriginal Peacekeeping Unit

The Aboriginal population of Ontario, based on estimates summarised by the Royal Commission on Aboriginal Peoples, is 143,100, of which 91,500 are Registered, 39,600 are Non-Registered, 12,800 are Metis and 900 are Inuit (vol. 1, p. 20). Almost half of the Native population of Ontario lives in Toronto. It is estimated that there are 65,000 Aboriginal people in the city, a diverse group of people, including a transient population.

The perceptions of the police by Native people in the city is consistent with those reported above, elsewhere in Canada, where the dominant response is negative:

> One thing that all Native people agree on is that there is a serious problem with policing in the Aboriginal community. There is a perception that the police are guilty of brutality, racism, false arrests, and numerous other offences against Native people. Compounding this is a great sense of helplessness—that there is no recourse for the Native community. There is no place to make a complaint and nobody will listen anyway (Mukwe Ode First Nations Consulting, 1992, cited in Henry *et al.*, 1995, p. 109).

This was recognised by Metropolitan Toronto Police, who at one time had no established links with the Aboriginal community in the city.

The first formal moves were made in 1989 when an Aboriginal officer, with both professional and voluntary involvement in his community, was assigned to duties by the then Chief Designate (William McCormack) with the Aboriginal community on a full-time basis. Following development and expansion of the role, the title of Chief's Native Liaison was assigned. Then, in September 1992, the Police Services Board supported the establishment of the Aboriginal Peacekeeping Unit. This unit was charged with responsibilities to enhance communication between Native people and the police, and deliver a police service that was sensitive to the existing and changing needs of the Aboriginal Community. The police held an opening ceremony for the Unit on April 27, 1993 (Metropolitan Toronto Police, 1993). The Unit then expanded to be staffed by three Aboriginal Officers with supporting staff.

Originally, the Aboriginal Peacekeeping Unit was on the eighth floor of police headquarters. Recognising that this was a barrier to access, the Unit was moved to the ground floor, at the back of the building, so that people wanting to make contact with the unit needed only to enter by the rear doors, turn right, and walk a few paces. By 1995, it was recorded that "over 800 members of the community have visited the office" (Metropolitan Toronto Police, 1995, p. 11).

The historical background of relations between the police and Aboriginal people in Toronto formed a difficult basis for the development of positive relations. One account notes:

Historically, mistrust, misunderstanding and overt and systemic racism contributed to the development of a strained relationship between the police and Aboriginal people (Ministry of Solicitor General, 1997, p. 10).

An internal review of relations between the police referred to officers being aware of problems such as substance abuse and poverty, problems which led to contact between the police and Aboriginal people (Metropolitan Toronto Police, 1995). The review refers to "historical and cultural barriers, which prevented Aboriginal people from interacting more positively with police" (p. 24) and records the view that "more must be done (by the police) to address the particular needs and concerns of Aboriginal people" (p. 25).

Members of the Unit have undertaken to change relations between the police and Aboriginal people. Formal and informal means have been used to educate Aboriginal people about the police and to educate the police about Aboriginal customs, values and behaviour. Activities undertaken by members of the Unit have included:

- educational work in schools
- presentations at training sessions delivered at C.O.Bick College (the police college for Metropolitan Toronto Police)
- presentations at community facilities
- recruitment activities
- representations to First Nations communities in the Province
- assistance and support to Aboriginal officers as mentors.

Recognition of the distinctive contributions of Aboriginal officers has contributed to the establishment of a protocol "to ensure an Aboriginal officer can be summoned to the scene of any potentially volatile situation involving Aboriginal people" (*ibid.*, 1995, p. 11). Another step identified in the internal review was to request that the Police Services Board approve the amendment of a Force Rule to allow Aboriginal members to wear their hair in traditional braids (*ibid.*, p. 11).

Activities such as the above require continuing liaison with Aboriginal people in Toronto, their effectiveness depending upon formal and informal negotiation and maintenance of a network of communications between the police, Aboriginal people and others in the City. By mid-1995, it was reported that "a two-way educational process is ongoing, whereby the community learns about the policing service and officers are informed of aboriginal customs, values and modes of behaviour" (*ibid.*, p. 10). This was facilitated by members of the Aboriginal Peacekeeping Unit who conducted regular police clinics on the premises of agencies working with and for Aboriginal people in the city. The objectives of the police included a qualitative change in relations between the police and Aboriginal people:

Through its efforts, the Unit is attempting to create a climate in which Aboriginal people will avail themselves of all available police services. They are encouraged to report crime and advised how complaints about police service may be remedied (*ibid.*, p. 11).

An example of a specific project targeted at Aboriginal people living on the streets in winter and needing assistance is illustrative. Through advertisements in community newspapers, people were invited to donate sleeping bags which were then collected by the police. Through partnership with the business community, these were cleaned and kept in store, with a number being stacked in the Aboriginal Peace Keeping Unit. They were then distributed to Aboriginal people on the streets in need of them during the winter months.

The development of the Aboriginal Peace Keeping Unit indicates some adjustment of a large metropolitan police service to the needs of Aboriginal people while leaving some questions about the majority of encounters between Aboriginal people and police services.

Native Women's Resource Centre: Toronto

This second case study concerns Aboriginal people's own organisation in cities, particularly focusing upon a women's organisation which provides resources for Aboriginal people while maintaining liaison with the police.

The issue of support for victims within the Aboriginal communities is of national concern. As an example taken from British Columbia, the Oppal Commission refers to many voicing:

...concern about the manner in which police often treat women and minorities. Of the approximately 1100 submissions received by this Inquiry, 26% related to violence against women as an issue...Some of the complaints that we continue to hear involve police attitudes, reluctance to become involved or recommend charges, failure to take complaints seriously and failure to understand the dynamics of the problem (Oppal, 1994, p. xv).

In 1984, Toronto has no facilities for Native women. A group of Native women began meeting to discuss what could be done to provide support and meet their needs and those of others in the city. In October 1985, a resource centre was established, the Native Women's Resource Centre, in a residential area close to down-town Toronto. The centre is housed in a former house and provides office and community facilities, a kitchen and a resource centre. Originally, the Centre was intended as a "drop in" centre, and it remains an essential place where Aboriginal women needing advice or assistance can call in for help. However, the roles of the Centre have developed and expanded. Through links with other agencies and increases in staffing, new programmes have been offered, including adult education upgrade classes, job readiness programmes, adult literacy classes, counselling, information, and referral work involving an intake worker, and pre-natal and post-natal programs provided by a nurse. Within ten years of the Centre's beginnings, a wide range of activities was underway, as summarised in one of the Centre's leaflets:

> Programs presently operating include client information and referral, a food bank, a clothing give-away, youth activities, circles, craft classes a Brighter Futures Program, for mothers of infants and young children, literacy development and a Student Advancement Program offering Grade 12 equivalency to selected native women on social assistance. In addition, special events are frequently sponsored such as winter solstice celebrations and health and wellness conferences for community members (*Introduction to the Native Women's Resource Centre*, no date).

Participation by Native women, as volunteers, in the initiation, management and provision of services and through the board of directors, is key to the purpose of the Centre. Its commitment to communicating traditional Native teachings and their relevance to the contemporary circumstances of women in the city is clear in the imagery, vocabulary and statements of their resources, the illustrations and the use of Ojibway and Cree in their publications. These publications include a booklet to assist victims of sexual assault, a pamphlet about the empowerment of women, and an anthology of Native women's writings. The Centre's belief in the value of traditional teachings is clear:

> The centre believes the traditional wisdom of the native people can effectively complement any assistance provided to native women so that they can develop a value system and a framework for living their lives as strong, capable leaders within their families, their places of work and their communities (*ibid.*).

At the same time the resources of non-Native culture are integrated with traditional Native perspectives. For example, a pamphlet about the empowerment of women has the title "The Healing Journey" (1994), includes in its introduction the statement, "It has never been more important for Aboriginal men, women, and children to regain what was once theirs." It also draws upon forms of analysis, role-plays, tasks and activities which are closely linked with training workshops on assertiveness and self-help.

Liaison with Metropolitan Toronto Police Services, originally through the Native Liaison Office and subsequently through other links, was described as an ongoing aspect of the work of the Centre. Communication and consultation included discussions with the most senior officers to the level of the Chief and Deputy Chiefs as well as with those in Community Services and the Aboriginal Peacekeeping Unit. In addition to regular, monthly meetings with the Aboriginal Peacekeeping Unit and a member of Community Services, there is an informal agreement that direct communications are possible at any time. From time to time, these communications have been used to inform police services of particular difficulties in relations between the police and Aboriginal people; of particular criticisms of the police by Aboriginal people; of Aboriginal perspectives on critical incidents not only in the city but also from further afield in the province; and as a channel of communications in circumstances of conflict. In summary, a respondent from the Centre said "police in the city are very good...they're open to working with us...they don't necessarily agree with us but we do agree a process." Another summary phrase, with reference to policing in the province, was "Toronto is probably the most anti-racist police force." It was suggested that the more remote the provincial police, "the more red-necked" their approach to Aboriginal people.

The police maintained permanent liaison with the centre and a number of officers had worked formally and informally to support its continuation. Key officers had maintained communications on a range of issues, reinforcing the work of the centre, which was dealing with people who were the victims of crime, and facilitating implementation of the vision of empowerment at the core of the Centre's work.

Within the broader context of these developments in Toronto, as in Canada as a whole, the community orientation of police services has increased. Arguably the rationale and mechanisms for the development of the Aboriginal Peace Keeping Unit and liaison with the Native Women's unit would not have come together without three strategic dimensions of change in police services in Toronto. These three dimensions are: (i) community policing, which has been progressively developed, piloted and implemented as a strategic initiative; (ii) a review of strategies for the implementation of Metropolitan Toronto Police race relations policy (completed in 1995); and, (iii) specific attention by the police to the issue of relations between the police and Aboriginal people in the City.

None of these initiatives has guaranteed permanency. Each has been contingent upon particular political and economic contexts; each has been an outcome of specific local negotiations and struggles.

Vancouver Police and Native Liaison Society

While British Columbia is represented as "a large body of land entirely surrounded by envy" (Eric Nicol, cited in Ministry of Industry, 1995, p. 10), and while Vancouver, as the largest urban centre within British Columbia, continues to expand and attract wealth, the location also draws in people with problems. Those problems are concentrated in a locality of the downtown-eastside part of Vancouver. Here there are people who have problems with legal and non-legal drugs, where HIV is prevalent and where the annual homicide rate is estimated at more than twenty times the average for Canada as a whole.

As a result of the concentration of individual and collective difficulties in this specific locality within Vancouver, efforts were made within the Police Department and amongst local Aboriginal people to remedy the predicament of Aboriginal people in the City. These joint efforts led to the establishment of a store-front centre, close to the Police Department building. It was recognised that Aboriginal people in the City, many of whom had come from distant parts of the country, included many victims of crime who were not coming forward to gain support. In some cases, they did not know their rights while in others, their reluctance derived from fear of further victimisation or other anxieties. Of the estimated 67,000 Aboriginals in greater Vancouver, including only about 1,000 on the Musqueam reserve to the south of the City, a considerable number, difficult to estimate precisely since it included a transient population, were at any one time in and around the downtown eastside. "Why do they come to skid row?" said a community worker, "they just gravitate here!"

The store-front serves as a base for Victim Assistance Services. There are three Aboriginal staff, assisted by volunteers. Two constables from the Vancouver Police Department's Native Liaison Unit also work at the centre. The centre is managed by an executive committee, which steers, monitors and reviews the work undertaken and seeks to gain resources for the centre to continue. The staff provide information about a range of services available to victims of crime, including police investigations, court appearances and trial dates. In their own words, as summarised on a leaflet disseminated by the Unit:

The Vancouver Police Native Liaison Society is there to:

• Prevent crime and violence through counselling, education, intervention and referrals.
• Improve communication between the police, Native peoples, and downtown community groups.
• Reduce the fear of crime and reporting crime.
• Increase Native involvement in crime prevention.

Questions posed in a leaflet issued by the Vancouver Police Native Liaison Society, as the Unit is termed, give an insight into the main areas of its work and the personal qualities of support provided, including individual counselling:

Have you:

• been the victim of an assault or a crime?
• witnessed or been involved in a crime?
• been thinking about reporting a crime?

Need help?
Want to talk to someone?
Want to help someone?

The cautious way in which Aboriginal people have responded to the centre was reported by a police officer who was a founder of the service. He described how sometimes two Aboriginal people would come into the office, tentatively talking about general issues, and then, after about half an hour of discussion, one of them would get up to leave, to go elsewhere. This departure, leaving one person alone to raise the problem which spurred the visit, would only occur if the reconnaissance by the two visitors had successfully established confidence in the staff of the centre.

The three full-time case workers have now established a network of contacts amongst Aboriginal people in the City and provide a wide range of formal and informal support. Sometimes they are called upon to pick up victims and take them to court. Most commonly, those needing help in this way are victims of spousal abuse or common sexual abuse. "Bad love is worse than no love" said one of the community workers, telling of the support necessary for single mothers in the City, geographically isolated from their families and in many cases estranged from support back home.

Sometimes they provide help for children who have left foster-care. During the week before they were interviewed, the workers in the Unit assisted a 12-year-old boy who had run away from a foster home. Several issues regarding Native children were of concern to the workers at the centre. The fostering of Native children was a cause of contention. It was estimated that 70-75% of children in care are First Nations children. It was felt that the arrangements for foster care continued the tradition of the residential schools by operating in ways that divided children from their parents, with the method of funding, including the provision of a spending allowance for children, contributing to the separation of families. One worker referred to a conversation with someone who benefited financially from the arrangements for foster care, reporting that she had said, "Our kids are your cash cow." Reinforcing care about the family tragedies involved, another worker said "Mothers Day is one of the worst days in the year."

The education of Native children contributed to the situation, with low teacher expectations. One respondent typified the educational experience of Aboriginal children as follows: "Our kids get Basket Weaving 101, that's it!" In her view, streaming and banding contribute to Native children leaving school with low qualifications and with a high likelihood that they were destined for welfare.

Children and young people were amongst the many clients who were HIV positive. These included cases of a 12-year-old who had been working as a prostitute; a 17-year-old young man needing counselling after being informed of the result of tests; and a man who had recently moved to the City who had picked up the virus after moving in with someone soon after his arrival, not knowing of her condition. Sometimes, the combination of living conditions, state of health and drug dependency meant as one community worker put it that "this is a candy store for someone who wants to do something bad."

Centre workers were frequently asked by relatives to locate missing persons who had left reserves and come to the city. Success was quite frequent despite the transient nature of the Aboriginal people in the City because of the extensive contacts and underlying trust in the informal communications between the people there. Some are found on the streets, and have followed the injunction, for example, as one respondent expressed it in interview "to get in touch with your Mother." Others have been located within the justice system. Sadly, other missing people have been found through contacts with a hospital morgue, when assistance has come too late.

The Vancouver Police Native Liaison Society store-front, moved after a few years, when the Vancouver Police Department itself moved to new police headquarters, into a suite of offices on the ground floor of the old police building (still used as a police station). Prior to the move, people were consulted about the effects of the move and police and Native liaison workers reported that there was little, if any, adverse reaction to the possibility of transfer. The interior of the Unit provides offices for confidential counselling.

The Aboriginal identities of the Unit are immediately apparent on entry. Its walls are decorated with illustrations drawn, painted and printed by Native people. The centrality of Native traditional wisdom is also evident in the Unit's logo, a graphic depiction of an eagle, represented in a circular design in red and black, and described on a poster as follows:

> Robert Davidson's 1979 print Eagle depicts an eagle in the outer segment of the circle and a frog in the middle circle. The eagle represents protection, the outer self that the world sees.

The frog represents the inner self, the heart, the gut reaction. We must allow the feelings to show, to help the outside. Without the inner frog, the eagle isn't complete. If you take the frog away, the eagle has no mouth.

The workers at the Unit evaluate the work of the store-front regularly. The complex task of providing help to those on the streets, to victims of crime, to those with health problems, and those separated from their families, is not readily evaluated. The logging of cases indicates a continuing need for the Unit's services. A senior police officer involved in establishing the Unit said in interview that he had anticipated, at the time the unit was established, that it might need to operate for a few years and might then no longer be necessary. However, continuing experience with the problems of Aboriginal people in the City reinforces the current view that the need for the store-front is permanent. The problems of Aboriginal people in the City cannot be mopped up by a single organisation of dedicated workers. They are being re-created through the operation of larger, structural and local forces and the underlying causes do not, in the view of the members of the Unit, appear to be diminishing.

Conclusions

This chapter has drawn evidence from diverse empirical and theoretical materials to illustrate some of the key features of the circumstances facing Aboriginal people in the cities. Three main themes have been addressed. First, the continuing urbanisation of Aboriginal people has been summarised and the characteristics of the urban Aboriginal population outlined. While there is a high incidence of poverty, a higher proportion of women and young people in the cities, and a high proportion of single parent families, there is also evidence of diversity in the Aboriginal population. Questions were raised in this section about Aboriginal identity in a context of migration and change. Second, Aboriginal people's experience of criminal justice was highlighted as an example of a particularly critical issue. Within this, the experiences of women and of the victims of crime were considered together with the possibility of incorporating Aboriginal traditions into the criminal justice system. Finally, through examination of case studies in two Canadian cities, the emergent themes of Aboriginal experience in the city, Aboriginal identity and traditions and Aboriginal experiences of criminal justice were explored in a qualitative way. These case studies have shown how Aboriginal people, including Aboriginal women in particular, are shaping new relationships in urban areas. In doing so, they are drawing upon Aboriginal and non-Aboriginal traditions, re-negotiating power relationships and synthesising the components of new identities. While obvious contradictions exist between the activities of some sections of the non-Aboriginal institutions with which they co-operate and others; and while change may only be partial, nevertheless, it is clear that there are some measurable practical achievements of the work of these Aboriginal people.

The Royal Commission on Aboriginal Peoples drew attention to the absence of organization among urban Aboriginal people and the absence of coherent or co-ordinated policies:

Following three decades of urbanization, development of a strong community still remains largely incomplete. Many urban Aboriginal people are impoverished and unorganized. No coherent or co-ordinated policies to meet their needs are in place, despite the fact that they make up almost half of Canada's Aboriginal population. They have been largely excluded from discussions about self-government and institutional development. Aboriginal people in urban areas have little collective visibility or power (*RCAP*, 1996c, p. 531).

The Royal Commission identified the need for resources to support policy development and implementation:

It is clear that they urgently require resources to support existing organizations and create new institutions to enhance their cultural identity (*ibid.*).

The case studies above illustrate how positively resources can be used to support Aboriginal people in the city, creating paths for social inclusion and rendering Aboriginal people visible in their dealings with the non-Aboriginal institutions of the city.

References

Bernier, R. (1997) "The Dimensions of Wage Inequality among Aboriginal Peoples" *Statistics Canada* (No. 109).

Clatworthy, S. J. (1995) "The Migration and Mobility Patterns of Canada's Aboriginal Population" research study prepared for RCAP.

Clatworthy, S.J. *et al.* (1995) "Patterns of Employment, Unemployment and Poverty" (Part One) Final report presented by *Four Directions Consulting Group* to the Royal Commission on Aboriginal Peoples.

Dickson, S. (1993) *Hey Monias! The Story of Raphael Ironstand*, Vancouver: Arsenal Pulp Press.

Driedger, L. (1996) *Multiethnic Canada: Identities and Inequalities*, Toronto: Oxford University Press.

Indian Policing Policy Review (1990) *Task Force Report*, Ottawa: Indian Affairs and Northern Development.

Jackson, M. (1988) "Locking Up Natives in Canada" Report of the Canadian Bar Association Committee on Imprisonment and Release; reprinted in *U.B.C. Law Review*, vol. 23, 1989.

Jackson, M.A. (1994) "Aboriginal Women and Self-Government" in Hylton, J.H., Editor, *Aboriginal Self-Government in Canada: Current Trends and Issues*, Saskatoon: Purich Publishing.

LaPrairie, C. (1994) *Seen But Not Heard: Native People in the Inner City*, Ottawa: Department of Justice of Canada.

LaRocque, E. (1997) "Re-examining Culturally Appropriate Models in Criminal Justice Applications," in Michael Asch, *Aboriginal and Treaty Rights in Canada: Essays on Law, Equality, and Respect for Difference*, Vancouver: University of British Columbia Press.

Luke, C. and Luke A. (1998) "Interracial Families: Difference Within Difference," *Ethnic and Racial Studies*, vol. 21, no. 4, July, pp. 728-753.

McMillan, A.D. (1988) *Native Peoples and Cultures of Canada: An Anthropological Overview*, Vancouver: Douglas and McIntyre.

Metropolitan Toronto Police (1993) *Annual Report*.

Ministry of Solicitor General (1997) *Building Bridges: Off-Reserve Policing.*

Ministry of Industry (1995) "Canada: A Portrait," *Statistics Canada*, Ottawa.

Miller, J. R. (1996) *Shingwauk's Vision: A History of Native Residential Schools*, Toronto: University of Toronto Press.

Monture-OKanee, P.A. and Turpel M. E. (1992) "Aboriginal Peoples and Canadian Criminal Law: Rethinking Justice," *U.B.C. Law Review* (Special Edition: Aboriginal Justice, p. 249).

Native Women's Resource Centre of Toronto (1994) *The Healing Journey*, Toronto.

Oppal, W.T. (1994) *Closing the Gap: Policing and the Community*, Report of the Commission of Inquiry into Policing in British Columbia.

Quigley, T. (1994) "Some Issues in Sentencing of Aboriginal Offenders" in Gosse, R., Henderson, J. and Carter, R. *Continuing Poundmaker and Riel's Quest*, Presentations Made at a Conference on Aboriginal Peoples and Justice, Saskatoon: Purich Publishing.

Royal Commission on Aboriginal Peoples (1996a) *Bridging the Cultural Divide*, Ottawa: Minister of Supply and Services.

Royal Commission on Aboriginal Peoples (1996b) *Report of the Royal Commission on Aboriginal Peoples, Volume 1, Looking Forward, Looking Back*, Ottawa: Minister of Supply and Services.

Royal Commission on Aboriginal Peoples (1996c), *Report of the Royal Commission on Aboriginal People, Volume 4, Perspectives and Realities*, Ottawa: Minister of Supply and Services.

Satzewich, V. and Wotherspoon, T. (1993) *First Nations: Race, Class and Gender Relations*, Scarborough: Nelson Canada.

Statistics Canada (1998) *The Daily*.

Stl'atl'imx Nation Tribal Police and Stl'atl'imx Tribal Police Board (1995) *A Short History*, Lillooet: British Columbia.

Todd, F. and Todd, R. (1997) *Police Community Partnerships: Bridging Solitudes*, Report to the Canadian High Commission in the United Kingdom.

Wannell, T. and Caron, N. (1994) "A Look at Employment-Equity Groups Among Recent Postsecondary Graduates: Visible Minorities, Aboriginal Peoples and the Activity Limited," Labour Market Outlook and Sectoral Analysis Branch, Human Resources Development Canada, *Statistics Canada*, report no. 69.

Chapter 5

Aboriginal Peoples: Health and Healing

Geoffrey Mercer

Introduction

Throughout the twentieth century, the health status of the Aboriginal population, whether assessed by mortality or morbidity rates or other indicators of general social malaise, has been significantly worse than for the rest of Canadians. Aboriginal peoples have been denied control of their own communities and lives, and have felt helpless in the midst of wide-ranging social and political injustices. Not until the 1970s did the growth of political protest impress governments with the need for a change in Aboriginal-state relations in order to address these deep-seated inequalities, including the significant "health divide." Indeed, a central objective of these Aboriginal campaigns has been to link action against the sources of ill-health with a wider healing process that restores Aboriginal rights and self-government.

This chapter will examine the emergence of "health and healing" in recent policy debates. It will: first, outline the sorry legacy of Aboriginal ill-health during the twentieth century; second, outline the changing trajectory of health policy; third, explore the central features of a wide-ranging critique and the promotion of a "new strategy," as presented in the *Report of the Royal Commission on Aboriginal Peoples* (*RCAP*, 1996b, 1996c); and finally, examine specific recommendations for health services, together with the initial government proposals for a "renewed partnership" in the health care system.

A Sorry Legacy

The contact with Europeans is widely accepted as disastrous for the health of Aboriginal Peoples: with the population decimated by infectious diseases, and the environment and its resources increasingly diminished and polluted (Young, 1988). The pattern of ill-health is maintained through the twentieth century, with much higher mortality rates among Aboriginal peoples compared with the rest of the Canadian population.

There have been important reductions in Aboriginal mortality rates, particularly over the last three decades, but a significant health divide remains because of parallel improvements for all Canadians. Thus, the Infant Mortality Rate (IMR) for Registered Indians in the late 1980s was one-sixth of what it was in the 1950s, while the Inuit IMR declined even more sharply. Again, recent figures show a fall in the IMR for Registered Indians from 28 to 11 per 1,000 live births between 1979 and 1993 but this was matched by a decline from 11 to 6 in the overall Canadian rate. These patterns are replicated across most measures of health status and well-being:

- life expectancy at birth in 1990 was 7-8 years less for First Nations than for Canadians as a whole—ranging from 66.9 years for men to 74 years for women, compared with national rates of 73.9 and 80.5 years respectively;
- mortality rates for registered Indians in the late 1980s were the highest for all age groups, with infant mortality (at 14 and 20 per 1,000 births for Registered Indians and Inuit) more than twice the national rate;
- the causes of mortality demonstrate significant contrasts: accidents, violence and self-injury are particularly high, with the Aboriginal suicide rate six times more than the Canadian average (and eight times higher among Aboriginal females aged 15-24 years);
- levels of infectious diseases are much higher in the Aboriginal population (with the incidence of tuberculosis rate almost seven times greater); while visual, hearing and communication impairments, degenerative and life threatening conditions (particularly diabetes and heart disease) are more prevalent and/or increasing at a faster rate (including HIV/AIDS and cancer);

- higher rates of utilisation of health services, and longer lengths of stay in hospital; and
- higher levels of social malaise, as instanced by rates of alcoholism, drug and solvent addiction, accidents, violence and self-harm, child and sexual abuse (Young, 1994; RCAP, 1996b).

The data base on which these conclusions are drawn is far less reliable for the Aboriginal than the non-Aboriginal population. The Department of Indian Affairs and Northern Development (DIAND) is responsible for those First Nations people (Registered Indian and Inuit) living on reserves or in northern communities for whom the federal government has constitutional jurisdiction. In contrast, census data have recently shifted to self-definition as the criterion for Aboriginal status. Indeed, both data sets are characterised by changes in collection and reporting practices, particularly in their recording of morbidity levels and patterns. Consequently, for most of the twentieth century, the health status of the non-status Indian and Métis populations, who comprised two-thirds of those claiming Aboriginal ancestry in 1990, is largely undocumented. The Aboriginal Peoples Survey, 1991 fills in some of the gaps but it contains its own shortcomings (particularly of under-enumeration).

This paucity of national statistics offers a revealing, if negative, commentary on the federal approach to Aboriginal health. It is only in the last quarter of the twentieth century that the extent and character of Aboriginal ill-health has been widely acknowledged as a failure of the Canadian state that required something more than *ad hoc* and piecemeal initiatives at the local level.

Identifying the Failures of Aboriginal Health Policy

The policy response to the high levels of disease and social malaise which separated Aboriginal Peoples from the rest of Canadian society in the 1950s concentrated on controlling the worst excesses, not least where these threatened the non-Aboriginal population (as with TB). This incorporated the extension of mainstream services that followed a medically-dominated, disease-oriented approach, that denied Aboriginal people involvement in planning or organisation. This contrasted with Aboriginal arguments that health is integral to self-government, and for some a treaty right (although the promise to provide a "medicine chest" clause was only spelled out in Treaty 6). For their part, Aboriginal organisations interpreted this as an entitlement to a broad range of primary, secondary and tertiary health services, whereas the federal government has historically adopted a minimalist reading, something more equivalent to a first aid kit.

The separation of the Aboriginal population from its traditional ways of life and healing practices has reinforced its dependence on "mainstream" medical services, institutions and professional experts. Hence, the "health system" for First Nations in the twentieth century has been dominated by non-Aboriginal practitioners and extra-community institutions, such as DIAND and the Medical Services Branch (MSB), along with their non-Aboriginal "experts." While the assimilationist rationale for the forced removal to and abuse of Aboriginal children in residential schools has attracted widespread condemnation, the denigration of traditional health knowledge and practitioners has attracted far less criticism. Aboriginal health practice was formally replaced by a rudimentary medical system. By the 1950s, this comprised 18 regional hospitals, 65 health centres and 33 nursing stations, although most were minimally resourced (Waldram *et al.*, 1995). These facilities were supplemented by the transportation of sick people and pregnant women away from their families and communities to hospitals in urban centres. These were generally experienced as unsympathetic, if not actually hostile, to the provision of culturally-appropriate care (Kaufert and Forsyth, 1994).

The low priority accorded to Aboriginal health policy is further illustrated by the changing location and status of "Indian Affairs" within the federal bureaucracy. In 1936, health policy was taken over by the Department of Mines and Resources, then responsibility was transferred in 1945 to the newly established Department of Health and Welfare, before in 1962 the Indian Health Services Directorate was subsumed within the Medical Services Branch that dealt with all those groups not subject to provincial jurisdiction (Young, 1988). This left the Department of Indian Affairs and Northern Development responsible for policies in such areas as housing, drinking water and sewerage, and economic development. However, while the significance of initiatives in these areas for public health was recognised for most Canadians, federal policies for Aboriginal peoples seemed to largely ignore the connections.

Inter-governmental disputes, dating back to the Constitution Act, 1867, have also plagued Aboriginal health policy making. While section 91(24) identifies federal jurisdiction for "Indians, and Lands reserved for the Indians," section 92 allocates the establishment and delivery of human services to the provinces. This meant that health policy action has been characterised by recriminations between the two levels about which of them has failed to meet its constitutional obligations. Since the introduction of Medicare, the federal government has reimbursed the costs for First Nations people and also provided those living off-reserve with a range of non-insured health benefits (including dental, eye glasses, medical aids, prescription drugs and transportation). However, while First Nations have claimed that these benefits are portable off-reserve, the federal government has treated this as a policy decision, rather than a right.

The Métis and non-status Indian populations, who fall outside the Indian Act, notwithstanding their inclusion in section 35 of the Constitution Act, 1982, are part of the provincial jurisdiction. They are therefore entitled to the same health services as any other resident of a province, although these rights have been widely ignored in practice. The rise of an urban-based and diverse Aboriginal population has presented increasing dilemmas for policy-makers. However, provinces and metropolitan governments have been loathe to fund Aboriginal-specific programmes.

Nor did the national debates about health care, surrounding for example, the Royal Commission on Health Services (Hall Report, 1964), the 1970 Federal Task Force on the Cost of Health Services (Canada, 1969), and the passage of the Canada Health Act, 1984, dwell on the shortcomings or difficulties facing Aboriginal health care. Federal leverage on the organisation and delivery of health care and associated social welfare programmes by the provinces was reinforced through its significant role in cost-sharing under the Established Programs Financing (EPF) scheme, and the Canada Assistance Plan (CAP). This legitimated monitoring how far the provinces met the central objectives of Medicare. Nonetheless, the federal government did not extend the same concern for basic standards to health service performance in Aboriginal communities. Instead, it seemed more intent on controlling costs, by restricting Aboriginal entitlement for non-insured medical benefits and the reimbursement of health care for those who had moved off-reserve.

With the growth of protests about their overall treatment by Canadian governments, Aboriginal organisations became increasingly vocal in their criticisms of health services and policies. In one of the most comprehensive rebuttals, the Manitoba Indian Brotherhood, in its 1971 document, *Wahbung: Our Tomorrows*, identified external control as the major issue:

> The effectiveness of the health services programs has historically been hampered by both the lack of understanding and the lack of involvement of Indian people. Externally controlled hospitals and nursing stations, externally developed programs of curative or preventive medicine have left little room for local participation (Manitoba Indian Brotherhood, 1971, p. 172).

Aboriginal participation in health programmes advanced slowly and unevenly. This spanned individual health centres, health education and promotion campaigns, and the James Bay and Northern Quebec Agreement 1975. These did not amount to a concerted federal plan, but were triggered by the pressures to deal with land claims, and gathering political demands by Aboriginal peoples for the redress of constitutional wrongs. These protests ran parallel to the resurgence of conflict between Quebec and the rest of Canada, with calls to recognise the province's distinct position within Canada, if not political independence. Attempts to respond to Quebec's demands generated a variety of innovative constitutional and other political proposals, including the Constitution Act 1982. These, in turn, gave a further impetus to campaigns for Aboriginal rights and self-government.

Health Transfer Policy

The immediate catalyst to a reformulation of Aboriginal health policy was protests at the government plans to reduce health care funding in 1978 (particularly non-insured health benefits). In an effort to explain its position, the federal government spelled out what were termed the "three pillars" of its First Nations health policy:

- an emphasis on community development, including the improvement of underlying socio-economic conditions;
- reaffirmation of the traditional trust relationship between First Nations and the federal government; and

- integration with the "mainstream" of the Canadian health care system (Favel-King, 1994).

This statement did not go far enough for some: the *Report of the Advisory Commission on Indian and Inuit Health Consultation* (Berger, 1980) argued for greater Aboriginal participation in programme design and service delivery. The federal response included an offer to transfer administrative responsibility for specific programmes, such as the National Native Alcohol and Drug Abuse Programme (NNADAP), and the Community Health Representative Programme (CHRP), introduced in 1980-81. In addition, a five-year Community Health Demonstration Project was introduced in 1982 to promote the transfer of community health services in order to:

- enable First Nations to "design health programmes, establish services and allocate funds according to community health priorities";
- reinforce the accountability of First Nations to their members; and
- promote adherence to health programmes (Favel-King, 1994).

Evaluation of the programme has been mixed (Beavais, 1988; Young and Smith, 1992), and largely depends on whether it is judged in terms of a shift in control over health policy to First Nations, or against the more modest DIAND preference for the delegation of administrative responsibility for specific programmes. Nevertheless, applications from First Nations gathered momentum, so that by March 1996, 141 First Nations had concluded agreements and 237 were in pre-transfer negotiations (RCAP, 1996b).

Peguis Case Study

A case study of the development of community health services in Manitoba's largest reserve, Peguis First Nation, located approximately 170 kilometres north of Winnipeg, illuminates some of the key issues raised by the health transfer initiative (Cohen and O'Neil, 1994). The Peguis proposal for funding in 1987 acknowledged that the Health Transfer Initiative did not provide the level or range of control demanded:

...the ideal that is envisioned would be an arrangement enshrined in the self-government concept. The concept would see us establishing our own institutions and systems independent of government interference save fiscal appropriations by virtue of entitlement under our treaty, Aboriginal and inherent rights (Peguis First Nation, 1987).

However, the perceived opportunities to improve on what was currently available and build for future Aboriginal control outweighed these doubts. The Peguis negotiated their transfer agreement in July 1991. They were well-positioned to enter the initiative early as they had accumulated over ten years' experience of participation in the administration of local health services. On the positive side, the Peguis concluded that the transfer programme gave them a greater sense of "ownership" of community health programmes. It is further credited with improving the level of funding for health services, as well as increasing fiscal flexibility, so that locally-defined service needs could be given a higher priority. This included the enhancement of traditional healing services.

On the debit side, key features of the programme militated against full Peguis control. These included restrictions on levels of funding and the range of programmes covered, with non-insured health services a noteworthy omission. Health budgets were frozen at the time of transfer and based on the number of registered band members then living on the reserve, which ignored migration patterns (Assembly of First Nations, 1988). This also inhibited matching programmes to local preferences, or changing health needs, as where Fetal Alcohol Syndrome or HIV/AIDS cases increase post-transfer. All of this disadvantaged Aboriginal communities compared to other Canadians. It did not mean that innovative developments were impossible, but significantly, where the Peguis addressed one of their priorities—mental health provision—it was done outside the transfer initiative.

In addition, not all of the local community wanted to move away from mainstream medical services, and there was some anxiety that the "traditional" route was being forced on local people. Conversely, some traditional healers feared that even partial integration would lead to greater non-Aboriginal regulation. The Peguis compromised by including traditional healing as a service option.

Criticisms that the programme offered only a partial step forward towards Aboriginal control are echoed in the experience of many other First Nations (Young and Smith, 1992; Tremblay, 1995). There were also widely expressed fears that, by agreeing to the principle of health transfer, Aboriginal peoples were undermining their treaty right to health, and tacitly accepting a move from federal into provincial jurisdiction (Assembly of First Nations, 1988). This was widely depicted as a federal objective that stretched back to the 1960s (Speck, 1989). A further concern was that, as part of the overall government commitment to welfare state retrenchment, the Medical Services Branch was "trimming" non-insured health benefits, such as eye examinations, dental care, drug prescriptions, and aids to independent living. It appeared that the federal/treaty obligation was being diminished by changing economic conditions and the political trend towards restructuring government activities.

Addressing Culturally Inaccessible Services

Mainstream health services were often berated by Aboriginal clients because of their exclusively eurocentric approach. This lack of attention to the specific cultural needs and concerns of Aboriginal people is illustrated in a case study of models for delivering primary care, referral and crisis intervention in urban settings, such as walk-in clinics, hospital emergency rooms and primary care practices (McClure *et al.*, 1993). City centre walk-in clinics and hospital emergency rooms, which are usually open from 12-24 hours a day, provide the main source of primary and acute care. For example, the Westside Clinic in downtown Saskatoon is widely used as a "drop in" centre by Aboriginal people in contrast to the rest of the population (Waldram, 1990; Waldram and Layman, 1988). In Winnipeg, the Health Sciences Centre and St. Boniface General Hospital perform similar "drop in" functions (Kaufert with Forsyth, 1994). The relatively "open door" character of these facilities is the main attraction, although few provide anything like the range of culturally sensitive services available to most reserve populations.

In the 1980s, an emerging alternative was the community health centre (CHC). This offered a generic programme approach geared to a specific, multi-cultural population base. Thus, Klinic Inc. Community Health Centre in Winnipeg was established for a diverse inner city population (including 12% with an Aboriginal background) to deliver programmes ranging from crisis intervention, reproductive health, drug abuse, HIV testing to sexual abuse. However, a user survey in the mid-1980s identified various linguistic and cultural barriers, with too few Aboriginal staff, and strained practitioner-client relationships. Over the last decade, Klinic has endeavoured to make its services more culturally sensitive and has increased its recruitment of Aboriginal staff (Kaufert with Forsyth, 1994).

The demand for linguistically accessible and culturally appropriate services within mainstream services is also evident in the growth of medical interpreters. The first dedicated interpreting service for Aboriginal patients in a Canadian urban hospital was set up in Winnipeg in 1971 (Kaufert with Forsyth, 1994). It demonstrated a wide range of misunderstandings and conflicts with mainstream staff over hospital procedures and regulations. The interpreter's role became increasingly merged with that of patient advocate/ culture broker. This ranged from requests to disconnect fire alarm systems for "smudging" ceremonies in the patients' rooms, to persuading hospital staff to allow patients to discontinue "western" medications immediately prior to commencing traditional treatment (O'Neil 1988; Kaufert and O'Neil 1990). This led to the Manitoba government supporting a two-year training programme for interpreters leading to qualification as a "Native Liaison Worker." It emphasised assertiveness and communication skills, understanding medical terminology, family violence and crisis counselling, inter-cultural mediation and health education (Kaufert with Forsyth, 1994).

A further instructive study of an initiative to deliver medical care in a culturally appropriate way is provided by the Innuulisivik Maternity Centre (Fletcher and O'Neil, 1994). Until the 1950s, births in the Nunavik region were assisted by traditional birth attendants. With the growth of permanent "village" communities and the building of nursing stations, professional nurse-midwives acquired a higher profile. Then, in the early 1970s, federal health administrators decided that all births involving women from Hudson Bay coast communities should take place in a hospital setting. This reflected prevailing medical opinion about the most effective way to counter the region's high infant mortality rate. However, there was minimal local consultation, and the isolation of Inuit women from their families and communities was found a very stressful experience and widely criticised as a form of coercive assimilation.

Over time, an alliance of Inuit women and non-Inuit health care providers and administrators, backed by a community consensus across the region, persuaded the federal government to set up a regional Maternity Centre (against medical opposition).

Ultimately the Innuulisivik Maternity Centre is a laboratory in which two different cultural perspectives on pregnancy and birth meet. A hybrid form of health care service delivery is evolving in which both culture groups provide differing perspectives. The Maternity Centre provides a model for co-operative management of health care that redresses perceived injustices of the past and contributes to a larger process of social and cultural renewal as well as the reacquisition of political power (Fletcher and O'Neil, 1994).

In summary, the period between the 1960s and 1980s witnessed mounting condemnation of the extent and entrenched character of social and health inequalities, and the alienation of Aboriginal peoples from mainstream services. This encouraged support for increased Aboriginal involvement in programme planning and delivery, and greater awareness of the need for culturally appropriate and accessible service provision. Yet the transfer of administrative responsibilities for health programmes was slow and limited. In this respect it mirrored broader frustrations at the failure to address historic injustices which characterised Aboriginal-state relations (Frideres, 1993; Satzewich and Wotherspoon, 1993).

A "New Strategy": The Royal Commission Report

The continuing failure of constitutional debates to find a new way forward in Aboriginal-state relations was given renewed urgency by the spectre of violent confrontations following the Mohawk stand-off at Oka. This led to the setting up of a Royal Commission on Aboriginal Peoples in 1991. Its deliberations gave focus to the widest spectrum of Aboriginal grievances, with "health and healing" a continuing theme. The Royal Commission Report (RCAP, 1996a, 1996b, 1996c, 1996d) outlined a comprehensive Aboriginal health strategy that built on established grievances and criticisms. Its main objectives comprise:

- **equity**—equal outcomes in health status, and access to health services;

- **holistic approach**—recognition that body, mind, spirit and emotions are inter-connected, in individual and community approaches to health, as well as guiding integrated service provision;
- **Aboriginal control of services**—top-down, non-Aboriginal control does not work since it is rooted in alien values and priorities; and
- recognition of the important **diversity** across Aboriginal communities, based on community needs, and appropriate service provision (RCAP, 1996b, pp. 223-4).

Confronting Health Inequalities

In developing its analysis of Aboriginal ill-health, it was argued that policy-makers had to address the whole range of social and historical injustices experienced by Aboriginal peoples:

> The Innu are sick and dying because of a well-documented syndrome of ill health brought on by the enforced dependency and attempted acculturation of an entire people…for the Innu, health and ill health are profoundly political issues, inseparable from social and economic considerations…the real health system will be one which will allow Innu society to function properly again, one which will remove foreign domination, and one which will offer the Innu respect as a distinct people (Peter Penashue, quoted in RCAP, 1996b, p. 315).

The reasons for the manifest inequalities between social groups have attracted considerable policy interest world-wide. Contending explanations centre on: artefactual/measurement biases; social selection (biological) differences; culture/behaviour and lifestyle issues; and materialist or structuralist accounts. These are not meant to be mutually exclusive, and a key Canadian contribution to these debates has been the notion of a "health field" where human biology, the environment, lifestyle and health care organisation all exert separate and combined effects (Lalonde, 1974). This has been taken forward in World Health Organisation (WHO) discussions about "Achieving Health For All By the Year 2000" which identified the following key principles: equity; health promotion; community participation; multi-sectoral collaboration; primary health care; and international co-operation (WHO, 1985).

Equity in health care suggests, "equal access to available care for equal need; equal utilisation for equal need; equal quality of care for all" (Whitehead, 1992:434). It follows that certain pre-requisites for health must be assured. However, achievement of the substantive rights of citizenship still eludes Aboriginal Peoples (Frideres, 1993). The RCAP Commissioners broadly accepted arguments about the primacy of material or socio-economic explanations of the inequalities in health between Aboriginal Peoples and other Canadians (Kirmayer *et al.*, 1994; Aitken and Mitchell, 1995), while recognising the contribution of other factors. However, they offer little analysis of health inequalities across the Aboriginal population, as this relates to different structural factors and socio-economic circumstances and conditions within and between communities, except for an overview of the particular issues confronting Aboriginal women.

The Royal Commission pays particular credence to arguments that 90 percent of the determinants of health are "non-medical," and that increased expenditure on health services does not bring continuing improvements in health status (Lalonde, 1974; McKeown, 1976). The exaggerated claims for biomedicine are countered by identification of an overlap between western science and traditional knowledge such that: "Principles of health and healing long held by indigenous cultures are now being confirmed by scientific research" (RCAP, 1996b, p. 220). Policy attention is thus re-oriented to countering the "new determinants of health"—which similarly resonate with traditional Aboriginal thinking:

- poverty and social assistance (particularly high levels of poverty, unemployment and welfare dependence);
- adequacy of the built environment (notably problems of clean water supply, sanitation and poor standard housing) and community infrastructure; and
- environmental degradation (the impact of pollution and contamination on traditional food sources, ways of life and ties to the land) (RCAP, 1996b, p. 166).

This list highlights the importance of greater inter-sectoral collaboration in policy-making, both between government departments and across the several levels of government. The Report also strongly commends the promotion of "healthy lifestyles" and making "healthy choices." Nevertheless, it is acknowledged that,

the social problems facing Aboriginal people today are proving more resistant to change than are their physical health problems (RCAP, 1996b, p. 123).

Holistic Approach

The mainstream health care system has been contemptuous of Aboriginal health beliefs and practices. Ill-health and social malaise have been explored as individual/community failings. This disregards Aboriginal Peoples' historical experience of discrimination and maltreatment which has encouraged low individual and community self-esteem. Mainstream health policy for Aboriginal communities is characterised by a piecemeal approach, concentrating on *ad hoc* programmes for specific problems—such as teenage pregnancies, suicide, drug addiction, child and sexual abuse.

In contrast, the Aboriginal definition of "health" extends beyond medically defined health outcomes to highlight physical, mental, emotional and spiritual well-being (Favel-King, 1994). It is located in traditional culture and spirituality.

The Native concept of health...is said to be holistic because it integrates and gives equal emphasis to the physical, spiritual, mental and emotional aspects of the person. The circle is used to represent the inseparability of the individual, family, community and world...The circle (or wheel) embodies the notion of health as harmony or balance in all aspects of one's life...[Human beings] must be in balance with [their] physical and social environments...in order to live and grow. Imbalance can threaten the conditions that enable the person...to reach his or her full potential as a human being (Feather, 1991, pp. 1-2).

This approach informs the Aboriginal emphasis on "community healing" and the search for causes well beyond individual circumstances. It demands a wide-ranging political, economic and cultural programme for the regeneration and support of Aboriginal communities and their ways of life. It also encompasses a positive orientation towards health. This echoes the definition adopted by the World Health Organization in 1948: "Health is a state of complete physical, mental and social well-being, [not] the absence of disease or infirmity."

More recently, the WHO has argued for an emphasis on health as a "resource" which enables people to manage and change their surroundings. In embracing this theme, the Federal Health Minister, Jake Epp, identified three main challenges in the pursuit of "health for all": reducing inequalities, increasing prevention and enhancing coping (Epp, 1986, 1988). The mechanisms to achieve these goals comprise: self-care, mutual aid and the establishment of healthy environments. There are also three implementation strategies: fostering public participation; strengthening community health services; and co-ordinating healthy public policy. This framework provided an obvious stimulus for the Royal Commission Report, although inter-sectoral collaboration on health issues remains an elusive goal in mainstream provision, while entrenched medical and other professional interests are resistant to shift the power balance in health service provision to user and community groups. Again, the proposed decentralisation of decision making, to local Health Boards for example, may lead to policies that contradict the national standards demanded by the Canada Health Act. For Aboriginal Peoples, significant structural and political changes in Canadian society are necessary before the rhetoric of "health for all" comes near to being a practical reality.

Aboriginal Control

Any proposal for movement towards Aboriginal control of health policy becomes embroiled in the constitutional conflicts between different levels of government over responsibility for health policy. The status quo is condemned as unjust and ineffective, and conducive only to a "policy vacuum." Innovative solutions are demanded, but most require redesigning established jurisdictions and responsibilities (Cassidy and Bish, 1989; Favel-King, 1994). As yet, the several levels of government have been reluctant to make the radical changes necessary to satisfy demands for Aboriginal self-government. Given that First Nations have denounced moves to "relegate" them to a provincial responsibility, the most likely proposals to achieve general support entail some extension of Aboriginal self-government, with greater federal and provincial government sharing of responsibility, as well as funding.

There are also specific issues surrounding the upgrading of Aboriginal involvement in urban governments (RCAP, 1993, p. 10). For example, should First Nations governments extend their jurisdiction to cover members off-reserve—as has happened with the Siksika Nation which has significant numbers living in the Calgary area? Should the urban population initiate separate (and parallel) governing agencies and frameworks, perhaps an urban-level Aboriginal government? The diversity of the urban Aboriginal population, and the determination of Métis communities in particular, to avoid being incorporated into a wider "status-blind" organisation presents a considerable challenge. In most large Canadian cities, Aboriginal organisations involved in health and social welfare activities have multiplied, either providing services directly to clients, or in association with the mainstream sector. By the early 1990s, metropolitan centres such as Toronto and Winnipeg had as many as 40 such Aboriginal organisations, although these were often relatively small-scale, poorly funded and in competition for clients (RCAP, 1996c, p. 555).

One suggestion for cutting through the constitutional morass is contained in proposals for an Aboriginal Health Act. This would re-define the responsibilities of each level of government, monitor/enforce performance targets, and set out the healing philosophy underpinning Aboriginal services. However, there is yet little agreement on the form that urban Aboriginal government might take, and allowance will have to be made for the various populations served and their contrasting circumstances. Different suggestions include: the retention of political linkages with bands; a focus on province-wide federations or treaty organisations; and the development of land-based governments. Some urban-based groups argue that their interests have not been best served by reserve governments or existing Aboriginal political organisations. As a result, separate and more "organic" organisations have been developed to support Aboriginal social and cultural needs, including umbrella bodies such as URBAN in Vancouver, the Native Canadian Centre in Toronto and the Aboriginal Council of Winnipeg.

Recognition of Aboriginal Diversity

The baseline for Aboriginal demands in the 1990s is that health policy and services have failed Aboriginal people, with particular problems facing the urban Aboriginal population. According to the *Aboriginal Peoples Survey* (1991), the Registered Indian, Inuit and Métis totalled 720,000, of whom around 45 percent (or 320,00) lived in urban areas. Although it is widely assumed that this population is highly mobile, it includes a substantial proportion who are long-term urban residents. These groups demonstrate a common pattern of social disadvantages, including a high rate of poverty, poor housing and a wide-ranging experience of racism and discrimination (McClure *et al.,* 1993, p. 32).

The Aboriginal urban population also presents some of the most acute health care dilemmas, while also lacking the same organisational, human or funding resources available to those living on reserves or in northern communities. A novel attempt to develop a new model for the delivery of primary health care is the Aboriginal health centre. The first of these in Canada, Anishnawbe Health Toronto (AHT), was established in 1988, and has been followed by initiatives in other metropolitan centres, such as Vancouver and Winnipeg, to adapt this to their own context and Aboriginal population (Kaufert with Forsyth, 1994). The Aboriginal health centre seeks to emulate the transfer of health services that have been negotiated with First Nations reserve communities. Although not endowed with a secure or extensive funding base, this model, whether standing alone or as part of a broader community or "friendship" centre, has become recognised for its "culturally sensitive, efficient and effective service provision" (RCAP, 1996a, p. 980).

However, its development exemplifies a general dilemma for policy makers of how to balance the "retraditionalisation" of services with the delivery of innovative programmes in a culturally appropriate manner to all sections of the Aboriginal population. Traditional healing is undergoing a resurgence, but healers remain in short supply and are unequally distributed around the country. In addition, access is controlled, most notably by restrictions on Medicare reimbursement to First Nations, and the travel costs of healers. Other barriers to be overcome include a lack of enthusiasm veering towards outright opposition from established professionals, as well as suspicion from traditional healers that training and practice will be controlled by "western" medical professionals (Gregory, 1989). There are particular concerns about the referral of patients by mainstream practitioners because of the lack of professional accreditation and regulation of traditional healers. This spotlights contrasting views on whether "traditional" and "western" systems of healing and medicine should be equal, merged or separate.

Translating Theory into Practice

The basic objective has been to identify ways in which the demands for equity, holism, control and diversity can be translated into effective services. The RCAP Report proposes a ten-year strategy based on:

- the re-organisation of health and social service delivery through a system of Aboriginal-run healing centres and healing lodges;
- an Aboriginal human resources development strategy, including traditional healing;
- adaptation of "mainstream" services to affirm participation of the Aboriginal population as individuals and collectively; and
- enhancement of an Aboriginal infrastructure program to address community development issues—particularly clean water, safe waste management and adequate housing (RCAP, 1996b, pp. 110-11, p. 231; RCAP, 1996c, p. 59).

Healing Centres and Lodges

The perceived shortcomings of mainstream services has hastened the development of Aboriginal "healing" centres as an immediate priority. These are identified with a comprehensive and multi-disciplinary range of services, and aim to:

- develop public education about health and healing;
- encourage community involvement in health and healing;
- promote healthy lifestyles; assessing local health needs;
- assess local health needs, and participate in local and regional health planning;
- collaborate with other service agencies;
- provide education and training opportunities; and

- liaise with Aboriginal and non-Aboriginal agencies outside the community (RCAP, 1996b, pp. 240-41).

A network of residential healing lodges is also proposed. These would focus on family and community healing. Those experiencing alcohol and drug addictions, and abused women, would have the opportunity for treatment/ refuge close to their communities in a "safe haven." The way forward is difficult and strewn with potential conflicts between family and individual rights—but "radical" initiatives to re-activate community healing mechanisms are being explored, notably to eliminate the high level of sexual abuse which has arisen in Aboriginal communities over the last century.

To take on these roles, the new centres require adequate funding, and the federal government's health transfer policy will need to be revised to overcome inter-governmental and inter-departmental barriers to integrated service delivery. Inspiration is taken from initiatives such as the Strong Earth Woman Lodge in Manitoba and a new Aboriginal Health and Wellness Centre in Winnipeg, which provide both primary care and Aboriginal healing based on Native spirituality, traditional knowledge and practices. In Ontario, the provincial government introduced a five-year Aboriginal Healing and Wellness Strategy in 1994 to foster innovative developments, including healing centres and lodges. Funding of $33 million has been provided through programme funds, federal allocations and provincial operating grants. Other provincial proposals included the transfer of general programme administration to First Nations governments, but this foundered on federal reluctance to concede health as a treaty right.

One of the most compelling examples of a culture-based, multi-service health centre is Anishnawbe Health Toronto (AHT). It was set up as a non-profit corporation in 1989, and governed by a board of directors elected from and by the Aboriginal community. Its staff include registered nurses, counsellors, street workers, AIDS education workers, registered nurses, physicians and other administrative and support workers. Core funding is provided by the Ontario Ministry of Health and supplemented by various project funding from the City of Toronto and other provincial government ministries (Anishnawbe Health Toronto, 1990; Ontario Ministry of Health, 1994). The broad aim of AHT is to facilitate healing/ empowerment by enhancing client understanding of Aboriginal history and cultures—through access to ceremonies, elders, traditional healers, teachings and so forth (Anishnawbe Health Toronto, 1988). AHT includes biomedical and traditional healing services. Its clients are drawn from long-time residents and new arrivals to the city, while some clients travel on a regular basis from Aboriginal communities outside the city to participate in traditional programmes (Anishnawbe Health Toronto, 1990).

Through the 1990s, Anishnawbe Health has increasingly emphasised "culturally-based," holistic services utilising traditional healers, elders and teachers, with non-Aboriginal professionals playing a secondary role. However, the AHT budget for traditional healers was only $45,000, or less than one-sixth of that allocated for orthodox physicians, and patient demand far exceeds the supply of experienced traditional healers in the Toronto area. One highly successful experiment involved bringing in an Ojibwa medicine man for two, five-day sessions of diagnosis and treatment. AHT reports that on each visit about 100 people were treated, some of whom travelled hundreds of miles from rural areas of the province. Yet the cost to the Centre was only $30 per person (Anishnawbe Health Toronto, 1990).

Other programmes include an elder counselling service, traditional talking circles, Aboriginal language classes, writing workshops, issue-focused weekend workshops, HIV-AIDS awareness and testing, new mothers and seniors, and community services including an extensive "Street Patrol" by staff and volunteers who provide food, blankets, condoms and a needle exchange. It employs two physicians who hold clinics at many locations around the city and are on call 24-hours a day, as well as nurses who provide family support services, after school programmes and the like. In total, some 2,500 people per week use Anishnawbe Health services. AHT has also become active as a North American clearinghouse for Aboriginal health education materials (George and Nahwegahbow, 1994).

Urban Aboriginal people are increasingly looking to community healing initiatives such as AHT to regain their political, social and economic health. This has also underpinned the development of "friendship centres," with more than 100 established across the country in the early 1990s—often supported by some federal funding (RCAP, 1996c). These play an important role for urban dwellers both as a referral service and a community gathering place. The RCAP argued strongly that the National Association of Friendship Centres should have a more significant role in service delivery (RCAP, 1996c, pp. 564-7). However, the status-blind approach of such organisations is challenged in the Prairie provinces where the significant Métis community has argued that this sidelines its specific interests. More generally, the growth of these and other community initiatives is constrained by jurisdictional disputes and funding difficulties.

Human Resources Strategy

Historically, cultural and linguistic differences have been used to exclude Aboriginal people from a variety of careers where universal certification is imposed. The shift towards traditional healers and more culturally appropriate services will also be frustrated without effective action to: recruit and train Aboriginal people as planners, administrators and front-line health practitioners; develop distinct Aboriginal institutions which apply Aboriginal knowledge; and open up mainstream services at all levels.

The need to increase the number of qualified Aboriginal practitioners in health and social services is generally accepted. It was estimated in the mid-1990s that there were only 50 Aboriginal physicians—around 0.1 per cent of all physicians. A similar under-representation exists in nursing and across other health professional groups (and at degree level generally), particularly of qualified Inuit staff. Hence the ambitious target of 10,000 Aboriginal professionals to be trained over a 10-year period (RCAP, 1996b). This general under-representation is reinforced by a manifest vertical segregation in the health sector, with those few Aboriginal staff over-represented in the less well-qualified, lower paid and lower status "health care assistant" posts, where they have little influence over service design or delivery. Again, only about 20 of the estimated 60 Aboriginal nurses in Quebec work primarily with Aboriginal people. Thus, most Aboriginal communities routinely interact with non-Aboriginal staff, who typically have little familiarity with Aboriginal cultures, or stay for short periods.

A list of issues which need to be addressed (or which generalise from existing University-based schemes) includes:

151

- specific admission and retention targets for Aboriginal students;
- pre-professional and pre-admission preparation programmes;
- an organised system of financial, academic, personal and family supports;
- innovative strategies to provide continuing support for Aboriginal students;
- support for innovative forms of programme delivery; and
- involvement Aboriginal Peoples in programme planning (RCAP, 1996b, p. 280).

Although the RCAP Commissioners stress the "success" of the community health representative (CHR) programme, it has attracted criticism which serves as a salutary warning to over-optimism. The main concerns are that: CHR staff mostly focus on health promotion and education; they have no clear lines of accountability; there are far too few CHRs to meet the demand; staff retention has been a problem, with little support provided for professional advancement; and CHR services are available only to First Nations people and Inuit living on their traditional lands.

More specifically, in order to support traditional knowledge and expand its application to the health and social problems facing Aboriginal peoples, an organisational infrastructure and an adequate funding base must be secured. Steps also have to be taken to preserve the oral tradition, extend understanding and respect for traditional ways, encourage apprenticeships, and control access to knowledge considered sacred.

Adaptation of Canadian Institutions

Mainstream health services have a continuing role to play in the "renewed relationship" demanded by Aboriginal peoples. The development of Aboriginal controlled services will take time, but some will still want to use western medicine and institutions. This will require action and co-operation from the several levels of government as well as professional organisations, including:

- affirmative action and employment equity hiring policies;

- specialised and fully-funded Aboriginal Units staffed by Aboriginal employees within mainstream institutions/ programmes (emulating the RCMP Indian Special Constable Programme);
- cross-cultural awareness/education programmes for non-Aboriginal staff;
- Aboriginal input into mainstream planning decisions (as part of the promotion of Aboriginal rights to self-determination); and
- inclusion of Aboriginal customary practices (RCAP, 1996b, p. 296).

In addition, in order to enhance the cultural appropriateness of mainstream services, the RCAP argued that it will be necessary to:

- increase Aboriginal staffing levels and involvement in day-to-day operations;
- develop strategic plans for increased Aboriginal involvement;
- examine the barriers to Aboriginal involvement;
- develop anti-racist programmes;
- provide an interpreting service and information/advocacy assistance;
- ensure Aboriginal control of health needs assessment;
- develop promotion and preventive services before crisis arises; and
- establish a monitoring and evaluation system to ensure the effectiveness and efficiency of services (RCAP, 1996b, pp. 306-7).

The development of culturally relevant health services stands as part of a wider process of cultural revitalisation and renewal. Culture-specific health knowledge and beliefs must be accepted as valid and integral to the organisation and delivery of health services.

Any "new strategy" must be backed up by adequate funding to initiate and maintain the significant development of services necessary to "bridge the health divide." The background context is not encouraging. Over the period from 1981-82 to 1995-96, total federal expenditure tripled, but social and health expenditures increased at an even faster rate, with a sharp rise in the last ten years. In an attempt to impose some fiscal restraint, EPF and CAP have been amalgamated into a single block arrangement called the Canadian Health and Social Transfer. The delivery of programmes to Aboriginal peoples is a particular target for cost cutting, insofar as the per capita cost is much higher for those living in remote communities. However, an effective "new strategy" will require additional funding, particularly in the early years, to reflect the higher need and depressed health status of Aboriginal peoples.

Although the overall fiscal cost of Aboriginal social and economic disadvantage (to national exchequer and in terms of individual lost incomes) is calculated at $1 billion, or about 1 percent of GDP (RCAP, 1996d, p. 48), the RCAP Report confidently predicts that savings on health budgets (and government finances) will amount to $450 million in 2016, rising continuously over the longer term (RCAP, 1996c, Table 3.3). It optimistically predicts that as Aboriginal control and confidence builds up, the demand for health care will diminish, but as a British audience will know, similar claims at the inception of the National Health Service proved illusory, and restraints on government expenditure remain high on the Canadian political agenda.

Enhancement of Aboriginal Infrastructure

The formal federal government response to the Royal Commission recommendations on health care has been positive. It accepted the need for a strategy to begin the "process of reconciliation and renewal with Aboriginal Peoples" in *Canada's Aboriginal Action Plan* which was published in January 1998. This includes: an acknowledgement of past mistakes and injustices; an emphasis on the need for reconciliation, healing and renewal of partnerships based on mutual respect and recognition; and developing joint plans for the future. It stresses the importance of strengthening Aboriginal governance and communities, and developing a new fiscal relationship, while also confirming the importance of public health and community healing approaches. One of the first initiatives has been the commitment of $350 million over a ten year period to generate community healing schemes for all Aboriginal Peoples affected by the abuses of the residential school system. The single organisation focus represents a significant attempt to overcome the fragmentation that has historically bedevilled Aboriginal health policy.

A recent initiative has been the setting up of the Aboriginal Healing Foundation in March 1998. This is an Aboriginal-run organisation directed to support and extend traditional healing and community-based programmes, while recognising the diversity of needs within and between Aboriginal communities. Its goal is to facilitate innovative partnerships across sectors and governments, at national, regional and local levels. A further development is an Aboriginal Health Institute to provide a data and information base (following the mainstream emphasis on "evidence-based decision making"), that will support research on the health needs of the Aboriginal population and disseminate examples of culturally appropriate good practice. It is also expected to promote the recruitment and training of Aboriginal health professionals.

The *Report of the RCAP* has given new momentum to existing programmes or extended them in imaginative ways, as much as introduced entirely new policy proposals. Thus, the Aboriginal Head Start programme, which had been established in 1995 for urban and northern Aboriginal communities to enhance child development, was extended in October 1998 to on-reserve children. The Building Healthy Communities community initiative that was introduced in 1994-95 with the aim of developing community health services to First Nations has acted as a similar stimulus. It has encouraged the exploration of ways to merge programme-specific funding into community-based health service agreements so that more effective action could be taken to support a community's priorities. The objective of increasing flexibility in developing community-based services also underpinned a pilot project which allows transfer of the administration of non-insured health benefits to selected First Nations.

The government has also explored ways in which eligibility to participate in health programme administration can be extended to a wider range of Aboriginal communities. The Royal Commission recommended that, in rural areas, communities of 250 people, or 1,000 where these were more dispersed, and in urban areas, a population of 1,000, should be sufficient for involvement. It was calculated that this would extend participation in the planning and delivery of health care to 44 urban and four non-urban communities.

Conclusions

Healing, in Aboriginal terms, refers to personal and societal recovery from the lasting effects of oppression and systemic racism experienced over generations. Many Aboriginal people are suffering not simply from specific diseases and social problems, but also from a depression of spirit resulting from 200 or more years of damage to their cultures, languages, identities and self-respect (RCAP, 1996b, p. 109).

In this sense, "healing" is about restoring "physical, social, emotional and spiritual vitality" to Aboriginal peoples. The debate is not just about an improved health care system but a better kind of society. This review illustrates that significant steps in respect of health policy have been taken in the final quarter of the twentieth century—against the back-drop of a major re-assessment of Aboriginal-state relations. However, it also indicates that much ground still needs to be made up, both towards the ultimate goal of self-determination and in closing the significant health divide between Aboriginal peoples and the rest of the Canadian population.

From a positive perspective, initiatives have been implemented to increase the participation of Aboriginal people in the design, management and delivery of health care. A considerable boost has been given to traditional medicine and healing, and progress has been made in introducing accessible and appropriate services, and generally re-shaping the mainstream health and social welfare provision. The health transfer policy has encouraged important reforms and advanced wider Aboriginal participation (although particular difficulties arise with the urban, non-reserve based and Métis population). The transfer programme also illustrates how much more needs to be done before a comprehensive health policy of, by and for Aboriginal peoples is accomplished. Most particularly, wide-ranging action is still required to effect the necessary improvements in the material and environmental conditions experienced by Aboriginal peoples. There is also little sign of an agreement on the necessary radical constitutional changes that will provide the political framework in which the different levels of government work together to support Aboriginal health and healing. Of course, the outcome and trajectory of health debates must also wait on whether progress is made towards resolving other sovereignty and jurisdictional/rights struggles in Canada.

In its attempt to confront undue pessimism about the possibilities for change, the RCAP Report is at times overly optimistic about the potential for generating social change and overcoming political opposition. As an illustration, the RCAP plans for recruitment of Aboriginal personnel to the health care system rely on levels of government funding, inter-sectoral and professional collaboration, as well as a restricted (or uncompetitive) labour market for Aboriginal labour. It seems more likely that the scale of the changes recommended will defy their projected achievement dates.

Yet the central objective should not be lost: to translate the current rhetoric of reconciliation and locate Aboriginal peoples within a Canada that they feel committed to, and which in turn sustains their distinctive position.

References

Aitken, G. and Mitchell, A. (1995) "The Relationship between Poverty and Child Health: Long-Range Implications," *Canadian Review of Social Policy*, no. 35, Spring.

Anishnawbe Health Toronto (1988) *A Proposal to Establish a Community Health Centre*, Toronto: Anishnawbe Health Toronto.

Anishnawbe Health Toronto (1990) *Anishnawbe Health Toronto-Budget Proposal 1990-1991*, Toronto: Anishnawbe Health Toronto.

Assembly of First Nations (1988) *Special Report: The National Health Transfer Conference*, Ottawa, Assembly of First Nations.

Beavais, D. (1988) "Autochtonisation des services de santé: réalité ou utopie?" in S.Vincent and G. Bowers, Eds. *James Bay and Northern Québec*, Montréal: Recherches amérindiennes au Québec.

Berger, T. R., Commissioner (1980) *Report of the Advisory Commission on Indian and Inuit Health Consultation*, Ottawa: Minister of Supply and Services Canada.

Bolaria, B. Singh and Dickinson, H.D., eds. (1994) *Sociology of Health Care in Canada*, 2nd ed., Toronto: Harcourt Brace and Co.

Canada. (1969) *Task Force Reports on the Cost of Health Services in Canada*, Volumes 1-3, Ottawa: Queen's Printer.

Canada. Health and Welfare (1992) *Aboriginal Health in Canada*, Ottawa: Minister of Supply and Services.

Canada. Health Canada. (1996) *Health Programs Analysis, First Nations and Inuit Health Programs*, Ottawa: Indian Health Information Library.

Cassidy, F. and Bish, R.L. (1989) *Indian Government: Its Meaning in Practice*, Lantzville, B.C.: Oolichan Books.

Cohen, B. and O'Neil, J.D. (1994) "Health Services Development in an Aboriginal Community: The Case of the Peguis First Nation," unpublished research study for Royal Commission on Aboriginal Peoples.

Epp, J. (1986) *Achieving Health For All: A Framework for Health Promotion*, Ottawa: Minister of Supply and Services.

Epp, J. (1988) *Mental Health for Canadians: Striking a Balance*, Ottawa: Health and Welfare.

Favel-King, A. (1994) "The Treaty Right to Health," unpublished research study for Royal Commission on Aboriginal Peoples.

Feather, J. (1991) *Social Health in Northern Saskatchewan: Discussion Papers for Working Group on Social Health*, Saskatoon: University of Saskatchewan Northern Medical Services.

Fletcher, C. and O'Neil, J.D. (1994) "The Innuulisivik Maternity Centre: Issues Around the Return of Inuit Midwifery and Birth to Povungnituk, Quebec," unpublished research study for Royal Commission on Aboriginal Peoples.

Frideres, J. (1993) *Native Peoples in Canada: Contemporary Conflicts*, 4th ed., Scarborough, Ontario: Prentice-Hall.

George, P. and Nahwegahbow, B. (1994) "Anishnawbe Health," unpublished research study for Royal Commission on Aboriginal Peoples.

Gregory, D. (1989) "Traditional Indian Healers in Northern Manitoba: An Emerging Relationship with the Health Care System," *Native Studies Review*, vol. 5, no. 1.

Hall Report (1964) *Royal Commission on Health Services*, Ottawa: Queen's Printer.

Kaufert, J.M. with Forsyth, S.M. (1994) "Health Status, Service Use and Program Models among the Aboriginal Population of Canadian Cities," unpublished research study for Royal Commission on Aboriginal Peoples.

Kaufert, J.M. and O'Neil, J.D. (1990) "Biomedical Rituals and Informed Consent: Native Canadians and the Negotiation of Clinical Trust," in G. Weisz, Ed. *Social Science Perspectives on Medical Ethics*, Dordrecht: Kluwer Academic Publishers.

Kirmayer, L. *et al.*, (1994) "Emerging Trends in Research on Mental Health Among Canadian Aboriginal Peoples", unpublished research study for Royal Commission on Aboriginal Peoples.

Lalonde, M. (1974) *A New Perspective on the Health of Canadians*, Ottawa: Information Canada.

Manitoba Indian Brotherhood (1971) *Wahbung: Our Tomorrows*, Winnipeg: MIB.

McClure, L., Boulanger, M., Kaufert, J., Forsyth, S. eds. (1993) *First Nations Urban Health Bibliography: A Review of the Literature and Exploration of Strategies*, Monograph Series No. 5, Northern Health Research Unit, University of Manitoba.

McKeown, T. (1976) *The Modern Rise of Population*, London: Edward Arnold.

O'Neil, J.D. (1986) "The Politics of Health in the Fourth World: A Northern Canadian Example," *Human Organisation*, vol. 45, no. 2.

O'Neil, J.D. (1988) "Referrals to Traditional Healers: The Role of Medical Interpreters," in D.E.Young, Eds. *Health Care Issues in the Canadian North*, Edmonton: The Boreal Institute for Northern Studies.

Ontario Ministry of Health (1994) *New Directions: Aboriginal Health Policy for Ontario*, Toronto: Government of Ontario.

Royal Commission on Aboriginal Peoples (1993) *Aboriginal Peoples in Urban Centres: Report of the National Round Table on Aboriginal Urban Issues*, Ottawa: Minister of Supply and Services.

Royal Commission on Aboriginal Peoples (1996a) *Report of the Royal Commission on Aboriginal Peoples, Volume 2. Restructuring the Relationship*, Ottawa: Minister of Supply and Services.

Royal Commission on Aboriginal Peoples (1996b) *Report of the Royal Commission on Aboriginal Peoples, Volume 3. Gathering Strength*, Ottawa: Minister of Supply and Services.

Royal Commission on Aboriginal Peoples (1996c) *Report of the Royal Commission on Aboriginal Peoples, Volume 4. Perspectives and Realities*, Ottawa: Minister of Supply and Services.

Royal Commission on Aboriginal Peoples (1996d) *Report of the Royal Commission on Aboriginal Peoples, Volume 5. Renewal: a Twenty-year Commitment*, Ottawa: Minister of Supply and Services.

Satzewich, V. and Wotherspoon, T. (1993) *First Nations: Race, Class, and Gender Relations*, Scarborough: Nelson Canada.

Shah, C.P. and Farkas, C.P. (1985) "The Health of Indians in Canadian Cities: A Challenge to the Health Care System," *Canadian Medical Association Journal*, 133.

Speck, D.C. (1989) "The Indian Health Transfer Policy: A Step in the Right Direction, or Revenge of the Hidden Agenda?" *Native Studies Review*, vol. 5, no. 1.

Statistics Canada (1993) *1991 Aboriginal Peoples Survey: Language, Tradition, Health, Lifestyle and Social Issues*. Ottawa: Statistics Canada.

Tremblay, A. (1995) "L'organisation de la santé dans une réserve montagnaise," *Recherches amérindiennes au Québec*, XXV (1).

Waldram J. (1990) "Physician Utilization and Urban Native People in Saskatoon, Canada," *Social Science and Medicine*, vol. 30, no. 5.

Waldram, J.B., Herring, D.A. and Young, T.K. (1995) *Aboriginal Health in Canada: Historical, Cultural and Epidemiological Perspectives*, Toronto: University of Toronto Press.

Waldram, J. B. and Layman, M. M. (1988) *Health Care in Saskatoon's Inner City: Report of the Westside Clinic-Friendship Inn*, Department of Native Studies, University of Saskatchewan, Saskatoon, Saskatchewan.

Whitehead, M. (1992) "The Concepts and Principles of Equity and Health," *International Journal of Health Services*, vol. 22, no. 3.

World Health Organization (1984) *A Discussion Document on the Concept of Principles of Health Promotion*, Copenhagen: WHO.

World Health Organization (1985) *Health For All By the Year 2000*, Geneva: WHO.

Young, D.E. and Smith, L.L. (1992) *The Involvement of Canadian Native Communities in their Health Care Programs: A Review of the Literature Since the 1970s*, Edmonton: Circumpolar Institute and Centre for the Cross-Cultural Study of Health and Healing.

Young, T. K. (1988) *Health Care and Cultural Change: The Indian Experience in the Central Subarctic*, Toronto: University of Toronto Press.

Young, T.K. (1994) "Measuring the Health Status of Canada's Aboriginal Population: A Statistical Review and Methodological Commentary," unpublished research study for Royal Commission on Aboriginal Peoples.

Chapter 6

Canadian Aboriginal Justice Circles: Restorative Alternatives to Justice or Political Compromise[1]

David S. Wall

Introduction

A disturbing recent trend within the criminal justice policies of many western societies has been for governments to "play the crime card" (Roberts, 1998, p. 420) and introduce more repressive penal policies in order to placate public and political pressure. Such strategies, ultimately, serve to negate the move that gained momentum during the early part of this decade[2] to reduce the use of imprisonment and therefore the costs of incarceration. The most apparent consequence of "playing the crime card" is that more and more individuals become incarcerated, thus loading their country's respective economies with crippling financial burdens. Furthermore, the longer term impact of those retributive policies is arguably to accelerate the processes of social exclusion with regard to offenders and thus further increase levels of social injustice. Unless checked, these trends in criminal justice policy could eventually damage the very social structures that they purport to protect. These trends tend to hit minority or marginalised groups the hardest. In Canada, one group that has been harshly treated historically by successive criminal justice policies, and the criminal justice system, has been the indigenous or Aboriginal peoples. Not only have they suffered generations of hardship, but they are disproportionately represented within the various stages of the criminal justice system and particularly within its correctional institutions (Harding, 1991; Quigley, 1994; RCAP, 1996).[3]

Against this background, policy makers and criminologists have begun to explore a range of alternatives to the conventional criminal justice processes. Alternatives combine current developments within general criminological thinking, such as restorative justice, with traditional processes of conflict resolution. This combination seeks to remove individuals from the criminal justice system by repairing, through a local peace-making process, the social and relational damage that they have caused and by eventually relocating them in their communities of origin.

In five parts, this paper will, firstly, contextualise criminal justice policy with regard to indigenous peoples. The second part will look at the various models of Aboriginal[4] justice circles which attained popularity during the 1990s as one of various alternative forms of delivering criminal justice. The third and fourth parts will explore the strengths and weaknesses of justice circles. The fifth and final part will draw some conclusions as to whether justice circles constitute alternatives to, or exits from, justice.

Contextualising the Concept(s) of Aboriginal Justice and Aboriginal Justice Policy

There exists a rich literature on Aboriginal justice policy.[5] Therefore, focus of the discussion here will be to establish the main threads of the debate which underpins the debate over the justice circles.

Many treatments of the debate over aboriginal justice see justice circles as the triumph of the traditional over the modern, yet the devolved model of justice can actually be seen to represent the opposite. The governance of the Canadian criminal justice system, like that of many modern bureaucracies, is split between the central and local governments. To use Osborne and Gaebler's (1992) much used metaphor, policy making, or "steering," takes place at a federal level whilst the administration, or "rowing," takes place at a provincial[6] and territorial level. Though grossly oversimplified, this division between steering and rowing is still useful because it illustrates the intended direction of policy (Crawford, 1996, p. 221). But the analogy is slightly complicated by the fact that the justice circles represents the "rowing" of justice, but with a local hand also placed on the tiller. Justice circles seek to adapt central criminal justice policy to local community norms and in this sense they do not represent a departure and celebration of the past. Rather, they represent the continuance of the present.

Ever conscious of the politics of criminal justice, policy makers are often motivated by the desire to resolve any contradictions that might exist within the administration of a criminal justice system. One such contradiction, in Canada and also in other former colonial countries,[7] exists with regard to the historical ill-treatment and over-representation of Aboriginal peoples within their criminal justice systems. Consequently, a prime concern of policy makers, especially since examples of injustice generate considerable publicity and public concern, is the need to ensure the correct treatment of Aboriginal peoples within the present and future criminal justice processes along with the need to reconcile past differences and harsh treatments. The resolution of these injustices is important in order to allow countries to further develop.

Such developments contrast with former, hegemonic, policy initiatives. Until recent years, it had long been the practice in former colonial societies to encourage a policy of "integrationalism" towards their Aboriginal peoples (see Palys, 1993). In Canada, one of the main symbols of this integrationalist policy was the residential school to which many, although not all, Aboriginal children were sent. The policy in these schools was to "kill the Indian in the child" in order to force integration (RCAP, 1996: vol. 1, chapter 10, s3). Some of the regimes in these residential schools have subsequently resulted in criminal and civil litigation. The need to resolve these cases and other cases involving Aboriginals outside the courts has encouraged Canada to look at more restorative means of resolving these cases rather than simply going through the courts and having the victim suffer the prospect of further, secondary, victimisation (Marshall, 1999, p. 23).

Recent thinking amongst Canadian justice policy makers has moved towards "accommodationalism" and towards developing ways that enable two legal cultures to operate together within a multi-cultural environment. Consequently, the Aboriginal issue sits fairly high on the policy maker's agenda and drives the debate over Aboriginal justice. The first school of thought argues for fairness in the justice process for Aboriginal peoples. Arising from these arguments is the proposal to develop a separate Aboriginal criminal justice system (Dussault, 1998; John Howard Society of Alberta, 1992; *Current*, 1990) much along the lines of the traditional systems that used to exist before the domination of western culture. So the justice circle is both a traditional form of dispute resolution, but, importantly, seeks to embody the values of customary law. The second school of thought seeks a slightly different strategy than the first in that it seeks to take desirable, or useful, aspects of Aboriginal culture and apply them for the benefit of the dominant culture. Put to one side here, is any discussion relating to the conceptual minefield that tends to arise with the use of such concepts, particularly the debates over cultural imperialism, for this is not the forum for such debate. This school of thought is attracted by Aboriginal forms of criminal dispute resolution, which not only seek to address the root problem rather than the symptoms and therefore effect a more permanent solution, but could be used to inform the development of the criminal justice systems of western societies. One of the main problems with this debate is that the two schools of thought become confused, with the outcome that current Canadian political and social guilt regarding the historic treatment of the Aboriginal peoples is cross-hatched with the growing trend in administrative politics to seek and place great value upon new ideas and solutions: the constant search for the magic bullet.

So, the arguments for encouraging the development of Aboriginal methods of dispute resolution are quite powerful. By focusing upon objects which Aboriginal people relate to, especially within their communities, the alternative methods increase the input and involvement of indigenous people and communities in justice processes and decisions. They also increase the quality of the decisions made, and also their outcomes, which arise from criminal justice processes that involve Native people. Finally, and most importantly, the community-based process not only empowers Aboriginal people by returning to them some control over criminal justice processes, but it also increases the overall legitimacy of the criminal justice processes amongst Aboriginal peoples (Nuffield, 1996).

Aboriginal Justice Circles

> Communities from Hastings in Dakota County to Whitehorse in Canada's Yukon Territory are digging deep into the past to find a remedy to recurring criminal justice behaviour that our justice system can't seem to fix (Adams, 1998).

Aboriginal Justice Circles are a very popular example of the practical articulation of restorative justice policy (Marshall, 1999 p. 15).[8] But they can be distinguished from other, earlier, forms of restorative justice by that fact that they "dig deeper into the underlying offender" (Adams, 1998) and seek to achieve the goals of reintegrating the offender and healing the wounds that they have created within their community. In their purest form, justice circles engender a concept of Aboriginal justice which is quite different from contemporary understandings of criminal justice. Aboriginal understandings of justice are shaped by Aboriginal cultures in which social order is traditionally bound around the local community. At the heart of these understandings are three important characteristics which mark Aboriginal justice as different and pose problems for the execution of western adversarial justice, especially with regard to due process and to the establishment of the mens rea and actus rea. The lack of a concept of guilt in the conventional adversarial sense causes considerable problems for the investigation of a complaint and also the prosecution of an offence. Furthermore, the impact of the offence is strongly felt by the local community that is also victimised. Consequently, the offence is perceived as taking place against the community rather than the state, which causes further problems for traditional court-based resolution, especially as traditional Aboriginal justice seeks a form of resolution that is geared towards community harmony (Green, 1995). There exist many examples of the operation of justice circles, within publications on Aboriginal justice alternatives by the Canadian Department of Justice (1995), the Canadian Church Council on Justice and Corrections (1996) and Scott (1997).[9] And their popularity has recently spread into the USA (Adams, 1998).

At this point in the discussion, it is important to establish why these schemes should have developed in Canada and not elsewhere. This is largely due to the establishment, during the past two decades, of a supportive legal infrastructure followed by equally supportive case law. Firstly, Canada's impressive array of human rights instruments (Hucker, 1999 p. 54) has provided a fertile environment for the development of such initiatives. The main driving force here is the constitutionally entrenched Charter of Rights and Freedoms[10] which not only affirms basic civil and political rights, but contains an equality clause (s.15,1) which is augmented by federal and provincial human rights codes that provide redress for victims of discrimination (*idem*). Secondly, this human rights framework is strengthened by Canada's respect for its multi-cultural population, both generally but also as expressed in various funding initiatives, such as the Aboriginal Community Corrections Initiative (see later). More specifically, the

Canadian Multiculturalism Act[11] encourages the preservation of Canada's many diverse cultures. Thirdly, these areas of legislation have caused the Canadian courts to become broadly sympathetic to the objectives of the Charter of Freedoms. With this legal infrastructure in mind, we can then understand the nature of the development of case law, such as the decisions in the land mark cases of *R. v. Moses* (*idem*) etc., (see below) when Judge Barry Stuart laid down rules for the usage of sentencing circles in his decision. The powers of the court were later tested in *R. v. Morin* (1994, 1995, 1996) and since the early 1990s there has developed quite a sizeable body of case law relating to sentencing circles.[12] These decisions have been facilitated by further legislative developments in the criminal procedural code as it relates to judicial discretion. Bill C-41, which came into force in September 1996, allows the judiciary more discretion in sentencing.

Typically, a sentencing circle will take place where an offender has either admitted guilt or has been convicted by a court. Either the offender can start off the process by agreeing to submit to the sentencing circle, or it can be suggested by the court with the agreement of the offender. Once the circle has agreed jurisdiction over the case, and the offender has also agreed to abide by the eventual ruling of the circle, then sentences might range from a length of supervised probation, a term of isolation or even imprisonment (Wheelright, 1998). Such circles have been used on many occasions during the past decade or so since they were first introduced. Indeed, there is some debate amongst the members of the judiciary as to when they were first introduced, as evidence suggests that the ideas were considered for some time before the current models were developed. Barnett, for instance, claims to have first used a sentencing circle type approach in 1978 (Barnett, 1995, p. 1). However, within the context of the current debates, the use of sentencing circles became more popular following the case of *R. v. Moses* (1992).

Justice circle projects vary considerably in terms of their levels, and types, of engagement with both the individual and the community. The two main sources of this variation are firstly, the type or level of community involvement, particularly with regard to which members of the community are actually involved in the process in a substantive way. In some projects, for example, the main decisions are taken only by the Elders,[13] whilst in others the main decisions are made by the community as a whole. In both cases, a member of the judiciary is present (see later).

The second source of variation originates from the varying functions of the circle. Some circles will deal purely with aspects of sentencing, which appears to be the most common variant, whereas others will focus upon community healing. But others, albeit a minority, will deal with functions as diverse as parole or even basic discretionary gatekeeping decisions like cautioning. In practice, it is quite common for one or more of these functions to be combined, most typically the sentencing and healing functions. This is particularly the case where the healing function involves the relocation of the offending individual within his or her community, as is the case, for example, in the Hollow Water Holistic Circle Healing project. The Hollow Water project deals mainly with cyclical sexual abuse within families and devotes considerable time to the reintegration of the offender(s) back into the community (Berma, 1997; Hollow Water First Nation, 1997; Solicitor General, Canada, 1997; Wheelright, 1998). In principle, the healing circle relates to the traditional Aboriginal practice of healing through a circle, whereas the sentencing circle is a latter-day derivative of the former. However, in practice confusion between the two is quite common. Crnkovitch, for example, found that the judge in the case that she observed used the terms healing circle and sentencing circle interchangeably, even though the circle was very different than the traditional Aboriginal healing circle (1996, p. 159, fn 1).

The process by which the circle usually takes place (because schemes vary) involves the offender admitting responsibility for his or her actions and then giving an explanation to both the primary victim and also the secondary victim, the community. Such explanations may often also accompany an element of restitution, where appropriate, either financially or via labour or services. The frequently lengthy discussions will also tend to involve some consideration of the means by which the offender can be metered out a meaningful punishment, often a short prison term followed by reparation and then reintegration into the community at some future date after the punishment has been expended.

Whilst it is common for the composition and organisation of the circles to vary according to local traditions, local arrangements and of course, the offences being dealt with, there are some common themes which characterise the process and these are described here. The most obvious characteristic is that the hearing will be held in a circle, or where this is not physically possible, an inner and outer circle. Those in attendance will typically include the accused, the victims, chairperson, court translator, judge, elder male, member of the community council, relatives of the victim, relatives of the accused, crown prosecutor, mayor, community healthworker, social worker, probation officer and defence counsel (Crnkovitch, 1996, pp. 164-165). The emphasis throughout the circle process is to enable the various members of the community to express their feelings about the offender, the offence and also its impact upon them. Consequently, the judge tends to facilitate rather than direct the process, and in some circles, even this role might be taken on by a chairperson appointed by the circle.

Although the circle proceedings lack the formality of the court room, Aboriginal traditions are nevertheless followed and participants are only allowed to speak when they are passed "the feather" or similar token. The circle procedure usually develops through a number of pre-determined phases[14] which are marked by, for example, the offenders explaining their actions, or elders explaining the broader community perspective, or the victims describing the impact upon them. Finally, the offender's reintegration into the community will be discussed with the main parties concerned. This reintegration might be some form of probation which involves the offender reporting to a support group, which itself might be responsible to the judge who is responsible for the case.

Interestingly, both the strengths and weakness of the circles (see later) lie in their capability to adapt, or appear to adapt (see later), Aboriginal traditions to existing situations. Quigley has noted variations within justice circle models as to the degree to which they adopt the traditional format, arguing that it is important to differentiate between "process orientated" circles which do not necessarily incorporate traditional forms of sentencing and those which do (Quigley, 1994, p. 287; Chartrand, 1995, p. 875, fn3). In circle sentencing, the values of Aboriginal society gain prominence, emphasising rehabilitation rather than punishment; promoting harmony within the community in a way that respects Aboriginal values and processes of dispute resolution, and thus allowing the community to heal itself. Importantly, for the current debates over the delivery of criminal justice policy, it can also provide a diplomatic compromise by giving local communities an important stake in the criminal justice process, whilst also retaining the sovereignty of the state as the process is overseen by a judge, who, guided by the will of the community, has the final word.

An Account of a Sentencing Circle

Before exploring the particular strengths and weaknesses of justice circles, it will be useful to develop a clearer picture of the dynamics of a circle. The following, draws heavily upon Crnkovitch's account of a circle in an Inuit community. It is in no way representative of the operation of justice circles. Indeed, it was the first circle to be held in Nunavik. However, it does give a very useful qualitative account of the process and assist the reader. Furthermore, it also illustrates some of the tensions that can develop within and during the process and which are discussed in greater detail in a later section. The justice circle was to consider a sentence for a wife abuser. The offender's wife, of course, was the victim of the abuse.

The judge opened the ceremony by clarifying his role and that of the other participants before emphasising the equality of participation. The purpose of the circle is to "break down the dominance that traditional court rooms accord lawyers and judges" (*R v Moses*, 1992, p. 366, Crnkovitch, 1996, p. 165). However, in the final analysis, a tension will always exist between this supposed equality and the fact that the judge is not obliged to follow the advice of the circle. In practice, the few accounts that exist of the operation of circles suggest that the judge does tend to follow the community will. Crnkovitch observed that once the judge had explained the various participant's roles, a male elder spoke about the general experience of the Inuit, who were involved in this case, within the Canadian criminal justice system. He was followed by members of the offender's family.

The Judge did not want to be seen to be directing or chairing the discussion, but as a consequence, the circle lost its structure. "The victim did not know what was going to happen to her in the circle. She told me that she was afraid and thought that she had to be there because she was going to be a witness at a trial" (Crnkovitch, 1996, p. 165). Crnkovitch believes that the judge could have provided the needed structure without dominating the proceedings (*ibid.*, p. 166). He was even reluctant to ask people to introduce themselves on the basis that he was afraid that such a request might appear to be meddling. Even so, the proceedings tended to be dominated by a few participants; the judge, the mayor, the chair of the Inuit Justice Task Force, the sister of the victim, the community healthworker and the offender. The latter only spoke five times, but at length.

The discussions were not as free flowing as might have been expected. This was partly due to the organisation of the circle but also because of the language barriers within the group attending the justice circle. Whilst a court interpreter was present, her role was taken over by the chair of the Inuit Justice Task Force, who kept interpreting and summarising the discussions. Consequently, states Crnkovitch, "The impact of the speaker's comments, especially the emotion and feeling behind the words, were likely to be lost" (*ibid.*, p. 167).

Crnkovitch felt that the dominance of the judge and lawyers in the traditional court process was simply replaced by the dominance of those who were influential within the community, namely, the chair of the Inuit Justice Task Force, a respected Inuit political leader and the mayor. Consequently, Crnkovitch observed that the least defined role of all in the circle that she observed was that of the victim. There was virtually no discussion of the harm suffered by the victim (who was the offender's wife). Furthermore, the participants appeared willing to assist the offender so long as he was willing to be helped. So, she implies, the rational, non-adversarial and polite tone of the conversation during which and participants remained calm contributed towards the offender

Indeed, at times the discussion concentrated so much on the structural issues affecting the offender's life, unemployment, drink, etc., that it implied that he, and not his wife, was the principal loser in the case. Indeed, these characteristics were referred to as his problem. However, the family violence worker did mention the need for the victim to have her own source of support should her husband begin assaulting her again. What is interesting about Crnkovitch's account is the way in which ownership of "the problem" shifted during the course of the proceedings to members of the circle, and at times, "This shift in focus implied that some degree of blame or responsibility for the abuse was being placed upon the victim" (*ibid.*, p. 167).

The outcome of the sentencing circle was that the judge pronounced a sentence that had been created by the group and which had been based upon the proposals of the mayor and also the offender. The punishment in this case was not custodial. Rather, the accused had to restrict his alcohol consumption and meet regularly with a selected support group. This support group would, at a predetermined time, then report back the accused's progress to the judge. Crnkovitch reported that at the end of the proceedings, the victim appeared relieved that it was over: "She appeared relieved and simply said. 'It was good'" (*ibid.*, p. 169).

The Strengths of the Justice Circle

The strengths of the justice circle are expounded in much of the contemporary literature (see R v Moses, 1992; Quigley, 1994; Green, 1995; 1998); the main issues are briefly discussed here. One of the leading proponents of sentencing circles, Judge Barry Stuart, has articulated in some detail, the benefits of circle sentencing in his judgement in *R. v. Moses* (1992) (also see Chartrand, 1995, p. 876). Stuart argued that the circle process merges the values of both First Nations and also western governments, thus providing a fundamental challenge to the monopoly of the professionals who are involved in, and determine, the criminal justice processes. Not only does it promote a sharing of responsibility by encouraging participation in the criminal justice process by the victim, the offender and, importantly, the victim's community. It also enhances the transfer of information between the state institutions, the victim, community and offender and facilitates a creative search for new options. Consequently, it extends the focus of the criminal justice system beyond that of the courts and police, and creates a constructive environment for the resolution of criminal justice problems by generating a greater understanding of justice system limitations (*ibid*). More specifically, it impacts upon the following areas.

Judiciary and Court Process

As stated earlier, the justice circle strives to preserve the principle of judicial independence in that in the final analysis the judge's decision still remains, but that decision is strengthened by the fact that it has been influenced by the local community view on the case under discussion.

Victim

The victims' views about their experiences of victimisation are heard, either through victim impact statements or a personal statement to the circle. Their views are rarely heard in the conventional criminal justice system.

Offender/Victimiser

The offender is reconceptualised as a victimiser and has to explain his or her actions to the victim. Consequently, the victimiser not only takes responsibility for his or her actions, but is also encouraged to understand the full impact of how those actions have affected the victim, the victim's family, their own family and also members of the community at large. In a wider context, the offenders are less likely to re-offend, thus alleviating their own suffering at the hands of the criminal justice system but also reducing the overall numbers of indigenous people within both the criminal justice system and its correctional insitutions.

Community

In many cases the wider social network [the community] of the victim, and in some cases, also the victimiser, is also victimised. On the one hand, the community wants an explanation for the victimiser's actions, whilst on the other hand, the same community will have to decide whether or not to take the victimiser back and if so, on what terms.

The Weaknesses of the Justice Circle

Much of the debate in favour of the justice circle approach involves the denigration of the existing system. However, it is simply wrong to say that the present system(s) does not also seek some of the goals of restorative justice, such as reparation and to some extent even restoration to the victims. It is also fairly true to say that any such goals have been tempered by limited resources and also fears of public/

media reactions and their political backlash. Furthermore, it is often hard to dissagregate the issue of Aboriginal rights from the broader debate over criminal justice. More specifically, there are a number of distinct weaknesses.

Overall High Operating Costs

Justice circles are very expensive to operate and, rather like crime prevention measures, they are hard to quantify in cost-benefit terms as they can last from 4 to 14 hours each. In cost benefit analysis terms, their costs are largely up front, as it is argued that they have a lower rate of recidivism. However, their costs and benefits may cut across the budgets of a number of different sectors, the courts, social services, police, corrections, supervision agencies and so on. Consequently, they require a very large, perhaps paradigmatic, leap of faith to even be given a chance of working. In addition to high operating costs is the local dependence upon state-driven funding initiatives.

Growth is Driven by State Funding Models

Underpinning the rise in popularity of restorative justice ideas such as justice circles has been an increase in the availability of federal funding to support such projects. Whilst it might be wrong to describe this as an example of supplier induced demand (Wall, 1996), in the same way that the availability of legal aid has, for example, proliferated the demand for publicly funded legal services, the availability of funding has nevertheless increased. An example of such a funding initiative is the Aboriginal Community Corrections Initiative,[15] run by the Aboriginal Corrections Policy Unit of the Solicitor General of Canada. The initiative encourages proposals from First Nations, community groups or Aboriginal organisations that have a mandate and capacity to provide services to offenders within a restorative/ healing process. Without such initiatives, justice circles would not likely have proliferated as they have. However, the main concern here is not the proliferation of justice circle projects but the way in which the funding models tend to be project driven.

Reliance Upon a Contestable Concept of Community

Central to the success of the justice circle is the practical existence of a coherent community. The justice circle approach requires an almost blind acceptance of the structure and culture of traditional Aboriginal communities. Yet, this belief goes against the grain of the literature on community which is largely critical. Crawford, for example, charts the political career of what he terms "appeals to community" (Crawford, 1996). In addition to problems with the concept and ideology of community are some very specific concerns about Aboriginal communities in general which affect the operation of the justice circle, particularly as no two communities are alike. Consequently no one solution will work in all communities. Four key areas of concern have to be taken into account when considering community-based alternatives to justice.

The first concern is the level of social cohesion, or social breakdown, which exists within the community. As a rule of thumb, communities subject to a relatively low degree of social breakdown will be less likely to experience difficulties in realising some of their aspirations towards justice (Nuffield, 1996, p. 10). Conversely, the opposite will occur. So, a community in which theft is the main crime problem will have fewer justice challenges than one in which sexual abuse and drugs are the main problem.

The second concern is the community's degree of integration with, or isolation from, the rest of society. A community's levels of integration into, and geographical isolation from, a larger society will affect its ability to develop its own initiatives.

The third concern relates to the human resources available within, and to, the community. For justice circles to work, other members of the community, "circle-keepers...a corps of volunteers in the community to shepherd the process" (Adams, 1998), have to be developed. The big question is who should these people be, how should they be chosen? The level of key human resources varies from community to community, particularly in terms of their elders structures, the capacity for training and also the extent to which traditional ways are still observed and practised. "Even where traditional practices and resources are still strong, some problems facing modern indigenous communities may be beyond the capacity of some practitioners to solve them" (Nuffield, 1996, p. 13). One possible problem that could arise here is the capacity of the community to reach a programme of punishment that is realistic and also falls within the Charter of Rights and Freedoms. Some examples of traditional punishment, for example, banishment to remote places, have been criticised as extremely harsh and as a human rights infringement.

The final, and perhaps the most problematic, of these concerns is the distribution of power or influence among community members (*ibid.*, p. 11). In some communities, disproportionate distributions of power leave some members disempowered, especially women and youth. Both groups are, for example, frequently excluded from key processes within the community to the point that they are unlikely to participate fully in the justice system either as victims, witnesses, or even as offenders (see Crnkovitch, 1993; Nuffield, *op. cit.*). This disproportionate distribution of power therefore challenges the ability of the justice process to yield a fair and equitable outcome: "whatever that may mean within the community's reality" (Nuffield, *op. cit.*). A further concern here is the lack of clarity as to the position of non-Aboriginals, especially members of other recognised minority groups, who live within the community, either as participants of the circle or their treatment as an offender.

So, it is questionable as to whether or not community exists in a form that would sustain the (great) expectations made of the justice circle. Whilst there is considerable evidence to suggest that Aboriginal communities are to a certain extent defined both externally and also geographically, the degree to which they also contain an internal coherence which leads to the cultural reproduction of the community varies. It cannot, therefore, be assumed that there exists the level of gemeinschaft or internal coherence that justice circles require. In this sense, they are a further example of the expression of the ideology of community as a policy tool in order to bridge contradictions.

Acceptance of the Community View is at the Discretion of the Court

The function of the circle is to advise the judge. It has an advisory, rather than statutory role. Consequently, one of its weaknesses is that the judge is not obliged to take the advice of the circle. In most, if not all, cases, however, the judge enters into a prior agreement with the circle that he or she will accept the community view. Of course, this weakness could also be interpreted as a strength in cases where the members of the circle want to impose what the judge feels is an unreasonable sentence.

The Problem of Justifying Positive Discrimination

Justice circles seek to address very specific injustices that are experienced by Aboriginal peoples within the criminal justice system. Indeed, the over-representation of Aboriginal peoples within the Canadian criminal justice system is, as stated earlier, often used to justify the shift towards more traditional methods of resolution (Harding, 1991; Quigley, 1994; RCAP, 1996). Consequently, the solutions they seek are ultimately divisive in a society that embraces multi-culturalism because they do not deal with the general over-representation of visible minorities, especially afro-Caribbean blacks, within the prison system (Roberts and LaPrairie, 1996, p.78; LaPrairie, 1997, p. 39; 1998b, p. 446). Therefore any broader programme of alternative criminal justice processes would need to be framed in such a way as to embrace the dynamics of the many injustices that exist within the criminal justice process.

LaPrairie has questioned the simplistic and uncritically accepted assumption that Aboriginal over-representation within the Canadian criminal justice system is simply a matter of institutional racism (1997, p. 39). She has argued that the debate over Aboriginal justice, and especially debates over the form of those alternatives, has lacked empirical study and has, instead, tended to draw upon anecdotal evidence from advocates of various Aboriginal justice projects. The Hollow Water Holistic Circle Healing project, for example, features very prominently in most discussions of justice alternatives (RCAP, 1996; Wheelright, 1998). LaPrairie's main concern is that in light of the many claims to the effectiveness of circle sentencing, no systematic empirical evaluation has been conducted. This lacunae is in contrast to other sentencing innovations, such as computerised sentencing databases, which have been exposed to rigorous scrutiny (Brodeur, 1987), but for circle sentencing, "all we have are the assurances of advocates" (Roberts and LaPrairie, 1996, p. 82). She observes that the debates over Aboriginal alternatives to justice, such as circle sentencing have, with some consistency, tended to make the following assumptions.

Firstly, the primary reason for over-representation of Aboriginal people in Canadian prisons is systematic racism and discrimination in criminal justice processing and the bases for this are historical and involve race and culture conflict (1998b, p. 446). Secondly, any problems with the criminal justice system experienced by Aboriginal peoples are unique to them and other similar economically situated people do not suffer similar problems. Thirdly, the experience of all Aboriginal people is similar, regardless of where they live.

Whilst she does not question the fact that a large number of Aboriginal people are caught up in the criminal justice system, LaPrairie does, however, question the accuracy of these three assumptions and suggests that empirical research be carried out to answer the following, uncomfortable, questions. Is there a differential processing in the criminal justice system due to culture conflict and racial discrimination or are there actually higher levels of Aboriginal offending? Do Aboriginal people commit the kinds of offences that likely result in carcereal sentences? Are there criminal justice policies and practices that have differential impacts upon Aboriginal offenders because of their socio-economic conditions? Finally, is the experience of Aboriginals in the criminal justice system the same from province to province and in both rural and urban settings? Each of these questions needs to be thoroughly researched and an answered.

Such empirical research, she believes, will discover that a much more sophisticated set of processes are involved which give rise to the above outcomes (1998b, p. 446). She observes that there has been a fairly rapid decline in interdependency among people in Aboriginal communities due to historical processes which have reproduced the mainstream social structure without the accompanying institutional development. The reserves, for example, are not integrated into mainstream society because of the historical practices of exclusion and the second-class status that is generally ascribed to Aboriginals. Consequently, a large group of marginalised and un-integrated people exists in communities because of uneven distribution of resources. Such lack of integration is exacerbated by cultural dislocation and the decline of informal mechanisms of social control, particularly, where relevant, through exposure to a dysfunctional family life and childhood abuse.

Limited Impacts Upon Legal Cultures

The philosophy(ies) within which justice circles are voiced introduces a new form of legal discourse which symbolises a shift in the framework for negotiating the meaning of particular events "from a language of claims and rights that are typical of legal discourse to a language grounded in the shared interests, mutual experiences and inter-dependencies of parties" (Crawford, 1996, p. 339). Yet, justice circles are fairly piecemeal developments and as such they are unlikely to make much of an overall impact upon legal cultures that are deeply entrenched within an adversarial philosophy. In the quest towards achieving a workable alternative to the failings of the existing criminal justice system, do these alternatives actually provide the parties involved with enough access to knowledge and advice about the criminal justice processes? One of the major criticisms of the existing criminal justice systems is that they are controlled by professionals whose interests, it is claimed, overshadow the real victims of the offence, even though such allegations are hard to prove (see Bevan, *et al.* 1994; Wall, 1996). Thus, devolving parts of the administration of justice process back to communities, reintroduces elements of laity and localism into those processes with the alleged, result that a more satisfying justice outcome is achieved. But this move back to tradition, localism and laity, places the criminal justice professionals in a rather contradictory position, especially the lawyer whose primary role is to act on behalf of the client and serve as a balance and a check against the might of the state. At one level, the minimal purpose of the defendant gaining access to justice (access to the expert services of a lawyer) must be to ensure that due process, and the protections that it affords, takes place (Young and Wall, 1996, p. 25). At the constitutional level, the purpose of gaining access to justice is to ensure that Canadian citizens, like those in many other western jurisdictions, can uphold their constitutional right to a fair trial.

What is the precise role of the lawyer in the process? Chartrand (1995) argues that the role of the lawyer is severely compromised by the principles of the justice circle. He contends that lawyers cannot exercise their duties impartially and effectively because of the potential contradiction that arises between the lawyers' adversarial role as counsel and the non-adversarial nature of the circle sentencing process. He further argues that there comes a point in the circle process at which the lawyer's protection of the client threatens the circle sentencing process by diminishing the role of the community, especially where the lawyer appeals directly to the judge. By allowing community involvement in decision-making with regard to their clients, lawyers disregard their commitment to act in the client's interest (Chartrand, 1995, p. 874). So, the alternatives serve to realign the traditional boundaries of the criminal justice professionals within the justice process.

Chartrand argues that Law Societies need to provide guidance to practicing lawyers when confronted with the option of having a circle sentencing process for their clients (Chartrand, 1995, p. 881). But, it is equally arguable that the legal profession is, as it always has been, fairly reflexive and that lawyers will do what they have always done and that is continue to re-negotiate the nature of the relationship between the profession, the client and also the justice process (see Paterson, 1996, p. 137). What is of perhaps greater concern is the nature of the justice circle as an alternative to justice and whether or not this constitutes an alternative or an exit from justice.

Conclusions: Restorative Alternatives to Justice or Political Compromise

This chapter has explored an increasingly popular alternative model for achieving local justice, the Aboriginal justice circle, which is currently gaining popularity within the Canadian criminal justice system and elsewhere. Justice circles represent an increasing trend towards the devolution of justice away from the state into the community. They are clearly seen as the way forward, especially as existing schemes appear to be failing badly. Whilst not necessarily cheap to operate, they are very proactive in that they seek to address the problem rather than the symptom and ultimately create cost savings in terms of both financial and human resources. Moreover, such schemes are extremely constructive in so far as they appear to meet broader societal ideals by addressing the victim's needs for justice as well as those of the local community, the victimiser and also the state. Existing systems largely address the latter at the expense of the former.

However, whilst the advantages of these alternative schemes seem considerable, there nevertheless exist some major concerns with regard to their operationalisability. The main concern is that in their quest to make peace between the various parties involved, they can bypass the formal criminal justice process and, of course, the balances and checks that the principle of due process, brings with it. As such, it is of concern that they provide an exit from justice, rather than alternative to it, and as such can leave both the victimiser, and also the defendant, vulnerable at various key points in the process, particularly with regard to ensuring that due process takes place. Although many of the cases in which these alternatives to justice are invoked will involve fairly minor infractions of the law, this is nevertheless a potential site for the miscarriage of justice. The UK research into cautioning, for example, greatly illustrates this phenomenon (Crawford, 1996, p. 313). Thus, the effective use of such policy requires mechanisms that will ensure the individual gets access to justice and has the latitude, where necessary, to make informed choices about options and directions. Some form of structure that provides a system of checks and balances is required to ensure that the legal needs of defendants are met. The justice circle, despite some assertions to the contrary, is still an alternative method of administering justice within the existing criminal justice system. As such, it is not an exit from justice, although concerns do exist with regard to access to justice matters.

This spin on the concept of restorative justice, or devolved or "satisfying justice," as it has been called (Department of Justice, 1995), is very attractive politically, as it seeks a middle ground which is the point at which all parties agree. It is a relatively new concept and differs from the largely state-centred models of justice that exist elsewhere. But its main advantage is that whilst "satisfying justice" is a compromise, it allows the various parties to engage the justice process at different levels, their level, rather than that of the state. Each party has different expectations of the criminal justice processes.

But we must not get too carried away. The debate over justice circles is normatively driven and takes place within a morally charged climate in which old ideas are seen as bad and new ideas are de facto good. Furthermore, the debate is also taking place against the politically charged backdrop of the fight for Aboriginal rights within a generation of Canadians who shoulder a considerable amount of guilt for their forebears.

To conclude, whilst the concept of a justice circle seems a very attractive proposition, it is extremely problematic. Its practical application is limited, but nevertheless very useful in some very complicated circumstances where a clearly defined community exists. Justice circles are best used to deal with specific issues within definable communities, for example, legacies of sexual abuse in Hollow Water. They can help break cycles of child abuse by enabling the community, the victims and victimiser come to terms with a problem and provide a forum to determine new terms of co-existence (Hollow Water First Nation, 1997). Indeed, it could be argued that the community consultation element would also suggest that the healing model might be *one* way of dealing with complicated issues, such as dealing with the reintegration of paedophiles in to a community, by working out some ground rules for living within a particular neighbourhood.

At the end of the day, we must have realistic expectations of alternatives such as justice circles. It is very important that those expectations are not shaped by the failure of social welfare policies elsewhere in the society. Equally important is the need not to mistake criminal justice policy for social policy. We must not lose sight of the fact that criminal justice is the coercive arm of the state. Because there will always be tension between justice and welfare, it is essential that a sense of realism prevails and that a balance is struck. But there is clearly a need for further research into the operation of the justice circle. On the one hand, we cannot simply deny the validity of the accounts describing positive experiences of the circle approaches. On the other hand, LaPrairie's quite extensive work in this area has demonstrated the need for independent (empirical) evaluations of the many projects that have developed.

Notes

1. My thanks go to Brian Tkatchuk, Kathleen Macdonald, Yvon Dandurand and the other members of the Center for Criminal Justice Police and Criminal Justice Reform and the University of British Columbia for their assistance.
2. See, for example, the rise and subsequent fall of the Criminal Justice Act 1991 in the UK. Also see Roberts (1998) for an overview of this debate.
3. There is some debate over the nature of Aboriginal over-representation within the criminal justice system. See discussion later in this paper, but also Roberts and LaPrairie, (1996) and LaPrairie (1997; 1998b).
4. The term Aboriginal is used interchangeably here with the term indigenous.
5. See the general bibliography.

6. The term provincial is used here to include the two territories.
7. For example, Australia, New Zealand, but also including the USA.
8. See Marshall (1999) for a comprehensive overview of the concept of restorative justice and also an overview of the various ways in which the concept is manifested in practice.
9. These publications contain a range of alternative schemes, of which the justice circles are one, but they or their derivatives are the most numerous.
10. Canadian Charter of Rights and Freedoms. Pt. 1 Constitution Act, 1982 being schedule B of the Canada Act 1982 (UK) 1982, c. 1 (see Hucker, 1999, p. 54).
11. S.C. 1988, c. 31.
12. For a good overview of this case law see <www.usask.ca/nativelaw/jah_scircle.html>
13. A discussion of the role of Elders within the circle can be found in *R. v. A.G.A.* (1998). Also see Church Council on Justice and Corrections, (1996) for a list of projects.
14. See for example the process in the Hollow Water Circles (Solicitor General, Canada, 1997; also at <www.csc-scc.gc.ca/Rjweek/english/resource/hollowe.htm>)
15. See <www.canada.gc.ca/depts/agencies/pco/aborguide/1-8_e.html>

Cases

R. v. A.G.A. [1998] Alberta Court of Queen's Bench. No. 282 March 17 (Elders involvement in the process).
R. v. Moses, (1992) 1 CNLR, (1992) 71 CCC (3d) 347, 11 CR (4th), 357. (See Benevides, 1994).
R. v. Morin, [1994] 1 CNLR, [1995] 4 CNLR 37, (1996) 101 CCC (3d) 124 (Sask. CA). (On the appropriateness of using sentencing circle).

References

Adams, J. (1998) "Circle of Justice," *Minnesota Star Tribune*, August 18, 1998.
Barnett, C. (1995) "Circle Sentencing," *Canadian Native Law Reporter*, vol. 3.
Benevides, H.J. (1994) "R. v. Moses and Sentencing Circles: A Case Comment," *Dalhousie Journal of Legal Studies*, vol. 3.
Berma, B. (1997) "Reflections on Community Holistic Circle Healing (CHCH)", Ottawa: Department of Corrections, <www.cscscc.gc.ca/Rjweek/english/resource/ hollowe.htm>.
Bevan, G., Holland, T. and Partington, M. (1994) *Organising Cost Effective Justice*, London: Social Market Foundation Memorandum no. 7.
Brodeur, J.P. (1987) *Evaluating Sentencing Databases*, Ottawa: Department of Justice.

Chartrand, L. (1995) "The Appropriateness of the Lawyer as Advocate in Contemporary Aboriginal Justice Initiatives," *Alberta Law Review*, vol. 33, no. 4.

Church Council on Justice and Corrections, (1996) *Satisfying Justice: Safe Community Options that Attempt to Repair Harm from Crime and Reduce the Use or Length of Imprisonment.* Ottawa: Church Council on Justice and Corrections.

Hollow Water First Nation, (1997) *Community Holistic Circle Healing: An Approach.*

Correctional Service of Canada, (1997) *Corrections in Canada*, Ottawa: Correctional Service.

Crawford, A. (1994) "Appeals to Community and Crime Prevention," Crime, *Law and Social Change*, vol. 22.

Crawford, A. (1996) "Alternatives to Prosecution: Access to, or Exits From, Criminal Justice?" in Young, R. and Wall, D.S., Editors, (1996) *Access to Criminal Justice: Legal Aid, Lawyers and the Defence of Liberty*, London: Blackstone Press.

Crnkovitch, M. (1993) "Report on the Sentencing Circle in C," in *Pauktuutit Inuit Women's Association: Brief to the Royal Commission on Aboriginal Peoples in Canada.*

Crnkovitch, M. (1996) "A Sentencing Circle," *International Journal of Legal Pluralism and Unofficial Law*, vol. 36.

Current, (1990) "An Aboriginal Justice System," *Currents*, vol. 6, no. 3.

Department of Justice (1995) *Putting Aboriginal Justice Devolution Into Practice: The Canadian and International Experience, Workshop Report*, July 5-7, 1995, Vancouver: Simon Fraser University: Department of Justice Canada.

Dussault, R. (1998) *Aboriginal People and the Criminal Justice System: A Long Shadow on a Just Society*, Aboriginal Studies Seminar, Canada House, London, November.

Green, R.G. (1995) "Aboriginal Sentencing and Mediation Initiatives: The Sentencing Circle and Other Community Participation Models in Six Aboriginal Communities," Unpublished LLM thesis, University of Manitoba: Winnipeg.

Green, R.G. (1998) *Justice in Aboriginal Communities: Sentencing Alternatives*, Saskatoon: Purich.

Harding, J. (1991) "Policing and Aboriginal Justice," *Canadian Journal of Criminology*, July, pp. 363-383.

Hucker, J. (1999) "Theory Meets Practice: Some Curent Human Rights Challenges in Canada," *Journal of Law and Society*, vol. 26, no. 1.

John Howard Society of Alberta, (1992) *Towards a Separate Justice System for Aboriginal Peoples*, Alberta: John Howard Society of Alberta.

LaPrairie, C. (1992) "Aboriginal Crime and Justice: Explaining the Present, Exploring the Future," *Canadian Journal of Criminology*, July.

LaPrairie, C. (1995) "Conferencing in Aboriginal Communities in Canada: Finding Middle Ground in Criminal Justice," *Criminal Law Forum*, vol. 6, no. 3.

LaPrairie, C. (1997) "Reconstructing Theory: Explaining Aboriginal Over-Representation in the Criminal Justice System in Canada," *Australian and New Zealand Journal of Criminology*, vol. 30.

LaPrairie, C. (1998a) "The 'New' Justice: Some Implications for Aboriginal Communities," *Canadian Journal of Criminology*, January.

LaPrairie, C. (1998b) *Review of Bridging the Cultural Divide: A Report on Aboriginal People and Criminal Justice in Canada* by the Royal Commission on Aboriginal Peoples, Social Policy and Administration, vol. 32, no. 4.

Marshall, T.F. (1999) *Restorative Justice: An Overview*, London: Home Office.

Nuffield, J. (1996) *Placing Indigenous Justice Developments in Context: Some Dimensions for Analysis of the Experience*, A background paper prepared for the Indigenous Justice workshop (Session 2.3) of the 11th Commonwealth Law Conference in Vancouver, August 27.

Osborne, D. and Gaebler, T. (1992) *Reinventing Government: How the Entrepreneurial Spirit is Transforming the Public Sector*, New York: Addison-Wesley.

Palys, T. (1993) *Prospects for Aboriginal Justice in Canada*, Vancouver: Simon Fraser University.

Paterson, A. (1996) "Professionalism and the Legal Services Market," *International Journal of the Legal Profession*, vol. 3, no. 1, pp. 137-168.

Quigley, T. (1994) "Some Issues in Sentencing of Aboriginal Offenders," pp. 269-296 in Grosse, R., Henderson J.Y., and Carter, R. (Eds) (1994) *Continuing Poundmaker and Riel's Quest: Presentations Made at a Conference on Aboriginal Peoples and Justice*, Saskatoon, Saskatchewan: Purich Publishing.

Roberts, J.V. (1998) "The Evolution of Penal Policy in Canada," *Social Policy and Administration*, vol. 32, no. 4.

Roberts, J.V. and LaPrairie, C. (1996) "Sentencing Circles: Some Unanswered Questions," *Criminal Law Quarterly*, vol. 39, pp. 69-83.

Royal Commission on Aboriginal Peoples (1996) *Bridging the Cultural Divide: A Report on Aboriginal Peoples and Criminal Justice in Canada: Synopsis of a Special Report by the Royal Commission on Aboriginal Peoples*.

Royal Commission on Aboriginal Peoples (1996) *Royal Commission on Aboriginal Peoples: Final Report*, <www.indigenous.bc.ca>.

Solicitor General, Canada (1997) *The Four Circles of Hollow Water*, Ottawa: Aboriginal Corrections Policy Unit, Solicitor General Canada (APC 15 CA, 1997).

Scott, J. (1997) Achieving Satisfying Justice: A Symposium on Implementing Restorative Models, Vancouver, March 20-23.

Wall, D.S. (1996) "Legal Aid, Social Policy and the Architecture of Criminal Justice: The Supplier Induced Demand Thesis and Legal Aid Policy," *Journal of Law and Society*, vol. 23.

Wheelright, J. (1998) "Generations of Sexual Abuse: How One Town is Breaking the Cycle," *Marie Claire*, November, pp. 108-114.

Young, R. and Wall, D.S. (1996) "Criminal Justice, Legal Aid and the Defence of Liberty," pp. 1-25, in Young, R. and Wall, D.S. *Access to Criminal Justice: Legal Aid, Lawyers and the Defence of Liberty*, London: Blackstone Press.

Other Useful References Relating to Aboriginal Justice

Auger, D. (1997) "Legal Aid, Aboriginal People, and the Legal Problems Faced by Persons of Aboriginal Descent in Northern Ontario," pp. 397-440, in McCamus, J.D. (1997) *A Blueprint for Publicly Funded*

Legal Services: Report of the Ontario Legal Aid Review, Volume 2, Ontario: Government of Ontario.

Bazemore, G. and Griffiths, C. (1997) Conferences, Circles, Boards and Mediations: Scouting the "New Wave" of Community Justice Decision Making Approaches, <www.cjprimer.com/circles.htm>

Berzins, L. (1997) "Perspectives on Achieving Satisfying Justice: The Challenge Before Us," *Interaction Newsletter*, vol. 9, no. 3, fall, 1997.

Benson, G. (1991) Canada (1991) *Developing Crime Prevention Strategies in Aboriginal Communities*, Ottawa: Solicitor General, Canada.

Crawford, A. (1997) *The Local Governance of Crime*, Oxford: Oxford University Press.

Dosanijh, U. (1997) *Strategic Reforms of British Columbia's Justice System*, Vancouver, B.C: Ministry of Attorney General, April.

Eid, E. (1997) *The Requirement to Provide Legal Aid under International Instruments*, Human Rights Law Section.

Friedland, M.L. (1997) "Governance of Legal Aid Schemes," in McCamus, J.D. (1997) *A Blueprint for Publicly Funded Legal Services: Report of the Ontario Legal Aid Review, Volume 3*, Ontario: Government of Ontario.

James, A. and Raine, J. (1998) *The New Politics of Criminal Justice*, London: Longman.

Howard, R. (1998) "How and Why Things Happen: Native Life in Canada," *The Globe and Mail*, July 8, 1998.

Indian Commission of Ontario (date unknown), *Indian Negotiations in Ontario: Making the Process Work*, Ontario: The Indian Commission of Ontario.

Kamien, T. (1995) Implementing Self-Government: An Examination of the Aboriginal Communities Act (Western Australia), Murdoch School of Law, <www.murdoch. edu.au/elaw /issues/v2n1/karmien.txt>.

McDonnell, R.F. (1992) "Contextualising the Investigation of Customary Law in Contemporary Native Communities," *Canadian Journal of Criminology*, July.

Mandamin, T. (date unknown) Harmony in the Community, <www.extension. ualberta.Ca/lawnow/harmony_.htm>.

Messmer, H. and Otto, H-U. (1992) "Restorative Justice: Steps on the Way Towards a Good Idea," pp. 1-12 in Messmer, H. and Otto, H-U. (eds) (1992) *Restorative Justice on Trial: Pitfalls and Potentials of Victim-Offender Mediation—International Research Perspectives*, London; Kluwer.

Ministry of Attorney General, BC (1998) A Restorative Justice Framework: British Columbia Justice Reform, Jan. 1998. <Www.ag.gov.bc.ca/public/ 98001.html> also see <www.ag.gov.bc.ca/public/98003.html>.

Ministry of Attorney General, BC (1998) "O'Connor Apologises to Complainants and First Nation Elders in Healing Circle," Ministry of Attorney General, BC Media Release June 17, Victoria, B.C.

Rudin, J. (1997) Legal Aid Needs of Aboriginal People in Urban areas and on Southern Reserves, in McCamus, J.D. (1997) *A Blueprint for Publicly Funded Legal Services: Report of the Ontario Legal Aid Review, Volume 2*, Ontario: Government of Ontario.

Simpson, J. (1998) "Consequences of Delgamuukw Decision Now Ticking in B.C.," *The Globe and Mail*, June 17, 1998.

Stenning, P.C. (1996) *Police Governance in First Nations in Ontario*, Toronto: Centre for Criminology.

Tomaino, J. (1997) "Guess Who's Coming to Dinner? A Preliminary Model for the Satisfaction of Public Opinion as a Legitimate Aim in Sentencing," *Crime, Law and Social Change*, vol. 27.

Von Hirsch, A. and Ashworth, A., Editors, (1998) *Principled Sentencing: Readings on Theory and Practice*, Oxford: Hart Publishing.

Chapter 7

Icons, Flagships and Identities: Aboriginal Tourism in British Columbia, Western Canada[1]

Heather Norris Nicholson

Welcome to our world.
Come share our pride.[2]
Catch the Native spirit.[3]

Introduction

Across Canada, web-sites, brochures and billboards invite browsers and passers-by to enter the distinctive cultural worlds of Canada's First Nations. From luxury resort hotels and archaeological sites to whale watching and powwows, Aboriginal Canada has become increasingly visible to the tourist. The emergence of Aboriginal interest in tourism has brought new diversity and impetus to an industry long associated with mountains, moose, Mounties and pioneer history. The traditions and distinctive artistic heritage of indigenous material culture seems to offer precisely the ingredients formerly lacking in Canada's tourism appeal.

These Aboriginal tourist-scapes of Canada should not be dismissed as further expressions of commodified cultures and economic assimilation into mainstream society (Cohen, 1993). Undoubtedly, tourism activity uses culture as a purchasable commodity and its encounters legitimise forms of cultural voyeurism, but can it also fulfil other goals? When tourism initiatives are situated within indigenous struggles for political autonomy, economic self-sufficiency and cultural recognition, their complex role within the negotiation of contemporary Aboriginal experiences and identities emerge. However, the elaborate government structure, which has evolved to promote indigenous tourism, still encodes other, more deep-rooted and problematic aspects of Canada's relationship with its First Nations.

This discussion identifies some of the multi-layered messages offered by Aboriginal tourism with reference to Cowichan Native Village on Vancouver Island. This site is set within a consideration of indigenous tourism in British Columbia and the overall growth of Canada's tourism industry. Marketing policies testify to broader political and cultural processes and disclose significant shifts in how Aboriginal people define themselves and are defined. The conclusion relates Aboriginal tourism to some of the wider issues facing both mainstream society and First Nations, and comments on tourism in the light of recommendations set out in the *Report of the Royal Commission on Aboriginal Peoples* (RCAP, 1996c).

Canadian Tourism and Indigenous Involvement

According to the World Travel and Tourism Council in 1996, tourism employs approximately 10 percent of the world's workforce in 204 million jobs and is now claimed to be the world's largest industry. Although the industry's decidedly complex nature means that precise figures may be difficult to verify, its competitive and volatile nature is indisputable. Notwithstanding tourism's susceptibility to economic fluctuations at both domestic and international level, governments favour tourism as an engine to economic development or diversification. Canada is no exception and, although the industry is marked by sharp swings which synchronise with the highs and lows of economic and business cycles, over half a million Canadians were directly employed in tourism in 1997. Total tourism spending reached $44 billion in 1997 and pumped nearly $8.8 billion into the Canadian economy in the first quarter of 1998. Within British Columbia, tourism's contribution to the provincial economy was shown by the $8.5 million spent by 21million overnight visitors during 1997.[4]

Fears of losing its share of the global market through the 1990s prompted Canada's tourism industry—at federal and provincial level—to widen both the image and appeal of all destinations. Changes in consumer tastes, leisure activities and tourists themselves—for instance, more mobile retirees and baby boomers with disposable income in search of speciality activities—placed growing emphasis upon nature, adventure tourism and cultural encounters ranging from historic places to lifestyles. Pragmatism and economic opportunism thus prompted both mainstream society and First Nations to greater involvement in tourism activity.

Arguably, beyond its economic appeal, tourism offers a meeting ground within which new identities and aspirations may be negotiated. Yet tourism activity seems fraught with the potential for collision between conflicting values both within and beyond Aboriginal communities, the dangers of collusion between different interest groups and the potential for unacceptable forms of compromise. Notwithstanding the economic expediency evident at different political levels, indigenous tourism is also claimed as a means to community development and a means to achieve cross-cultural understanding. But might the present enthusiasm for indigenous tourism provoke commercial rivalries among adjacent communities or serve up specially constructed tourist versions of Aboriginal identity which will hinder rather than foster inter-cultural understanding? Are such concerns minor in comparison to tourism's potential to generate economic and community development through creating much-needed local employment, training and role models which will promote self-esteem, socio-economic stability and better individual and community prospects?

The support for tourism in government circles and among some Aboriginal communities is prompted by different agendas, driven by broadly consensual to widely divergent motives. In an increasingly competitive global industry, the promotion of indigenous tourism represents economic opportunism at the government level and among managerial and entrepreneurial sectors of the Aboriginal population. Culturally-orientated tourism promises new marketing potential for Canada's tourism industry while offering Aboriginal peoples the means to define and redefine their identities, cultures and history on their own terms. Although government and First Nations both seem eager to gain from this marriage of convenience, the increasingly sophisticated ways of marketing Aboriginal culture also disclose many of the enduring inequalities between sections of indigenous and non indigenous society.

The Rise of Indigenous Tourism

In Western Canada, European fascination with the distinctive visual and material cultures of West Coast Nations prompted an early Aboriginal involvement in tourist activity (Francis, 1992). Visitors' thirst for spectacle, curiosity and collectibles introduced many changes in artistic output and cultural practice as a distinctive tourist souvenir art emerged. Some indigenous communities began the commercial production of masks, poles and chests—distinguished by their quality, size and subject matter—to satisfy collectors and travellers (Cole, 1985). Aboriginal guides, hunters and interpreters also emerged to assist nineteenth-century travellers and attest to the economic opportunism which accompanied early tourism even though such encounters were usually based upon unequal relations between visitor and local expert (Jansen, 1993).

Economic, cultural and socio-political inequalities constructed a fictive Aboriginal identity, which dominated tourism and advertising during much of the twentieth century. Aboriginal peoples continued to bring spectacle and exoticism to the cultural events which entertained Canada's increasingly immigrant and settler-dominated society. No longer paraded as the living relics of a disappearing race, the staged indigenous cultural presence at festivals was nonetheless part of the assimilationist approach underpinning successive government policies. The "saved" fragments of cultural practice provided visual public justification of the need for assimilation. The mismatch between the identities off-stage and on stage and screen were ignored or undetected by their audiences as most non-indigenous people rarely encountered or questioned the realities of marginalised Aboriginal existence.

Geographical and historical variables influenced which First Nations began to develop more pro-active roles in tourism activities that were initially confined mainly to transport, guiding and souvenirs. Opportunities were dictated by accessibility, proximity to other sites of tourism interest and relations with adjacent populations. For instance, on the outskirts of Calgary in Alberta, the T'suu T'sina (Sarcee) took part in the annual Stampede and further west, where the Trans-Canadian Highway crosses Lakoda (Stoney) lands at Morley, in the eastern foothills of the Rockies, facilities for scout camps were developed in the late 1960s (Norris Nicholson, 1992a, p. 60). This early encouragement of atracting non-Aboriginal visitors to reserve land recognised the importance of fostering cross-cultural under-standing through educational visits—a message taken up by many indigenous communities in later years.

Much of the impetus for First Nations tourism has emerged since the late 1970s and particularly within the last fifteen years (Murphy, 1985). Its growth parallels the rise of Aboriginal political prominence during the 1980s and indicates its acceptance by many community leaders as a means to achieve diverse socio-cultural, political and economic goals. As Aboriginal people challenged the structural inequalities entrenched in government policies, their struggle for political recognition as well as economic and social justice focused on the settlement of land claims (Richardson, 1989; Cassidy, 1991; Boldt, 1993). The recognition of legal claim to long-disputed land-bases signalled the first step towards greater economic self-reliance which, in turn, could help to break the vicious cycle of poverty, alienation and dysfunction which perpetuated under-development (Elias, 1991).

Land has both an economic and a cultural significance. Cultural assertion became part of the new political consciousness and discourse. The revival of cultural practice and renewed faith in spirituality offered guidance, strength and sources of inspiration. The repatriation of important confiscated ceremonial objects from museums into purpose-built facilities under community management reinforced the significance of material cultural artefacts (Clifford, 1997, p. 123). The distinctive visual identity of Aboriginal culture gained visibility in the quest for political recognition and greater economic self-reliance. New cultural interpretation centres sought to serve both community and visitor and fostered the start of culturally orientated tourism.

The rise of Aboriginal interest in tourism was timely for governments, as tourism became increasingly competitive during the 1980s. Across Canada, government funding, advisory services and training schemes encouraged community and rural-based tourism enterprises, including new Aboriginal businesses (BC, 1992-94). The subsequent, and at times over-hasty, promotion of uncoordinated tourism initiatives fulfilled different objectives: government agencies—at federal and provincial level—hoped that tourism might help to bring much-needed economic diversification while many First

Nations perceived tourism as a route towards greater economic autonomy. Tourism promised a way of participating in wider processes of change. Unsurprisingly, diverse representations of Aboriginality emerged as First Nations sought to negotiate places for themselves and their cultural identity in and through tourism.

Aboriginal Tourism Within British Columbia

British Columbia's tourism history illustrates how changing power relationships between Aboriginal groups and the dominant society intermesh with the politics of representation. Indigenous culture had first attracted visitors, researchers, collectors, photographers and artists to sites of Aboriginal significance from the later nineteenth century as shown by abundant writings, artwork, photographs and early film (see for example, Gidley, 1991; Clifford, 1991; Clifford, 1993). Participation of Aboriginal groups also occurred in annual parades and festivals in the provincial capital, Victoria and elsewhere. However, indigenous groups only began to develop a basis for sharing their culture more on their own terms during the 1970s.

A number of isolated tourism initiatives occurred in different parts of the province including the U'Mista Cultural Centre at Alert Bay which was associated with the return of Potlatch regalia and 'Ksan model village in Northern British Columbia. The problem of how to balance cultural integrity with economic opportunity soon revealed the dangers of insensitive tourism activity (Smith, 1994, p. 177; Whitt, 1995). The Native Brotherhood of British Columbia cautioned in 1980 against converting socially orientated cultural activities into tourism products. They warned that certain cultural activities had already lost their social role in succumbing to economic forces and tourist appeal (BC, 1980). Although still in an embryonic form, tourism was not well regarded, particularly by those who feared the consequences of greater public accessibility and commercialisation.

In contrast, a report by the federal government published in 1982, clearly sensed an economic opportunity as it dealt briefly with the "West Coast Indian Theme." After acknowledging "the exceptional nature of this Native Indian culture and its relatively low profile," the report continued:

The marketability of the West Coast Native Indian culture, its arts, crafts and ways of life is *quite high*...(and) should be explored (Canada, 1982; my emphasis).

The goal of economic self-reliance overcame many doubts about tourism over the next decade (Cassidy and Seward, 1991). Given tourism's capacity to reinforce economic dependency, necessity rather than choice probably prompted indigenous interest. Once wider societal trends place a monetary value on hitherto suppressed aspects of cultural identity and history, ignoring those commercial implications only opens opportunities for outsiders to assert new forms of economic control. A culturally orientated tourism offered the promise of desperately needed employment for some communities otherwise heavily dependent upon welfare. However fickle tourism might be, it could generate alternative sources of income no less vulnerable than such existing natural resource bases as fishing or forestry or the short-term commercial enterprises to which communities were beginning to turn.

Current prospects for indigenous tourism seemed promising as visitor surveys and reports urged for more distinctive marketing. Consultants advised that the industry should diversify away from the province's traditional reputation for spectacular scenery and the associated opportunities for outdoor activities:

The Super-Natural images cannot solely be used to market British Columbia...Instead, market studies of rubber-tire travellers suggest that Canada must offer American travellers a sense of foreignness, of different cultures and different ways of living (Kafka, White and Associates, 1988).

Since much of tourism's appeal lies in the desire for difference, it is unsurprising that the industry's adoption of indigenous culture became tinged with exoticism. The reorganisation of provincial tourism and its effective spread called for the invention of distinctive place-identities. Although pioneer history was deeply entrenched in popular Canadian culture, its echoes of the American West lacked promotional individuality. Meanwhile British Columbia's familiar wilderness motifs had become risky in the aftermath of controversial environmental campaigns (Furnis, 1997-98). Indigenous culture, suitably packaged, seemed to fill the gap, without a hint of how problematic those counter-histories might be. The provincial government promoters of West Coast Aboriginal tourism anticipated a new means to market their region. A distinctive tourism identity independent of the better known and widely spread Plains Culture traditions would help to distinguish provincial tourism from its neighbours and competitors.

> [T]here is a general perception of a lack of distinctive cultural identity and personality. It is precisely that cultural and historical void that Native tourism...[may] fill, in a way specific and unique to British Columbia (McGregor, 1984 cited in Zizka,1989, p. 4).

During the early 1990s, indigenous tourism development became a measure of wider political changes which rekindled hopes of settling Aboriginal land claims and calls for self-government (Richardson, 1989; Cassidy, 1991; Boldt, 1993). Prospects of gaining control over resources and a more secure economic future prompted capital investment projects in many Aboriginal communities. Provincial political leaders also grasped the implications as shown by the then Premier Mike Harcourt's comment to the British Tourism Industry in London in January 1992:

> Aboriginal tourism is going to grow quite dramatically as they move towards self-sufficiency in negotiations (*The Province*, January 30, 1992, p. A30).

The range of cultural products and tourist experiences being run by First Nations quickly began to diversify and indigenous artwork was used even in the promotion of non-Aboriginal facilities. Individuals set up some initiatives while others were community ventures. Locations could be on, adjacent to, or far from, Aboriginal community lands. Financial support included speculative ventures, grant-aid and reliance on charity donations. Evident variations in experience and expertise resulted in wide differences in promotion and management. Cultural content differed according to goals, attitudes and sensibilities of the individual(s) involved; some ventures placed emphasising education and cultural understanding, others targeting specific trends in such speciality tourism.

New forms of political and economic leadership encouraged imaginative development plans and investment strategies which ranged from tiny eco-tourism schemes and retail outlets to multi-purpose sites with lodges, galleries, gift shops, restaurants, craft centres and performance spaces (BC, 1991-94; Canada, 1993). Conference facilities and casinos were also considered by some First Nations and two multi-billion resort hotels were developed to "target different market segments with aims to highlight native culture, provide employment and to diversify investment portfolio."[5] Access to government management training, advisory systems, credit facilities and pump-priming project funding encouraged Aboriginal entrepreneurs eager to work in, from and for their communities.

Since not all First Nations had access to relevant expertise, some hired consultants from outside their communities or non-Aboriginal advisors who brought different visions of how tourism might be developed. Comparisons were drawn from elsewhere, initially from Hawaii—and more recently from Australia and New Zealand—in an enthusiastic flurry to embrace new opportunities.[6] Over-ambitious and unrealistic planning, insufficient or inappropriate preliminary research, financial mismanagement, poor staff relations and lack of clear direction occurred during this heady phase of expansion (Norris Nicholson, 1992b).

At the first Aboriginal Tourism Convention in early 1996 there were renewed warnings:

> Native tourism can degenerate into the kind of carnival freak show common in Florida, where handed-painted road signs point to Authentic Seminole Village, peopled by Mexicans in chicken feathers and war paint....We don't want to become third world entertainers and arts and craft sellers.[7]

Notwithstanding these concerns, British Columbia's indigenous tourism soon established a reputation for professionalism and quality of service. There was also acknowledgement that much growth—in many ways—would continue to occur: "I guess you could say that many aspects of Aboriginal Tourism are not in their infancy any more, but are now becoming toddlers."[8]

As Aboriginal tourism expanded, so did the need for strategic planning and attempts at co-ordination emanated from both Aboriginal and government sources. After a number of promising but short-lived initiatives, the Aboriginal Tourism Association of BC (ATBC), was launched in early 1997 "to represent all Aboriginal tourism businesses in BC" (O'Neil, 1997, p. 1). Regional developments were set within wider initiatives aimed at co-ordinated marketing: for instance, at federal level the Canadian Tourism Commission (CTC) set up in 1995 to revitalise Canada's promotion as an appealing, multi-facetted tourism destination, soon included an Aboriginal Programme. Its director's belief that "Aboriginal tourism can become the icon of Canadian offerings" within the next decade[9] was soon made explicit in a lavishly produced publication, *Live the Legacy*, (Canada, 1996b).

CTC's strategic plan for indigenous tourism, 1997-2007 had implications at the provincial level: for each region, it promoted cultural experiences through visitor facilities, travel agencies and themed resorts based on traditional architectural forms and motifs (Buhasz, 1997, p. 19). Media reports hailed this formative document as the industry's guiding vision for the next decade and claimed that indigenous involvement could satisfy two of the key requirements for late twentieth century tourism—culture and adventure.[10] CTC's rallying call to all the provinces was unequivocal: collectively, they were to make Canada the world leader in Aboriginal tourism.[11]

Further incorporation of British Columbia's indigenous tourism into a national industry occurred with the setting up of the Aboriginal Tourism Team Canada (ATTC) in early 1998, with the aim of bringing together all levels of government, industry and professional organisations. Its remit was to co-ordinate the promotion of indigenous tourism and to introduce systems of regulation and accreditation. ATTC received federal core funding from Aboriginal Business Canada, a division of Industry Canada as well as project funding from the Department of Indian and Northern Affairs. First Nations tourism in British Columbia, as elsewhere, thus became absorbed within bureaucratic and inter-ministerial structures of regional planning and financial administration.

By the late 1990s, Aboriginal community tourism planners operated within a system of tiered and multiple-agency policy-making and funding arrangements. These shared responsibilities replicate patterns of fragmentation and overlap, which occur in other spheres of government involvement in Aboriginal affairs. They also highlight the importance being attached to indigenous initiatives within Canada's tourism industry.

How did this activity fit within the wider socio-economic and politico-cultural agenda? Were government agencies and Aboriginal entrepreneurs colluding in what Adams has denounced as "contrived Aboriginal traditionalism," "cultural imperialism" and "cultural genocide" (Adams, 1997, p. 133)? Marketing Canada and its provinces through Aboriginality offers apparently uncontroversial images, which mask the more awkward aspects of recent government and public relations with First Nations groups. It is tempting to view indigenous tourism, however neatly packaged to reflect Aboriginal diversity, as a kind of cultural glue binding spaces and peoples. Certainly, through the 1990s, Canada's increasingly diverse and polarised economic, socio-cultural, ethnic and regional identities were reconfiguring notions of Canadianness in ways far exceeding the tradition duality of Canada-Quebec relations. During the same period, indigenous culture became far too important for the rest of Canada's tourism industry to ignore.

An evaluation of Aboriginal tourism must therefore acknowledge the consequences at different spatial scales as well as a variety of internal and external influences. Its incorporation in national policy-making may offer a fashionable marketing tool which boosts the promotion of individual regions and the overall appeal of Canada as a travel destination, but what are its effects at more localised levels? As global competition prompts attempts to standardise national tourism development, tourism impacts both positively and negatively upon local and regional cultures and economies.

Inevitably, sophisticated advertising increasingly reinforces the emphasis upon distinctiveness and uniqueness at individual Aboriginal tourism sites as their promoters seek to maintain a competitive edge over potential rivals. Can co-ordinated promotion foster collaboration and complementary tourism development or is it in danger of creating new forms of economic dependency? Might it also fuel inter-community divisiveness as initiatives compete for a relatively small segment of the overall tourism market? Does the desire for specialist niche marketing prompt a tendency towards inventing identities and local distinctiveness which may mask some of the complexities of contemporary Aboriginal experience and thus inhibit rather than enhance cross-cultural understanding? In seeking ways to try to evaluate some of these less tangible aspects of community-based initiatives, attention now turns to Cowichan Native Village. The following discussion draws upon site visits between 1990 and 1998 and interviews with past and present staff, including the staff manager, Bobbie Gabriel.[12]

Constructing Meanings in the Cowichan Valley

A series of historical and contemporary contexts help to define the emergence of indigenous tourism. Different agendas result from the interaction of economic, socio-cultural and political influences, which occur at several political levels. Meanings and identities are shaped by the various inter-connected contexts within which tourism operates: a project's stated and unstated aims, its uniqueness and relationship to similar activities, its links to other economic and social goals and perception of intending visitors, its ownership by the people it purports to represent and internal coherence all influence how messages conveyed by the site, staff and signs are understood.

This background highlights some of the influences that shape how Aboriginal cultural identity is portrayed at the Cowichan Native Village on Vancouver Island.[13] The Cowichan People are part of the Coast Salish Nation of southern British Columbia and Upper Puget Sound in Washington State. Although before contact with settlers the population was closer to 6,000, there are c.3,200 Cowichan members today. They claim to be the largest band in British Columbia and, in common with other First Nations, the population is young and rapidly expanding. After the severe dislocation and attempts to eradicate indigenous culture which occurred c.1850-1950, the Hul'qumi'num' dialect is becoming more widely spoken as part of a wider cultural recovery. Recent years have seen much economic growth. Long associated with trade through the production of Cowichan Sweaters and carving, community interests in tourism intensified in the later 1980s.

Cowichan Native Village was founded in 1990 on an accessible six-acre site adjacent to the Trans-Canadian Highway and beside the River Cowichan. Both the site and the southern quarter of Duncan, the adjacent non-Aboriginal settlement, occupy land belonging to the Cowichan Tribes. A series of cedar wood long houses, using traditional designs and building materials and named after different sites in the Cowichan Valley, provide visitor facilities which are staffed by a team of permanent and seasonal employees. After an initial welcome and tour, visitors may wander around freely between gallery and exhibition space, carving shed and handicraft demonstration areas, restaurant, cafe and retailing points.

A multi-media presentation, Great Deeds, made by a Vancouver production company with community members, provides a short historical overview and traditional music is broadcast across the site. Landscaped areas are dotted with recent carvings in both traditional and evolving art forms and include a story-telling and fire circle, barbecue pits and scattered seating areas. A scaled down version of the Cowichan river system introduces visitors to the continuing cultural importance of ethno-botany and offers a self-guiding trail among the native species beside the watercourse. During the summer, salmon barbecues are held everyday and the Coastal Salish Feast combines a dinner of traditional foods with a nightly performance using dance, masks and story-telling traditions to portray pre-contact Salish life.

In 1996, Cowichan Native Village was hailed as one of five national "flagship" Aboriginal tourism properties by the Canadian Tourism Commission (O'Neil, 1997, p. 2). Although the venture has encountered some of the problems mentioned earlier, its selection for national recognition assures publicity and a flow of visitors which make it appropriate as a focus for discussing Aboriginal tourism. Only one hour's drive north from Victoria, the site receives international visitors, particularly from the western United States and, until the Asian economic recession of the later 1990s, other Pacific Rim countries. European visitors are mainly from the UK and Germany although numbers from elsewhere in Europe rise annually. Apart from school parties, Canadian visitors tend to be from within the province or Ontario.[13] Aboriginal visitors tend to be fewer in numbers and often have professional interest in tourism-related activity.

According to Bobbie Gabriel, Cowichan Native Village juxtaposes aspects of traditional culture and artistic practice with modern heritage marketing. Orality and technology combine in the performance and multi-media shows; modern mass-catering meets traditional food preparation; gift shop, art gallery, exhibits, uniforms and advertising consciously strive to combine tradition with marketing styles based on the latest trends and practices within tourism and hospitality-related industries. Around the site, West Coast artists-in-residence—from beyond the Cowichan community—and their apprentices mix local and more diverse influences as they demonstrate their expertise, converse with visitors and produce work for sale or by commission.

The decision, in 1996, to change the site's well-known name from Duncan Native Heritage Centre to Cowichan Native Village discloses the complexities of tourist activities which try to be both an economic and political process. The site's logo, name and geographical association with the local town were swapped for a name and motif which reinforces cultural affiliation. Under the rubric of tourism, a subtle re-mapping of space and sharing of counter-histories occurred. The renamed parts of the Village express local language and pre-contact settlement history. Aboriginal orthography and an increasing use of family names assert a local uniqueness and challenge labels and imposed classification.

Yet, the specificity of distinctive place marketing does not quite fit with the inherent mobility and inter-cultural contact of many coastal communities! As family and community histories are reclaimed within wider processes of cultural renewal, people gain confidence in expressing identities which derive from an awareness of the close contact between many First Nations and their territories. So while, publicity claims that the site celebrates local cultural distinctiveness, carvers from First Nations further north are employed as their art traditions are too distinctive to omit from the Cowichan visitor experience. A narrow emphasis on locality makes neither cultural nor economic sense in a tourist region where, for the uninformed, poles and totems symbolise a broadly undifferentiated Aboriginal presence. Even in times of regional competition, the definition of local is highly flexible.

Indigenous tourism occurs in neither an economic nor a cultural vacuum. Notwithstanding the local emphasis, visitors also encounter some pan-Indian influences. According to surveys, some visitors are disappointed by the lack of Plains Culture—by far the most dominant cultural tradition in shaping modern representations of Indian's—but the site subtly encodes a wider ideological affinity. The Village shapes its own vision of a distinctive community by drawing upon broader evocations of Indianness, through art, music, story telling and particularly through language.

Since the expression of shared concerns and goals fosters notions of unity, elements of shared rhetoric are highly evident in contemporary indigenous life. As First Nations seek to reclaim political, economic and cultural recognition, the process of recovery assumes both a symbolic and literal level. Healing has become synonymous with empowerment and self-determination in a spiritual as well as societal sense. This vocabulary of healing which pervades site management practice sets the Village in an identifiable 1990s context of Aboriginal experience.

The site's mission statement, "to share and to build the pride of we the First people...to enhance the future of our native cultures" is seen, at least by some staff, as part of a wider community empowerment. The Village is presented as a microcosm of traditional values: while names and landscape design evoke pre-contact balance between natural resources and settlement and buildings attest to collaborative past lifestyles, cultural concerns inform management practice. Staff relations are informal and emphasise shared responsibilities, strengthening relations both within and beyond the community and providing a supportive environment for cultural and personal development.

The Village offers some staff their first experience of employment and opportunities to share ideas, meet others and members of other cultures. The management strives to offer a positive and protective work environment although culturally orientated tourism, by its very nature, brings public exposure to peoples whose histories may be full of cultural misunderstandings. As seasonal employees move between different functions, they develop a wide range of transferable experiences which foster fledging entrepreneurial or vocational skills. Cowichan offers a stepping stone to other career possibilities and further study. The site thus reveals the face of modern Aboriginal entrepreneurship as it combines aspects of tradition and modernity. It presents a source of community income generation, new employment, training opportunities and provides role models for younger Cowichan members.

Cowichan Native Village, according to Bobbie Gabriel, is neither living history nor a museum. Its current management sidesteps the issue of authenticity by acknowledging the importance of socio-cultural change. The site, as shown by the slogan, "Come share our Pride" is characterised as a point of cross-cultural contact—a means to engage both in a two-way process of recognition, respect and better understanding. Access to cultural and historical materials available on-site provides learning opportunities for both staff and visitors. Employees assert that cultural awareness, respect and sense of traditional ways have modern relevance: in short, the Village articulates representations of Aboriginality which are negotiable, inclusive and also unfamiliar to many non-Aboriginal visitors.

Implications

Tourists in Aboriginal Canada still travel in relatively uncharted territories which brim with complex and contradictory meanings. New guide books offer much needed orientation and help to sensitive non-Aboriginal visitors to historical and cultural contexts at many sites (Kramer, 1994; Coull, 1997). Tourism has constructed varied images and identities which are at times contradictory. Non-Aboriginal visitors may find that tourism offers ways to reconsider their preconceived notions of Indianness but does it present a coherent basis for greater understanding of indigenous experience? Can tourism anywhere provide a means to fulfil its oft-expressed goals of greater understanding through education and entertainment?

Tourism purports to offer accessible routes into bridge building between peoples, yet its appeal derives from constructed difference. The encouragement of a distinctive Aboriginal tourism within the marketing of Canada relies on the promotion of Otherness. Tourism requires a specificity of distinctiveness which may be subsumed within wider and more standardised promotion of cultural encounters. The tourism industry invites localised forms of tourism development yet it seeks to stimulate and meet tourist interests which often depend upon prior familiarity with more generic iconographies of Indianism.

At individual properties, management strategies and staff must decide how to balance local uniqueness and regional affiliation with broader appeals to a collective First Nations identity. Aboriginal tourism discloses how identities are constructed through spatial and temporal as well as socio-economic, cultural and political variables. The protection of cultural integrity against economic intrusiveness leads to selective exposure of local custom: Pan-Indianism, or its regional variations as on the West Coast, can be a protective mantle which diverts tourist attention from aspects of historical experience and culture that may be too painful, precious or problematic to put on show.

More widely circulated imagery and language help to orientate visitors, strengthen advertising and create instant recognition for individual tourism initiative within an increasingly competitive business environment. Evocations of community empowerment as well as spiritual or cultural renewal help to situate tourism activity within wider discursive contexts. Their familiarity may reinforce fictive notions of unity—reminiscent of what Anderson (1983) has termed an "imagined community"—which screen the diversities and divisions between and within First Nations.

Tourism offers opportunities to present alternative histories, as shown by the growth of heritage and cultural interpretation centres during the past two decades. At such sites, Aboriginal versions of past events and contemporary circumstances reach audiences from a wider background than do the content changes which have been made to some Canadian curriculum materials in recent years. Tourism histories, however under-written and lacking in detail, nonetheless signal different ways of shaping historical understanding. They are signposts to other historical possibilities and alternative voices. The exposure to other ways of telling, hearing and seeing may prompt some visitors to find out more.

Since the reclaiming of history is a political act, it has great significance for many communities as they reassert themselves. This was stated in the *Report of the RCAP* as:

...the determination of Aboriginal people to retain their cultures goes beyond nostalgia for an historical way of life (1996a, p. 619).

Recovering the past involves passing on understanding "for the sake of future generations," which extends far beyond any touristic purpose.

Tourism's alternative histories tend to be highly selective in their handling of past experiences. Aboriginal writers are already acknowledging that the uncritical rewriting of Aboriginal history may produce its own very different problems (Adams, 1997, p. 34; Wagamese, 1998, p. 6). They suggest that a focus upon pre-contact experiences may produce romanticised versions of Aboriginality which deny the actuality of indigenous experience. Idealising past experiences, however, is a familiar and perhaps necessary stage in the emergence of oppositional histories and post-colonial (or at least more liberated) identities. They remain fundamentally different from the bland histories of heritage marketing.

Wagamese (1998) suggests that over-emphasis of mythic pasts sets up unattainable role models, reinforcing self-doubt and cultural guilt. These concerns are relevant within tourism contexts where younger staff may encounter such historical representations. Fortunately, the significance increasingly attached to oral testimonies as sources of historical truth should ensure that memories and humour bring humanising touches to counter the somewhat "spiritually self-righteous" and "evangelical tones" which concern Wagamese. For visitors too, alternative histories, however simplified, still present useful perspectives which counter the pervasive misrepresentations which occur in popular culture.

The non-Aboriginal visitor who travels through Indian country via web-sites or tourism properties now meets images and messages which both challenge and reinforce old notions and stereotypes. Government encouragement—at federal and provincial levels—provide opportunities for economic and cultural activity that convey contradictory messages about contemporary Aboriginality. Were tourism to occur in isolation, then its potential to create new ways of racialising space and erecting mental barriers could be interpreted as a route towards cultural genocide, as put forward by Adams (1998). Arguably, seizing the opportunities made available by tourism is merely a late twentieth-century form of survival and adaptation.

Modern indigenous experience requires participation within both mainstream and Aboriginal worlds. Finding ways to meet the challenge of new opportunities without collusion or compromise is not straightforward, as perspectives on levels of acceptability and integrity vary. Effective indigenous tourism development will only occur through consensus on acceptable forms of cultural representation and within broader strategies of social, economic and community development. It is a pity that the *Royal Commission on Aboriginal Peoples* makes so little direct comment on tourism other than offering a passing, positive endorsement to tourism-related activity. A number of specific issues and recommendations have particular relevance to tourism activity and offer pointers for future research. These fall broadly under a number of headings, namely arts and heritage, education and youth.

If Aboriginal tourism is to be a sustainable and culturally sensitive activity, then the report's recommendations and reminders about appropriate development of heritage sites, full involvement of local people and greatly enhanced access to cultural and heritage education and training opportunities merit close attention and response from both within and beyond First Nations. Links between on-site training programmes and established accredited programmes through distance learning need to combine professional skill development with more analytical and comparative perspectives from beyond individual communities. The full range of employment opportunities for men and women within integrated tourism planning needs identifying so that skills may contribute elsewhere in community development.

Issues of identity, public understanding and youth opportunities are central to any consideration of tourism as an appropriate strategy for greater self-reliance among First Nations. In the final report (and throughout the preceding consultation process), Aboriginal youth testified to their hopes and also their desperate need for greater equity and opportunity. As a growth industry, the rise of indigenous tourism seems likely to play an increasing role in providing employment and kindling other related community initiatives and thus helping to mitigate economically motivated out-migration. It is incumbent upon present tourism professionals that this activity does not create cultural zoos which will only exacerbate the challenges facing First Nations as they negotiate their rightful place in Canadian society.

The report emphasises that the crucial task of "finding common ground between cultures" involves overcoming

...the stereotypes and erroneous assumptions held by both Aboriginal and non-Aboriginal people about each other's cultures. While Aboriginal people are confronted daily with the majority culture, non-Aboriginal people have few of the opportunities commissioners have had to share with the world view of diverse Aboriginal peoples and nations (RCAP, 1996a, p. 615).

Can tourism encounters, notwithstanding the prevailing reductive versions of reality, offer potential meeting grounds denied elsewhere by enduring processes of social, economic and spatial marginalisation? In a country which has long ignored the promises and terms once made and offered to Aboriginal peoples, the task of building a more positive relationship based on mutual recognition, respect, sharing and responsibility is vast (RCAP, 1996c, p. xi). In contrast to the uncertainty posed by Aboriginal land claims and goals of self-reliance, the sustainable development of tourism based upon long-term thinking rather than short-term opportunism might offer a relatively unthreatening means to challenge stereotypes and assumptions.

If such a transformation is to occur—rather than remain well-meaning rhetoric—then a reappraisal of how to accommodate multiple identities has to take place. Issues of identity are central to understanding many aspects of contemporary Canada. Quebec's sovereignty, the appraisal of multicultural policy, changing demographic trends and the experiences of Nunavut all pose challenges in making sense of Canadian identities. If Canada is to celebrate and draw strength from Aboriginal heritage—and not merely tourist dollars—it is timely to explore behind the sound bites of *icons* and *flagships* which are applied to First Nations tourism. Clearer understanding of how tourism policy and practice construct Aboriginal identities is one tiny step in the journey that faces indigenous peoples, Canadians and their visitors.

Notes

1. My thanks go to the staff, volunteers, artists and especially, Wuthqulwiit (Bobbie Gabriel), Assistant Manager at Cowichan Native Village (Duncan). Special thanks are also owed to Judy Hill, (Judy Hill Gallery, Duncan), Susan Andrews (Coordinator, Cowichan Valley Tourism) and Jennifer Jordan (Duncan-Cowichan Chamber of Commerce).
2. Duncan Heritage Centre, Cowichan Native Village—leaflets,1990-98, <www.cowichannativevillage.com>.

3. *Where Vancouver Island Magazine* (1998), front cover, Victoria, BC: Key Pacific Publishers.
4. Data from Canadian Tourist Information, <www.canadatourism.com/archive/tourism/commique/sep98/2sep98>.
5. *The Province*, 8 March 1992, p. C20; Full House, 1992, p. 3; ATA.PRIT.
6. Interviews, Cowichan Native Village; see also Harold Munro on proposal for a resort at Williams Lake which "would have a similar appeal to that of a Polynesian cultural centre in Hawaii...," *The Vancouver Sun*, 13 November 1993, ATA.PRIT; CTC Communique, November 1996, p. 9.
7. Parker, B., first President of CNATA, quoted in *The Financial Post Magazine*, February 1996, p. 7.
8. O'Neil, B., writing in *Business at the Summit*, February 1998, pp. 10-16; ATA.PRIT.
9. *The Globe and Mail*, 27 September 1997, pp. A13 and A19.
10. "Native Past in Demand," *The Province*, 18 May 1997, p. M3.
11. The setting up of the Aboriginal Tourism Corporation in the Spring of 1998 is further evidence of networking and partnership within indigenous tourism. See "Alliances in Vogue," *Rencontre*, vol. 21, no. 1, p. 18.
12. Site visits 1990-98, including interview with Wuthqulwiit (Bobby Gabriel).
13. Cowichan Native Village, Visitor satisfaction survey, August 1997.

References

Note: some materials lack full references and have been located within the Aboriginal Tourism Archive at the Pacific Rim Tourism Institute, Vancouver, British Columbia. They are marked ATA PRIT in the bibliography.

Adams, H. (1995) *A Tortured People. The Politics of Colonization*, Penticton: Theytus Books.
Anderson, B. (1983) *Imagined Communities: Reflections on the Origin and Spread of Nationalism*, London: Verso.
Boldt, M. (1993) *Surviving as Indians*, Toronto: University of Toronto Press.
Buhasz, L. (1997) "Going Native," *The Globe and Mail*, 27 September 1997 A19.
British Columbia. Ministry of Tourism and Ministry Responsible for Culture/First Nations Tourism Association (1993) *British Columbia First Nations Guide*, Victoria: Ministry of Tourism.
British Columbia (1980) *Travel Industry Development Study Agreement (TISDA). The Development of Native Tourism in British Columbia*, Victoria: Province of British Columbia.
British Columbia. Ministry of Small Business, Tourism and Culture, Ministry of Aboriginal Affairs & First Nations Tourism Association (1991-1994). *First Nations Products and Events. Guide to Native Sites, etc.*, Victoria: Ministry of Small Business, Tourism and Culture.

British Columbia. Ministry of Small Business, Tourism and Culture (1992-94) *Community Tourism Action Program Reports*, Victoria: Ministry of Small Business, Tourism and Culture.

Canada. Industry, Science and Technology Canada (1993) *Competitiveness in the 90s. Alliances with Aboriginal Business. Company Case Studies from British Columbia*, by Ellis, E. Ottawa: Industry, Science and Technology Canada.

Canada. Industry Canada. Aboriginal Business Canada (1996a) *Promoting the Growth of Canada's Aboriginal Businesses. New Directions 1996*, Ottawa: Ministry of Supply and Services.

Canada. Office of Tourism and Regional Economic Expansion (1982). *Province of British Columbia Tourism Development Strategy: The Vancouver Island Tourism Region*, Ottawa: Office of Tourism and Regional Economic Expansion.

Canada. Statistics Canada (1994) *Travel-Log Summer 1994. The Main Overseas Tourism Markets in Canada*, A report by Monique Beyrouti, Ottawa: Ministry of Industry, Science and Technology.

Canada. Tourism Canada. Canadian Tourism Commission. (1996c) *Live the Legacy*, Ottawa: Tourism Canada.

Cassidy, F. (ed.) (1991) *Reaching Just Settlements*, Lantzville: Oolichan Books.

Cassidy, F. and Seward, S.B. (1991) *Alternatives to Social Assistance in Indian Communities*, Lantzville: Oolichan Books & The Institute for Research in Public Policy.

Churchill, W. (1994) *Indians Are Us? Culture and Genocide in Native North America*, Toronto: Between the Lines.

Clifford, J. (1997) *Routes. Travel and Translation in the Late Twentieth Century*, Cambridge: Harvard University Press.

Clifford, J. (1991) "Four Northwest Coast Museums: Travel Reflections," in Karp, I. and Lavine, S. (Eds.) (1991). *Exhibiting Cultures: the Poetics and Politics of Museum Display*, Washington: Smithsonian Institution Press.

Clifford, J. (1993) "On Collecting Art and Culture," in During, S. (Ed.) (1993). The Cultural Studies Reader, London: Routledge.

Clifford, J.E. (1988) *The Predicament of Culture: Twentieth Century Ethnography, Literature & Art*, Cambridge: Harvard University Press.

Cohen, E. (1993) "The Study of Touristic Images of Native People: Mitigating the Stereotype of a Stereotype," in Pearce, D.G. and Butler, R.W. (Eds.) *Tourism Research, Critiques and Challenges*, London: Routledge.

Cole, D. (1985) *Captured Heritage. The Scramble for Northwest Coast Artifacts*, Seattle & London: University of Washington Press.

Coull, C. (1997) *A Traveller's Guide to Aboriginal British Columbia*, Vancouver: Whitecap Books/Beautiful British Columbia.

Elias, P.D. (1991) *Development of Aboriginal People's Communities*, North York: Captus Press.

Francis, D. (1992) *The Imaginary Indian. The Image of the Indian in Canadian Culture*, Vancouver: Arsenal Pulp Press.

Furnis, E. (1997/98) "Pioneers, Progress and the Myth of the Frontier," *BC Studies*, 115/116.

Gidley, M. (Ed.) (1991) *Representing Others. White Views of Indigenous Peoples*, Exeter: University of Exeter Press.

Helin, C. (1998) "Native Ruling Seen as Business Boon: an Interview with Aboriginal Lawyer, Calvin Helin," *Voice of BC Business. Newsletter of the BC Chamber of Commerce*, Spring issue.

Jansen, P. (1993) "Who's the Boss? Native Guides and White Tourists in the Canadian Wilderness, 1850-1914," paper presented at the British Association for Canadian Studies Annual Conference, Cambridge.

Kafka, J., White, S. and Associates, (1988) "Opportunities in the Tourism Industry," report prepared for Nicola Valley Development Corporation, April (ATA PRIT).

Kramer, P., (1994). *Native Sites in Western Canada*, Canmore: Altitude Publishing Canada Ltd.

McGregor, J. R. (1984, August) "Native Self-sufficiency, Renewal and Development," paper presented at an international conference, Vancouver (ATA PRIT).

McIlwraith, T. (1996) "The Problem of Imported Culture: the Construction of Contemporary Sto:lo Identity," *American Indian and Culture Journal*, vol. 20, no. 4.

Miller, J.R. (1989) *Skyscrapers Hide the Heavens*. Toronto: University of Toronto Press.

Murphy, P. (1985) *Tourism: A Community Approach*, New York: Methuen.

Nash, D. (1978) "Tourism as a Form of Imperialism," in Smith, V.L. (Ed.) *Hosts and Guests, the Anthropology of Tourism*, Oxford: Basil Blackwell.

Norris Nicholson, H. (1992a) "Cultural Tourism in Enterprising Times," *London Journal for Canadian Studies*, vol. 8 no. 2.

Norris Nicholson, H. (1992b) "Cultural Centres or Trading Posts," *Museums Journal*, vol. 8 no. 2.

Norris Nicholson, H. (1997) "Collision, Collusion and Challenge: Indigenous Tourism in Western Canada," in Murphy, P.E. (Ed.) (1997) *Quality Management in Urban Tourism*, Toronto: John Wiley.

O'Neil, B. (1997) "Aboriginal Tourism BC Open for Members!" *Aboriginal Tourism BC*, October 1 (2).

O'Neil, B. (1997a) "Flagship for Aboriginal Tourism Canada," *Aboriginal Tourism BC*, October 1 (2).

Parker, B. (1992) "Aboriginal Tourism in Canada. From Perception to Reality," in Reid, L.J. (Ed.) *Community and Cultural Tourism. Conference Proceedings*, Travel and Tourism Research Association/ Statistics Canada.

Richardson, B. (Ed.) (1989) *Anger and Renewal in Indian Country*, Toronto: Summerhill Press/Assembly of First Nations.

Royal Commission on Aboriginal Peoples (1996a) *Volume 1. Looking Forward, Looking Back*, Ottawa: Minister of Supply and Services.

Royal Commission on Aboriginal Peoples (1996b) *Volume 2, Part 2, Restructuring the Relationship*, Ottawa: Minister of Supply and Services.

Royal Commission on Aboriginal Peoples (1996c) *People to People: Nation to Nation. Highlights from the Report of the Royal Commission on Aboriginal Peoples*, Ottawa: Minister of Supply and Services.

Smith, D. H. (1994) "The Issue of Compatibility Between Cultural Integrity and Economic Development Among Native American Tribes," *American Indian Culture and Research Journal*, vol. 18, no. 2.

Wagamese, R. (1998) "Reconstructing Aboriginal History," *Windspeaker*, July, vol. 16, no 3.

Walker, E.G. (1987) "Native Involvement in Heritage Resource Development: A Saskatchewan Example," *Native Studies Review*, vol. 3 no. 2.

Watson, G.L. and Kopachevesky, J.P. (1994) "Interpretations of Tourism as Commodity," *Annals of Tourism Research*, vol. 21, no. 3.

Whitt, L.A. (1995) "Cultural Imperialism and the Marketing of Native America," *American Indian Culture and Research Journal*, vol. 19, no. 3.
Zizka, L. (1989) "Native Tourism in British Columbia," unpublished paper. Tourism Management Program, Capilano College, Vancouver.

Index